mind+machine

mind+machine

A Decision Model for **Optimizing** and **Implementing Analytics**

Marc Vollenweider

To my wife Gabi and our children Michèle,
Alexandra, Eric, and Mike

CONTENTS

PREFACE

Thank you for buying this book.

In 2015, after 15 years of operations in the field of research and analytics, we decided to adopt the notion of mind+machine at Evalueserve. We believe this marriage of the perceptive power of the human brain with the benefits of automation is essential because neither mind nor machine alone will be able to handle the complexities of analytics in the future.

The editorial team at John Wiley & Sons approached me in November 2015 to ask if I would like to write a book on how our mind+machine approach could help with the management of information-heavy processes—a topic that is of increasing interest to companies worldwide. We got very positive feedback from clients, friends, and colleagues on the idea, and decided to go ahead.

Mind+Machine is for generalist mainstream middle and top managers in business functions such as sales, marketing, procurement, R&D, supply chain, and corporate support functions, particularly in business-to-business (B2B) and B2C industries. We're writing for the hopeful beneficiaries and end users of analytics, and for people who might need to make decisions about analytics, now or in the future. The book is not a technical text primarily addressed to data scientists—although I firmly believe that even those specialists have something to learn about the primary problem in generating return on investment (ROI) from analytics.

We won't be looking at super-advanced but rare analytics use cases—there are specialized textbooks for those. Instead, we're looking at the *efficient frontier*, offering practical help on dealing with the logistics of managing and improving decision-making support and getting positive ROI at the same time.

After reading this book, you should know about key issues in the value chain of mind+machine in analytics, and be in a position to ask your data scientists, IT specialists, and vendors the right questions. You should understand the options and approaches available to you before you spend millions of dollars on a new proposal. You'll learn some useful things to demystify the world of analytics.

We're also proposing a novel approach, the Use Case Methodology (UCM), to give you a set of tangible and tested tools to make your life easier.

We've included 39 detailed case studies and plenty of real-life anecdotes to illustrate the applications of mind+machine. I'm sure you'll recognize some of your own experiences. And you'll see that you're far from alone in your quest to understand analytics.

What makes me want to put these ideas about the problems and solutions to analytics issues out in the world is conversations like these two.

The first words to me from a very senior line manager in a B2B corporation:

> "Marc, is this meeting going to be about big data? If so, I'll stop it right here. Vendors are telling me that I need to install a data lake and hire lots of increasingly rare and expensive statisticians and data scientists. My board is telling me that I need to do 'something' in big data. It all sounds unjustifiably expensive and complex. I just want to make sure that my frontline people are going to get what they need in time. I keep hearing from other companies that after an initial burst of analytics activity, real life caught up with them, the line guys are still complaining about delays, and the CFO is asking a lot of questions about the spend on big data."

During a meeting with the COO of an asset manager to define the scope of a project:

> "We do thousands of pitches to pension funds and other institutional investors every year. We have over 25 different data sources with quantitative data and qualitative information, with lots of regional flavors. However, we still put the pitches together manually and get the sign-offs from the legal department by e-mail. There must be a smarter way of doing this."

Why is analytics becoming such a controversial and challenging world? Why are managers either daunted by overhyped new initiatives and processes that they don't understand or frustrated by the feeling that there should be a better way to do something, given all this talk about better, bigger, brighter analytics?

Typical line managers want to get the right decision-making support to the right people at the right time in the right format. The proliferating number of analytics use cases and available data sets is not matched by an expansion in individuals' and companies' capacities to mentally and logistically absorb the information. Additionally, existing and new compliance requirements are piling up at a remarkable speed, especially in industries with a high regulatory focus, such as financial services and health care.

Analytics itself is not truly the issue. In most cases, the problem is the logistics of getting things done in organizations: defining the workflow and getting it executed efficiently; making decisions on internal alignment, the complexities of getting IT projects done, and other organizational hurdles that hamper the progress. These complexities slow things down or make projects diverge from their original objectives, so that the actual beneficiaries of the analytics (e.g., the key account manager or the procurement manager in the field) don't get what they need in time.

Many other issues plague the world of analytics: the proliferation of unintuitive jargon about data lakes and neural networks, the often-overlooked psychology of data analytics that drives companies to hold too dearly to the idea of the power of data and makes the implementation more complex than required, and the marketing hype engines making promises that no technology can fulfill.

Based on hundreds of client interactions at Evalueserve and with my former colleagues in the strategy consulting world, it became increasingly clear that there is a strong unmet need in the general managerial population for a simplified framework to enable efficient and effective navigation of information-heavy decision-support processes. Simplicity should always win over complex and non-transparent processes—the analytics space is no exception.

I want to demystify analytics. I'll start with the fundamental observation that terms such as big data and artificial intelligence are getting so much attention in the media that the bricks-and-mortar topics of everyday analytics aren't getting the attention they deserve: topics such as problem definition, data gathering, cleansing, analysis, visualization, dissemination, and knowledge management. Applying big data to every analytics problem would be like taking one highly refined chef's tool—a finely balanced sushi knife, for example—and trying to use it for every task. While very useful big data use cases have emerged in several fields, they represent maybe 5 percent of all of the billions of analytics use cases.

What are the other 95 percent of use cases about? **Small data**. It is amazing how many analytics use cases require very little data to achieve a lot of impact. My favorite use case that illustrates the point is one where just 800 bits of information saved an investment bank a recurring annual cost of USD 1,000,000. We will discuss the details of this use case in Part I.

Granted, not every use case performs like that, but I want to illustrate the point that companies have lots of opportunities to analyze their existing data with very simple tools, and that there is very little correlation between ROI and the size of the data set.

Mind+Machine addresses end-to-end, information-heavy processes that support decision making or produce information-based output, such as sales pitches or research and data products, either for internal recipients or for external clients or customers. This includes all types of data and information: qualitative and quantitative; financial, business, and operational; static and dynamic; big and small; structured and unstructured.

The concept of mind+machine addresses how the human mind collaborates with machines to improve productivity, time to market, and quality, or to create new capabilities that did not exist before. This book is not about the creation of physical products or using physical machines and robots as in an Industry 4.0 model. Additionally, we will look at the full end-to-end value chain of analytics, which is far broader than just solving the analytics problem or getting some data. And finally, we will ask how to ensure that analytics helps us make money and satisfy our clients.

In Part I, we'll analyze the current state of affairs in analytics, dispelling the top 12 fallacies that have taken over the perception of analytics. It is surprising how entrenched these fallacies have become in the media and even in very senior management circles. It is hoped that Part I will give you some tools to deal with the marketing hype, senior management expectations, and the jargon of the field. Part I also contains the 800 bits use case. I'm sure you can't wait to read the details.

In Part II, we'll examine the key trends affecting analytics and driving positive change. These trends are essentially good news for most users and decision makers in the field. It sets the stage for a dramatic simplification of processes requiring less IT spend, shorter development cycles, increasingly user-friendly interfaces, and the basis for new and profitable use cases. We'll examine key questions, including:

- What's happening with the Internet of Things, the cloud, and mobile technologies?
- How does this drive new data, new use cases, and new delivery models?
- How fast is the race for data assets, alternative data, and smart data?
- What are the rapidly changing expectations of end users?
- How should minds and machines support each other?
- Do modern workflow management and automation speed things up?
- How does modern user experience design improve the impact?
- How are commercial models such as pay-as-you-go relevant for analytics?
- How does the regulatory environment affect many analytics initiatives?

In Part III, we will look at best practices in mind+machine. We will look at the end-to-end value chain of analytics via the Use Case Methodology (UCM), focusing on how to get things done. You will find practical recommendations on how to design and manage individual use cases as well as how to govern whole portfolios of use cases.

Some of the key questions we'll address are:

- What is an analytics use case?
- How should we think about the client benefits?
- What is the right approach to an analytics use case?
- How much automation do we need?
- How can we reach the end user at the right time and in the right format?
- How do we prepare for the inevitable visit from compliance?
- Where can we get external help, and what are realistic cost and timing expectations?

- How can we reuse use cases in order to shorten development cycles and improve ROI?

However, just looking at the individual use cases is not enough, as whole portfolios of use cases need to be managed. Therefore, this part will also answer the following questions:

- How do we find and prioritize use cases?
- What level of governance is needed, and how do we set it up?
- How do we find synergies and reuse them between the use cases in our portfolio?
- How do we make sure they actually deliver the expected value and ROI?
- How do we manage and govern the portfolio?

At the end of Part III you should be in a position to address the main challenges of mind+machine, both for individual use cases and for portfolios of use cases.

Throughout the book I use numerous analogies from the non-nerd world to make the points, trying to avoid too much specialist jargon. Some of them might be a bit daring, but I hope they are going to be fun reading, loosening up the left-brained topic of analytics. If I could make you smile a few times while reading this book, my goal will have been achieved.

I'm glad to have you with me for this journey through the world of mind+machine. Thank you for choosing me as your guide. Let us begin!

ACKNOWLEDGMENTS

My heartfelt thanks to Evalueserve's loyal clients, employees, and partner firms, without whose contributions this book would not have been possible; to our four external contributors and partners: Neil Gardiner of Every Interaction, Michael Müller of Acrea, Alan Day of State of Flux, and Stephen Taylor of Stream Financial; to our brand agency Earnest for their thought leadership in creating our brand; to all the Evalueserve teams and the teams of our partner firms MP Technology, Every Interaction, Infusion, Earnest, and Acrea for creating and positioning InsightBee and other mind+machine platforms; to the creators, owners, and authors of all the use cases in this book and their respective operations teams; to Jean-Paul Ludig, who helped me keep the project on track; to Derek and Seven Victor for their incredible help in editing the book; to Evalueserve's marketing team; to the Evalueserve board and management team for taking a lot of operational responsibilities off my shoulders, allowing me to write this book; to John Wiley & Sons for giving me this opportunity; to Ursula Hueby for keeping my logistics on track during all these years; to Ashish Gupta, our former COO, for being a friend and helping build the company from the very beginning; to Alok Aggarwal for co-founding the company; to his wife Sangeeta Aggarwal for introducing us; and above all to my wonderful wife Gabi for supporting me during all these years, actively participating in all of Evalueserve's key events, being a great partner for both everyday life and grand thought experiments, and for inspiring me to delve into the psychology of those involved at all levels of mind+machine analytics.

—Marc Vollenweider

LIST OF USE CASES

PART I

THE TOP 12 FALLACIES ABOUT MIND+MACHINE

The number of incredible opportunities with great potential for mind+machine is large and growing. Many companies have already begun successfully leveraging this potential, building whole digital business models around smart minds and effective machines. Despite the potential for remarkable return on investment (ROI), there are pitfalls—particularly if you fall into the trap of believing some of the common wisdoms in analytics, which are exposed as fallacies on closer examination.

Some vendors might not agree with the view that current approaches have serious limitations, but the world of analytics is showing some clear and undisputable symptoms that all is not well. To ensure you can approach mind+machine successfully, I want to arm you with insights into the traps and falsehoods you will very likely encounter.

First, let's make sure we all know what successful analytics means: the delivery of the right insight to the right decision makers at the right time and in the right format. Anything else means a lessened impact—which is an unsatisfactory experience for all involved.

The simplest analogy is to food service. Success in a restaurant means the food is tasty, presented appropriately, and delivered to the table on time. It's not enough to have a great chef if the food doesn't reach the table promptly. And the most efficient service won't save the business if the food is poor quality or served with the wrong utensils.

The impact on a business from analytics should be clear and strong. However, many organizations struggle, spending millions or even tens of millions on their analytics infrastructure but failing to receive the high-quality insights when they are needed in a usable form—and thus failing to get the right return on their investments. Why is that?

Analytics serves the fundamental desire to support decisions with facts and data. In the minds of many managers, it's a case of the more, the better. And there is certainly no issue with finding data! The rapid expansion in the availability of relatively inexpensive computing power and storage has been matched by the unprecedented proliferation of information sources. There is a temptation to see more data combined with more computing power as the sole solution to all analytics problems. But the human element cannot be underestimated.

I vividly remember my first year at McKinsey Zurich. It was 1990, and one of my first projects was a strategy study in the weaving machines market. I was really lucky, discovering around 40 useful data points and some good qualitative descriptions in the 160-page analyst report procured by our very competent library team. We also conducted 15 qualitative interviews and found another useful source.

By today's standards, the report provided a combined study-relevant data volume of 2 to 3 kilobytes. We used this information to create a small but robust model in Lotus 1-2-3 on a standard laptop. Those insights proved accurate: in 2000, I came across the market estimates again and found that we had been only about 5% off.

Granted, this may have been luck, but my point is that deriving valuable insight—finding the "so what?"—required thought, not just the mass of data and raw computing power that many see as the right way to do analytics. Fallacies like this and the ones I outline in this part of the book are holding analytics back from achieving its full potential.

BIG DATA SOLVES EVERYTHING

From Google to start-up analytics firms, many companies have successfully implemented business models around the opportunities offered by big data. The growing number of analytics use cases include media streaming, business-to-consumer (B2C) marketing, risk and compliance in financial services, surveillance and security in the private sector, social media monitoring, and preventive maintenance strategies (Figure I.1). However, throwing big data at every analytics use case isn't always the way to generate the best return on investment (ROI).

Before we explore the big data fallacy in detail, we need to define analytics use case, a term you'll encounter a lot in this book. Here is a proposed definition:

"An analytics use case is the **end-to-end analytics support solution** applied once or repeatedly to a **single business issue** faced by an **end user** or homogeneous group of end users who need to make decisions, take actions, or deliver a product or service **on time** based on the **insights** delivered."

What are the implications of this definition? First and foremost, use cases are really about the end users and their needs, not about data scientists, informaticians, or analytics vendors. Second, the definition does not specify the data as small or big, qualitative or quantitative, static or dynamic—the type, origin, and size of the data input sets are open. Whether humans or machines or a combination thereof deliver the solution is also not defined. However, it is specific on the need for timely insights and on the end-to-end character of the solution, which means the complete workflow from data creation to delivery of the insights to the decision maker.

Now, getting back to big data: the list of big data use cases has grown significantly over the past decade and will continue to grow. With the advent of social media and the Internet of Things, we are faced with a vast number of information sources, with more to come. Continuous data streams are becoming increasingly

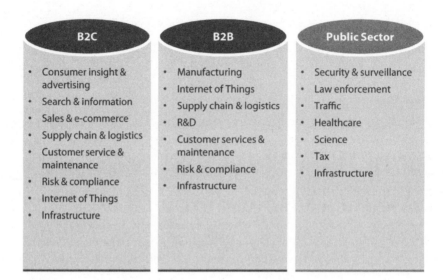

Figure I.1 Areas of Big Data Impact

prevalent. As companies offering big data tools spring up like mushrooms, people are dreaming up an increasing number of analytics possibilities.

One of the issues with talking about big data, or indeed small data, is the lack of a singular understanding of what the term means. It's good hype in action: an attractive name with a fuzzy definition. I found no less than 12 different definitions of big data while researching this book! I'm certainly not going to list all of them, but I can help you understand them by categorizing them into two buckets: the geek's concept and the anthropologist's view.

Broadly speaking, tech geeks define big data in terms of volumes; velocity (speed); variety (types include text, voice, and video); structure (which can mean structured, such as tables and charts, or unstructured, such as user comments from social media channels); variability over time; and veracity (i.e., the level of quality assurance). There are two fundamental problems with this definition. First, nobody has laid down any commonly accepted limits for what counts as big or small, obviously because this is a highly moving target, and second, there is no clear "so what?" from this definition. Why do all of these factors matter to the end user when they are all so variable?

That brings us to the anthropologist's view, which focuses on the objective. Wikipedia provides an elegant definition that expresses the ambiguity, associated activities, and ultimate objective:

> Big data is a term for data sets that are so large or complex that traditional data processing applications are inadequate. Challenges include analysis, capture, data curation, search, sharing, storage, transfer, visualization, querying, updating and information privacy. The term often refers simply to the use of predictive analytics or certain other advanced

methods to extract value from data, and seldom to a particular size of data set. Accuracy in big data may lead to more confident decision making, and better decisions can result in greater operational efficiency, cost reduction and reduced risk.

High-ROI use cases for big data existed before the current hype. Examples are B2C marketing analytics and advertising, risk analytics, and fraud detection. They've been proven in the market and have consistently delivered value. There are also use cases for scientific research and for national security and surveillance, where ROI is hard to measure but there is a perceived gain in knowledge and security level (although this latter gain is often debated).

We've added a collection of use cases throughout this book to help give you insight into the real-world applications of what you're learning. They all follow the same format to help you quickly find the information of greatest interest to you.

ANALYTICS USE CASE FORMAT

Context: A brief outline of where the use case comes from: industry, business function, and geography

Business Challenge: What the solution needed to achieve for the client(s)

Solution: An illustration of the solution or processes used to create that solution

Approach: Details on the steps involved in creating the solutions along with the mind+machine intensity diagram, illustrating the change in the balance between human effort and automation at key stages during the implementation of the solution

Analytics Challenges: The key issues to be solved along with an illustration of the relative complexity of the mind+machine aspects applied in solving the case

Benefits: The positive impact on productivity, time to market, and quality, and the new capabilities stemming from the solution

Implementation: The key achievements and the investment and/or effort required to make the solution a reality (development, implementation, and maintenance, as applicable), illustrated where possible

I wanted to include some of the more exciting projects currently under development to show the possibilities of analytics. In these cases, some of the productivity gain and investment metrics are estimates and are labeled (E).

Innovation Analytics:
Nascent Industry Growth Index

Context

Organization
Corporate innovation departments,
hedge funds, PE and VC firms

Function(s)
Companies investing in nascent
industries

Industry
Corporates and
financial services

Geography
Global

Business Challenge

- Build index to forecast probability of high near-future growth of specified
  nascent industries
- Read and interpret technical and business text from thousands of documents

Solution

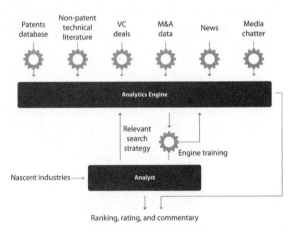

Nascent Industry Growth Index

Approach

- Developed proof of concept to manually
  create industry-agnostic index
- Set up team of 4 FTEs (Full-Time Equivalent)
  (1 each from analytics and IP, FS, and corporates)
- Deployed text analytics tool (KMX) to
  automate innovation intensity ranking
  through free-text patent searching.
- Created production platform to aggregate
  disparate data sets and semiautomate
  growth forecast index creation

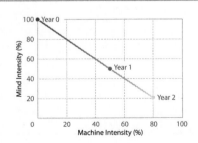

Analytics Challenges

- High variety of data sets to be integrated
- Iterative training of text analytics engine to accurately read large volumes of text
- Establishing judicious use of analyst involvement and time to screen relevant from irrelevant data
- Fine-tuning index over time to improve its accuracy in providing probability of high growth

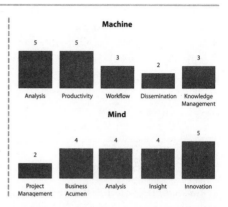

Benefits

Productivity	Time to Market	New Capabilities	Quality
• Reduces the need for an analyst by 50% to 90%	• Proof of concept built in 3 months • Product in 9 months	• Removed subjectivity in innovation prioritization criteria • Enabled faster prioritization of attractive markets and better judgment of next big industry wave	• Unmatched rigor in forecasting nascent industry inflection point • Initial accuracy is about 70%; improving with analyst intervention and iterative engine training

Implementation

- Proof of concept in 3 months with 6 FTEs
- Data warehousing, platform development, and testing for 6 months with 8 FTEs
- Thereafter, recurring engagement of 3 FTEs for 1 month per quarter
- Budget of USD 0.5 million in the first year
- Opex includes USD 0.1 million per year database cost and 2–3 FTEs

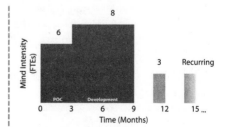

The big data hype has its origin in three factors: the appearance of new data types or sources, such as social media; the increasing availability of connected devices, from mobile phones to machine sensors; and the evolution of ways to analyze large data sets in short periods of time. The sense of possibility led to a proliferation of use cases. We cannot say how many of these untested use cases will survive. Ultimately, the question is not what *can* be done, but what *actually* delivers value to the end user.

Gartner predicts that 60 percent of big data initiatives will fail in 2017,[1] and Wikibon, an open-source research firm, maintains that the average ROI for big data projects is currently only about 55 cents on the dollar spent instead of the expected $3 to $4.[2] The latter assessment wasn't made by CFOs, but came directly from practitioners, who saw a "lack of compelling need" for big data in those use cases as a reason for the low returns. However, our experience is that CFOs are increasingly asking about the viability of such analytics.

For large companies, the investment in big data infrastructure and expertise can easily run into the tens of millions of dollars. It would seem obvious that prior to any such investment, the company would want to fully investigate the need, and yet in the 2012 BRITE/NYAMA "Marketing Measurement in Transition" study, 57 percent of companies self-reported that their marketing budgets were not based on ROI analysis.[3]

Measuring the ROI of analytics use cases is unfortunately not as easy as it sounds. This is especially true where companies have invested in infrastructure such as central data warehouses, software licenses, and data scientist teams. Properly calculating the desired impact at the use case level requires the corresponding governance and control, which is rare at this stage. In a series of initial interviews with companies that went on to become Evalueserve clients, seven areas were found to be lacking—in some cases, almost completely:

1. Governance structure for the data and use case ownership
2. Accountability for individual use cases, portfolio management, and associated economics
3. Clear definition of analytics use cases
4. Objectives and intended end user benefits for each use case
5. Tracking the actual results against the targets
6. Knowledge management allowing the efficient reuse of prior work
7. Audit trails for the people, timing, actions, and results regarding the code, data, and findings

That said, examples of excellent and highly focused big data use case management do exist. The use case *Cross-Sell Analytics: Opportunity Dashboard* shows solid accountability. The campaign management function of the bank continually measures the ROI of campaigns end to end, and has built a focused factory for a portfolio of such analytics.

An example of a much weaker big data use case was recently proposed to me by a US start-up engaged in human resources (HR) analytics. The example illustrates some of the fundamental issues with the current hype. An ex-consultant and an ex-national security agent suggested using a derivative of software developed for the surveillance field for recruiting analytics. Based on the previous five to 10 years of job applications—the curriculum vitae (CV) or resume and cover letter—and the performance data of the corresponding employees, a black-box algorithm would build a performance prediction model for new job applicants. The software would deliver hire/no hire suggestions after receiving the data of the new applications.

We rejected the proposal for two reasons: the obvious issue of data privacy and the expected ROI. Having done thousands of interviews, I have a very simple view of resumes. They deliver basic information that's been heavily fine-tuned by more or less competent coaching, and they essentially hide the candidate's true personality. I would argue that the predictive value of CVs has decreased over the past 20 years. Cultural bias in CV massaging is another issue. Human contact—preferably eye contact—is still the only way to cut through these walls of disguise.

The black-box algorithm would therefore have a very severe information shortage, making it not just inefficient, but actually in danger of producing a negative ROI in the form of many wrong decisions. When challenged on this, the start-up's salesperson stated that a "human filter" would have to be applied to find the false positives. Since a black-box algorithm is involved, there is no way of knowing how the software's conclusion was reached, so the analysis would need to be redone 100 percent, reducing the ROI still further.

It was also interesting to see that this use case was being sold as big data. It's a classic example of riding the wave of popularity of a term. Even under the most aggressive scenarios, our human resources performance data is not more than 300 to 400 megabytes, which hardly constitutes big data. Always be wary of excessive marketing language and the corresponding promises!

These are just two isolated use cases, which is certainly not enough to convince anyone trained in statistics, including myself. Therefore, it is necessary to look at how relevant big data analytics is in the overall demographics of analytics. To the best of my knowledge, this is not something that has ever been attempted in a study.

At first, it's necessary to count the number of analytics use cases and put them into various buckets to create a demographic map of analytics (Figure I.2). One cautionary note: counting analytics use cases is tricky due to the variability of possible definitions, so there is a margin of error to the map, although I believe that the order of magnitude is not too far off.

Cross-Sell Analytics:
Opportunity Dashboard

Context

Organization
United States retail bank

Function(s)
Regional managers
and financial advisers

Industry
Retail banking

Geography
United States

Business Challenge

- Identify target customers and interesting products without centralized customer portfolios
- Efficiently and securely distribute customer data to support opportunity identification
- Give regional managers optimal oversight of their financial advisers

Solution

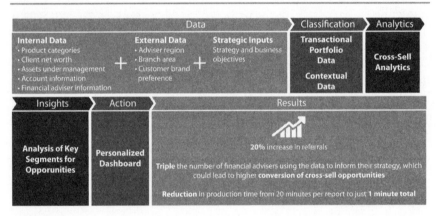

Data			Classification	Analytics
Internal Data · Product categories · Client net worth · Assets under management · Account information · Financial adviser information	**External Data** · Adviser region · Branch area · Customer brand preference	**Strategic Inputs** Strategy and business objectives	**Transactional Portfolio Data** **Contextual Data**	**Cross-Sell Analytics**

Insights	Action	Results
Analysis of Key Segments for Opporunities	**Personalized Dashboard**	20% increase in referrals **Triple** the number of financial advisers using the data to inform their strategy, which could lead to higher **conversion of cross-sell opportunities** **Reduction** in production time from 20 minutes per report to just **1 minute total**

Approach

- Created a dashboard to allow financial advisers to identify the best cross-sell opportunities and generate individualized reports with suitable products for their customers
- Began auto-generation of weekly opportunity summaries for managers
- Implemented filtering so financial advisers only see their customers' information and managers only see information for their region

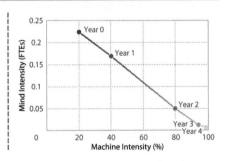

Analytics Challenges

- Decreasing data processing time to enable multiple iterations and replication across segments
- Working within financial advisory regulations regarding data security
- Ensuring only the necessary information reached the right person in the right format at the right time
- Providing appropriate monitoring for regional managers

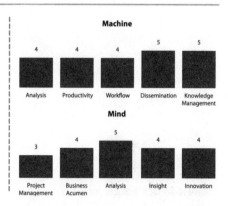

Benefits

Productivity	Time to Market	New Capabilities	Quality
• A 20% increase in referrals • Increased share of wallet for investment-only clients	• Report generation time down to 1 hour (from over 1 week)	• Stronger partnership for brokerage & retail banking divisions • Individualized reports for each financial adviser	• Increased efficiency and transparency for the financial adviser processes

Implementation

- Production time of 345 hours over 3 months (includes design, development, and testing)
- Rapid adoption: compared to their previous system, three times as many financial advisers use these reports to plan their cross-sell strategy

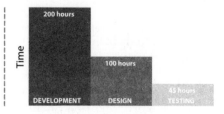

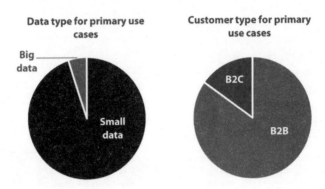

Figure I.2   Demographics of Use Cases

This map illustrates my first key point: big data is a relatively small part of the analytics world. Let's take a look at the main results of this assessment of the number of use cases.

1. Globally, there are a staggering estimated *one billion* implementations of **primary use cases**, of which about 85 percent are in B2B and about 15 percent in B2C companies. A primary use case is defined as a generic business issue that needs to be analyzed by a business function (e.g., marketing, R&D) of a company in a given industry and geography. An example could be the monthly analysis of the sales force performance for a specific oncology brand in the pharmaceutical industry in Germany. Similar analyses are performed in pretty much every pharmaceutical company selling oncology drugs in Germany.

2. Around 30 percent of companies require high analytics intensity and account for about 90 percent of the primary analytics use cases. International companies with multiple country organizations and global functions and domestic companies with higher complexity are the main players here.

3. The numbers increase to a staggering *50 to 60 billion* use cases globally when looking at **secondary implementations**, which are defined as micro-variations of primary use cases throughout the business year. For example, slightly different materials or sensor packages in different packaging machines might require variant analyses, but the underlying use case of "preventive maintenance for packaging machines" would still remain the same. While not a precise science, this primary versus secondary distinction will be very relevant for counting the number of analytics use cases in the domain of Internet of Things and Industry 4.0. A simple change in sensor configurations might lead to large

numbers of completely new secondary use cases. This in turn would cause a lot of additional analytics work, especially if not properly managed for reuse.

4. Only an estimated 5 to 6 percent of all primary use cases really require big data and the corresponding methodologies and technologies. This finding is completely contrary to the image of big data in the media and public perception. While the number of big data use cases is growing, it can be argued that the same holds true for small data use cases.

The conclusion is that data analytics is mainly a *logistical* challenge rather than just an analytical one. Managing the growing portfolios of use cases in sustainable and profitable ways is the true challenge and will remain so. In meetings, many executives tell us that they are not leveraging the small data sets their companies already have. We've seen that 94 percent of use cases are really about small data. But do they provide lower ROI because they are based on small data sets? The answer is no—and again, is totally contrary to the image portrayed in the media and the sales pitches of big data vendors.

Let me make a bold statement that is inevitably greeted by some chuckles during client meetings: "Small data is beautiful, too." In fact, I would argue that the average ROI of a small data use case is much higher due to the significantly lower investment. To illustrate my point, I'd like to present *Subscription Management: "The 800 Bits Use Case,"* which I absolutely love as it is such an extreme illustration of the point I'm making.

Using just 800 bits of HR information, an investment bank saved USD 1 million every year, generating an ROI of several thousand percent. How? Banking analysts use a lot of expensive data from databases paid through individual seat licenses. After bonus time in January, the musical chairs game starts and many analyst teams join competitor institutions, at which point the seat license should be canceled. In this case, this process step simply did not happen, as nobody thought about sending the corresponding instructions to the database companies in time. Therefore, the bank kept unnecessarily paying about USD 1 million annually. Why 800 bits? Clearly, whether someone is employed ("1") or not ("0") is a binary piece of information called a "bit." With 800 analysts, the bank had 800 bits of HR information. The analytics rule was almost embarrassingly simple: "If no longer employed, send email to terminate the seat license." All that needed to happen was a simple search for changes in employment status in the employment information from HR.

The amazing thing about this use case is it just required some solid thinking, linking a bit of employment information with the database licenses. Granted, not every use case is as profitable as this one, but years of experience suggest that good thinking combined with the right data can create a lot of value in many situations.

Subscription Management:
"The 800 Bits Use Case"

Context

Organization
Investment bank

Function(s)
Sell-side research

Industry
Financial services

Geography
Global

Business Challenge

- Collect and update subscription information by region, team, and analyst level
- Create a centralized information repository providing detailed subscription and license information
- Provide regular customized reports on usage and cost

Solution

Data sources

Internal database

Sourcing teams

Business managers

Subscription users

Define data and methodology to extract required data

Run codes to automate extraction process

Create dashboard with customization options

Approach

- Collated and analyzed the reporting requirements of client
- Consolidated the required data from multiple sources (internal database, sourcing teams, business managers, users)
- Automated the data extraction process
- Created dynamic dashboard to provide customized charts and tables on required parameters

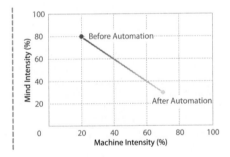

Analytics Challenges

- Extraction of required data from multiple files from various sources
- Ensuring consolidation of data in a single file through appropriate coding
- Delivering consistent and easy-to-read visualizations

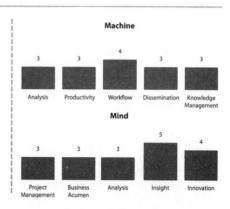

Machine

Analysis	Productivity	Workflow	Dissemination	Knowledge Management
3	3	4	3	3

Mind

Project Management	Business Acumen	Analysis	Insight	Innovation
3	3	3	5	4

Benefits

Productivity	Time to Market	New Capabilities	Quality
• Centralized view of all subscriptions • Savings: over USD 1 million per year	• 70% faster time to delivery	• Ready availability of terms and conditions • Self-certification from subscribers to confirm requirement • Optimized usage & spend recommendations	• Zero error rate due to automation of data extraction and consolidation

Implementation

- 1 FTE developed customized automation tool in 3 weeks
- Sent first version of the dashboard for two monthly reporting periods for feedback
- Incorporated feedback and implemented the final version at the start of the third reporting month

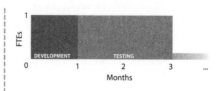

This use case illustrates another important factor: the silo trap. Interesting use cases often remain unused because data sets are buried in two or more organizational silos, and nobody thinks about joining the dots. We will look at this effect again later.

Summing up the first fallacy: not everything needs to be big data. In fact, far more use cases are about small data, and the focus should be on managing portfolios of profitable analytics use cases regardless of what type of data they are based on.

MORE DATA MEANS MORE INSIGHT

Companies complain that they have far more data than insight. In 2014, the International Data Corporation (IDC) predicted that the amount of data available to companies will increase tenfold by 2020, doubling every two years.[4] In one conversation, a client compared this situation to a desert with the occasional oasis of insight.

"Marc, we are inundated with reports and tables, but who'll give me the 'so what'? I don't have enough time in the day to study all the data, and my junior people don't have the experience to come up with interesting insights."

The ratio seems to worsen daily, as the amount of available data rises rapidly, while the level of insight remains constant or increases only slightly. The advent of the Internet of Things puts us at risk of making this ratio even worse, with more devices producing more data.

As the Devex consulting practice writes:

> Stanley Wood, senior program officer for data, evidence and learning at the Bill & Melinda Gates Foundation, has said that while large sums have been invested to collect various types of data, much of the results these efforts yielded were nowhere to be seen. In a previous interview, Wood even told Devex that one of the biggest points open data can help with is the waste of billions of dollars that have been spent in data collection.[5]

FT.com writes:

> According to Juerg Zeltner, CEO of UBS Wealth Management, a mass of information does not equal a wealth of knowledge. With global

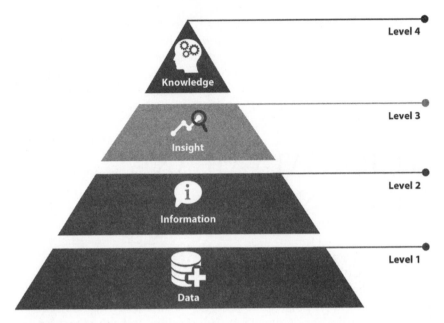

Figure I.3 Pyramid of Use Cases (Levels 1–4)

financial markets continuing to be volatile, the need for interpretation has never been greater.[6]

Before we proceed, let me introduce a simple but necessary concept for talking about data. It is quite surprising how confused the discussion of the term *data* still is, even among data scientists and vendors. In reality, there are four fundamentally different levels, depicted in Figure I.3:

- Level 1: Data—raw data and "cleansed" or "preprocessed" data

  This could be a sequence of measurements sent from a temperature or vibration sensor in a packaging machine, a set of credit card transactions, or a few pictures from a surveillance camera. No meaning can be gleaned without further processing or analysis. You may know the term *cleansing*, but this just refers to readying data for further analysis (e.g., by changing some formats).

  Returning to our restaurant analogy from the start of this section, raw data are like raw vegetables just delivered from the grocery store, but not really scrutinized by the chef. Data quality remains a very big issue for companies. In the 2014 Experian Data Quality survey, 75 percent of responding UK companies said that they had wasted 14 percent of their revenue due to bad data quality.[7]

- Level 2: Information—data already analyzed to some extent

    Simple findings have already been derived. For example, the sensor data has been found to contain five unexpected outliers where vibrations are stronger than allowed in the technical specifications, or an analysis of market shares has shown the ranking of a product's market share in various countries in the form of a table or a pie chart. The key point is that we have some initial findings, but certainly no "so what."

    In the restaurant analogy, the chef might have cut and cooked the vegetables, but they haven't been arranged on the plate yet.

- Level 3: Insight—the "so what" that helps in making value-adding decisions

    This is what the decision maker is looking for. In our restaurant analogy, the vegetables have now been served on the plate as part of the full meal, and the patron's brain has signaled this wonderful moment of visual and gustatory enjoyment.

    There is definitely some room to improve, as shown in a BusinessIntelligence.com survey sponsored by Domo: only 10 percent of 302 CEOs and CXOs believed that their reports provided a solid foundation for decision making,[8] and 85 percent of 600 executives interviewed by the Economist Intelligence Unit (EIU) mentioned that the biggest hurdle of analytics was to derive actionable insights from the data.[9]

- Level 4: Knowledge—a group of Level 3 insights available to others across time and space

    This is the essence of what analytics, and indeed research, aims for: insights have been made reusable over time by multiple people in multiple locations. The decision maker might still decide to ignore the knowledge (not everyone learns from history!), but the insights are available in a format that can be used by others. In the restaurant analogy, our guest was actually a reviewer for a major and popular food blog, magazine, or even the *Michelin Guide*. The reviewer's description informs others, sharing the experience and helping in decisions about the next evening out.

A core question that I am posing here is how these four levels of data relate to the concept of mind+machine: where does Mind have a unique role, and where can Machine assist? The short answer is that machines are essential at Level 1 and are becoming better at their role there. At Level 2, some success has been achieved with machines creating information out of data automatically. However, Levels 3 and 4 will continue to require the human mind for 99 percent of analytics use cases in the real world for quite some time.

It is interesting to see that companies are experiencing challenges across Levels 1 to 3, with a higher focus on Level 3. A 2013 survey sponsored by Infogroup and YesMail with more than 700 marketers showed that 38 percent were planning to improve data analysis, 31 percent data cleansing, and 28 percent data collection capabilities.[10] The survey did not include questions pertinent to Level 4.

To illustrate the variation in data volumes for each level, we'll take the use case of the chef explaining the process of cooking a great dish in various ways: in a video, in an audio recording, and in a recipe book. Let's assume that all these media ultimately contain the same Level 4 knowledge: how to prepare the perfect example of this dish.

A video can easily have a data volume between 200 megabytes (1 MB = 1 million bytes = 8 million bits) up to about 1 gigabyte (1 GB = 1 billion bytes = 8 billion bits) depending on the definition resolution. A one-hour audio book describing the same meal would be about 50 to 100 megabytes—roughly 4–10 times less data than the video—and the 10 pages of text required to describe the same process would be only about 0.1 megabytes—about 2,000 times less data than the video.

The actual Level 3 insights and the Level 4 knowledge consume only a very small amount of storage space (equal to or less than the text in the book), compared to the initial data volumes. If we take all the original video cuts that never made it into the final video, the Level 1 data volume might have even been 5 to 10 times bigger.

Therefore, the actual "from raw data to insight" compression factor could easily be 10,000 in this example. Please be aware that this compression factor is different from the more technical compression factor used to store pictures or data more efficiently (e.g., in a file format such as .jpeg or .mp3). This insight compression factor is probably always higher than the technical compression factor because we elevate basic data to higher-level abstract concepts the human brain can comprehend more easily.

The key point is that decision makers really want the **compressed insight** and the **knowledge**, not the raw data or even the information. The reality we see with our clients is exactly the opposite. Everyone seems to focus on creating Level 1 data pools or Level 2 reports and tables with the help of very powerful machines, but true insights are as rare as oases in the desert.

If you're not convinced, answer this question. Who in your organization is getting the right level of insight at the right time in the right delivery format to make the right decision?

Here is a funny yet sad real-life situation I encountered a few years ago. An individual in a prospective client's operations department had spent half of their working time for the previous seven years producing a list of records with various types of customer data. The total annual cost to the company, including overhead, was USD 40,000. When we spoke to the internal customer, we received confirmation that they had received the list every month since joining the company a few years previously. They also told us that they deleted it each time because they did not know its purpose. The analysis never made it even to Level 2—it was in fact a total waste of resources.

Regarding delivery, I can share another story. A senior partner in a law firm got his team to do regular reports on the key accounts for business development—or as they referred to it, client development. The team produced well-written,

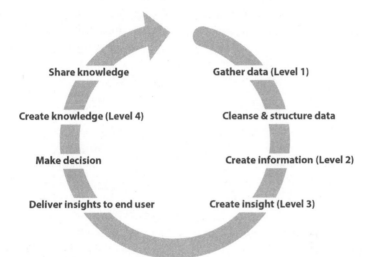

Figure I.4   The Ring of Knowledge

insightful 2–3 MB reports in MS Word for each account and sent them to the partner via email. However, he found this format inconvenient—he perceived scrolling through documents on his Blackberry to be a hassle and didn't even realize that his team summarized the key takeaways from each report in the body of the email itself.

In this case, the Level 3 insights actually existed but had zero impact: right level of insight, right timing, but wrong format for that decision maker. You can imagine what wasted resources it took to create these reports. This example also illustrates the need to change the delivery of insights from lengthy reports into a model where relevant events trigger insightful and short alerts to the end users, prompting them to take action.

These two examples show the need to understand the value chain of analytics in more detail. The value is created largely at the end, when the decision is made, while the effort and cost are spent mostly at the beginning of the analytics cycle, or the Ring of Knowledge (Figure I.4):

Step 1: Gather new data and existing knowledge (Level 1).
Step 2: Cleanse and structure data.
Step 3: Create information (Level 2).
Step 4: Create insights (Level 3).
Step 5: Deliver to the right end user in the right format, channel, and time.
Step 6: Decide and take action.
Step 7: Create knowledge (Level 4).
Step 8: Share knowledge.

If any step fails, the efforts of the earlier steps go to waste and no insight is generated. In our first example, step 3 never happened so steps 1 and 2 were a waste of time and resources; in the second, step 5 failed: the insight desert was not successfully navigated!

The insight desert is filled with treacherous valleys and sand traps that could block the road to the oasis at each stage:

- Steps 1 and 2: Functional or geographic silos lead to the creation of disparate data sets. Inconsistent definitions of data structures and elements exist with varying time stamps. Various imperfect and outdated copies of the original sources lead to tens, hundreds, or thousands of manual adjustments and more errors in the data.
- Step 3: Too much information means that really interesting signals get lost. There is a lack of a proper hypothesis of what to analyze.
- Step 4: There is a lack of thinking and business understanding. Data scientists sometimes do not fully understand the end users' needs. Contextual information is lacking, making interpretation difficult or impossible. Prior knowledge is not applied, either because it does not exist or because it is not accessible in time and at a reasonable cost.
- Steps 5 and 6: Communication problems occur between the central data analytics teams and the actual end users. Distribution issues prevent the insights from being delivered—the so-called Last Mile problem is in effect. There is an ineffective packaging and delivery model for the specific needs of the end user.
- Steps 7 and 8: There is a lack of accountability for creating and managing the knowledge. Central knowledge management systems contain a lot of obsolete and irrelevant content, and a lack of documentation leads to loss of knowledge (e.g., in cases of employee attrition).

Any of the aforementioned means a very significant waste of resources. These issues keep business users from making the right decisions when they are needed. The problem is actually exacerbated by the increasing abundance of computing power, data storage capacity, and huge new data sources.

What would a world of insight and knowledge look like? Our clients mention the following key ingredients:

- Less but more insightful analysis addressing 100 percent of the analytics use case
- Analytic outputs embedded in the normal workflow
- More targeted and trigger-based delivery highlighting the key issues rather than just regular reporting or pull analysis
- Short, relevant alerts to the end user rather than big reports deposited on some central system

- Lower infrastructure cost and overhead allocations to the end users
- No requirement to start a major information technology (IT) project to get even simple analyses
- Simple, pay-as-you-go models for analytics output rather than significant fixed costs
- Full knowledge management of analytics use cases, so that the world does not need to be reinvented each time there is a change

Innovation Scouting: Finding Suitable Innovations shows a good example of very large amounts of data being condensed into a high-impact set of insights, and knowledge being extracted to ensure learning for the future.

Currently, many companies follow the approach of first creating a central analytics team, generating a massive data lake with secondary copies of all possible data sources, and buying expensive software licenses before starting to think about the analytics problems and their governance.

The Use Case Methodology that will be discussed in Part III forces everyone to think about the business issue to be addressed first. Then the business issue gets disaggregated into its subissues in the form of an issue tree, and only then should there be any talk about the data needed to perform the analysis.

Interestingly, the issue tree analysis was already taught in the 1980s. The challenge then was to make the most from the available data, whereas today it is to find out how the business issue can be addressed using as little data and as few resources as possible. However, the methodology is still the same.

New data sources and ways to connect and analyze them can add a lot of value, but companies need to ensure that such analyses achieve the desired impact while maintaining a positive return on investment (ROI), rather than getting lost in the insight desert. More data definitely does not automatically imply more insight.

Innovation Scouting:
Finding Suitable Innovations

Context

Organization
Large consumer packaged goods
company

Function(s)
Open innovation and R&D

Industry
Consumer packaged goods

Geography
Global, HQ in the United States

Business Challenge

- Scout for new suppliers and innovation partners to speed up new product development
- Identify and track the latest innovations across product categories
- Screen and manage submissions received through the open innovation platform

Solution

Define challenge	Define the business challenge and the relevant success criteria
Conduct research	Use primary and secondary research, patent searches, and a host of internal productivity tools to conduct a thorough list generation exercise
Screen results	Screen results on the basis of relevant success criteria, and benchmark the results on a number of qualitative and quantitative parameters
Conduct due diligence	On a set of high-potential results, conduct due diligence to evaluate feasibility of use, partnership models, technical specifications, etc.

Approach

- Used an iterative combination of intellectual property and business research to ensure exhaustiveness of results from a market and technology perspective
- Developed robust framework to benchmark the results to ensure relevance and deliver automated ranking
- Defined processes and guidelines to shorten the time to accept or reject any lead

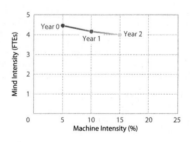

Analytics Challenges

- Global project management, coordination, and consistency of analysis across centers
- Developing standard processes to be followed for accepting or rejecting any innovation idea or solution
- Identifying approach to cross-reference results from intellectual property research and business insights to yield more valuable results

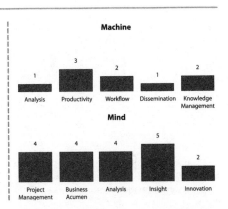

Benefits

Productivity	Time to Market	New Capabilities	Quality
• Decrease in groundwork time; more focus on strategic activities • Efficiency gains of around 15% • Provision of only the most targeted results saved time & effort	• Sped up the process of identifying high-potential solutions	• Support for business & intellectual property research and analytics • Management of open innovation portal • Services in non-English languages	• Exceptional quality recognized with innovation capability award by the client

Implementation

- 10 years of partnership with the client with ~3 years of continuous support in open innovation and scouting
- ~4 FTEs working across different centers to continuous monitoring and adhoc work
- High client involvement in year 1 to refine research parameters, clarify business-specific terminology, define processes, and so on
- Client involvement reduced to a minimum from year 2 onward

	Design and setup phase	Implementation
Client	High (to define processes)	Low
Solution team	High	High
	Year 1	Year 2 onward

FIRST, WE NEED A DATA LAKE AND TOOLS

First, we had databases, then data marts and data warehouses, and now we have data lakes. The term was probably coined by the CTO of Pentaho to contrast it with data marts, which are smaller repositories of derived attributes rather than the underlying data.[11] Data lakes are much larger repositories of raw data with the promise of unsiloed data. Maybe one day there will be data seas, data planets, and data galaxies.

The concept is always the same: collect copies of all internal and external data in a central repository and then perform all kinds of analytics. As PwC (formerly PricewaterhouseCoopers) stated in *Technology Forecast: Rethinking Integration*:

> Data lakes are big. They can be an order of magnitude less expensive on a per-terabyte basis to set up and maintain than data warehouses. With (open-source) Hadoop, petabyte-scale data volumes are neither expensive nor complicated to build and maintain. Some vendors that advocate the use of Hadoop claim that the cost per terabyte for data warehousing can be as much as $250,000, versus $2,500 per terabyte. . . . Accessibility is easy in the data lake, which is one benefit of preserving the data in its original form. Whether structured, unstructured, or semi-structured, data is loaded and stored as is to be transformed later. Customer, supplier, and operations data are consolidated with little or no effort from data owners, which eliminates internal political or technical barriers to increased data sharing.[12]

While having all data stored centrally sounds great, there are some fundamental issues with such approaches.

The risk of data graveyards: Sean Martin, CTO of Cambridge Semantics, says: "We see customers creating big data graveyards, dumping everything into Hadoop distributed file systems and hoping to do something with it down the road. But then they just lose track of what's there."[13]

While the actual Hadoop technology might be less expensive on a per-terabyte basis, the real cost is hidden in the various data scientist teams required to access, analyze, and distribute the data. The key question again comes down to the governance of analytics use cases.

Duplication of sources: Bringing all data to a central location implies the creation of massive numbers of copies of the original source data. This sounds far less dangerous than it actually is. There are three fundamental problems with this approach.

First, the dynamic nature of the hundreds and thousands of data sources means that **copies are outdated** by definition. The updating cycle cannot mirror every change instantaneously, necessitating large numbers of adjustments that often have to be made manually.

Second, the structures of the original sources vary depending on business requirements. Who makes sure that the copies are complete?

Finally, there is the oft-overlooked issue of the intellectual property rights for the original data. The proponents of data lakes are very proud to point out that they can easily store petabytes (1 PB = 1,000 TB) of unstructured or structured external data together with internal data. It is easy to understand that there are **significant intellectual property risks** for the external data. Where does it come from? Who owns it? Does the company have and continually maintain the licenses? If so, who in the company has the licenses: everyone or just a few power users? This can be an issue even when the data are thought to be internal. Where did the data actually originally come from? Did it come from a commercial database and get copied into the central repository without considering the aspect of intellectual property?

Without very strict governance, massive data lakes can be ticking time bombs. Don't get me wrong: every technology has its advantages and risks, and central repositories can work. But ask yourself: do you really believe that your company has the right skills in place to control all of these issues?

We would argue that companies with a core business centered on data have reached a high level of proficiency when it comes to data governance. However, what percentage of companies fit into this category? 1 percent? 5 percent? Gartner's report *The Data Lake Fallacy: All Water and Little Substance* lists several issues with data lakes.[14] One key aspect is the assumption that users know the context in which the data has been collected, including gaps, imperfections, and changes in the data structures later on. This assumption might be valid for central data scientists, but it is certainly not correct for the noncentral business users who get access. Big data initiatives

Virtual Data Lake:
A Use Case by Stream Financial

Context

Organization
Major organizations with multiple
jurisdictions & functions

Function(s)
Cross-functional

Industry
All industries, with significant data
(e.g., financial services)

Geography
Global

Business Challenge

- Provide executive management with an overview of all data, which is highly siloed, while still keeping ability to analyze data at lowest level of granularity
- Improve both data quality and timely delivery of insights in response to changing market circumstances
- Remove the need for a central data lake

Solution

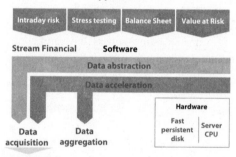

Applications

| Intraday risk | Stress testing | Balance Sheet | Value at Risk |

Stream Financial **Software**

Data abstraction

Data acceleration

Hardware

| Fast persistent disk | Server CPU |

| Data acquisition | Data aggregation |

Data sources

Data portal: Abstraction, federation, virtualization, integration, -as-a-service

Approach

- Used data virtualization to integrate data from multiple sources in a unified, logically virtualized schema for on-demand consumption
- Embedded data governance into the culture of the organization
- Enacted a disciplined change process that recognizes a federated model of data ownership and change responsibility
- Used a virtual data lake as the technology enabler

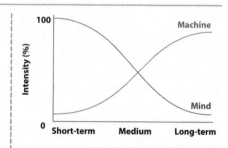

Analytics Challenges

- Each data source required to own and make data available in a form that allows querying, aggregating, or analysis across the organization
- Data owners are responsible for data quality and ensuring availability for wider organizational use
- Users are no longer allowed to keep local copies of other users' data—this was the root cause of data quality issues and process inefficiencies

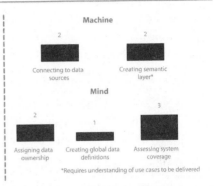

Machine

2
Connecting to data sources

2
Creating semantic layer*

Mind

2
Assigning data ownership

1
Creating global data definitions

3
Assessing system coverage

*Requires understanding of use cases to be delivered

Benefits

Productivity	Time to Market	New Capabilities	Quality
• Ability to query and join billions of rows of data across disparate and heterogeneous data sources • Use any analytics across heterogeneous data landscape	• Rapid reaction to new requirements for data sources and analytics • Product built incrementally delivering benefits in weeks	• Leverages existing systems and infrastructure rather than relying on greenfield development • Solve problems incrementally without years of requirements analysis	• Best quality data from the original source in a standardized manner without the need for physical database implementation

Implementation

- Solved real business problems in weeks and built incrementally without risk of redesign
- Started with desktop implementation and seamlessly moved to enterprise-wide scalability
- Budget of USD 0.5 million for year 1
- Capex of USD 0.1 million for software and data
- Potential savings of 50 to 75% from elimination of duplicate data and processes (based on previous experience)

Provided by Stephen Taylor, CEO of Stream Financial

(for which the data lakes were created in the first place) are especially vulnerable to this.

Increasingly, there are more use case-based, virtual alternatives to the massive data lakes that are inherently superior to the centralized approaches in many cases. Companies like Stream Financial in the United Kingdom or FireFly Information Management in Switzerland follow a virtual approach, not violating the integrity of the source. Rather than replicating sources, Stream Financial leaves them untouched and just provides fast access to the right data sets when the risk analysis is being performed. The fundamental advantages are:

- **Accountability:** The owners of the original data remain accountable for their data and its quality and cannot absolve themselves of this responsibility.
- **Transparency:** Drilling down to the most granular trade or position level is possible and gives end users a fully transparent view of the original source data.
- **Realistic ambition:** Many large organizations attempt to resolve their data problems by proposing a rebuilding of the entire systems architecture from scratch, which is far too difficult.
- **Local empowerment:** A softer but no less important benefit is that this approach empowers local teams since they retain ownership of the data.
- **Change facilitation:** Using a query-based rather than copy-based approach allows underlying data sources to continue to evolve, as they typically do, especially in the highly regulated financial services environment.
- **A posteriori:** To build a physical model in the database, most warehouse programs require a priori knowledge of all the possible questions required to be answered. The virtual approach adopts an a posteriori approach where all the data elements do not need to be established in advance. The end users do not need to know all of the possible questions they wish answered ahead of time. The infrastructure is more adaptable.
- **Cost and investment:** The central query engine is designed to run on vanilla hardware and uses highly compressed data. This allows superior performance to comparative appliances for a fraction of the cost. Moreover, there is no investment in duplication of storage.
- **Security and compliance:** The architecture facilitates following the necessary audit and compliance rules, which can be onerous in heavily regulated industries like financial services. Data can be anonymized on the fly, so queries on data sources where there are strict data privacy laws will be in compliance with those laws.

Of course, this virtual approach also needs governance, but it is architecturally designed around analytics use cases, and it avoids the pitfalls of trying to sail the data lakes. Your CFO will also like the benefit of this approach being intrinsically less expensive.

ANALYTICS IS JUST AN ANALYTICS CHALLENGE

Part I: The Last Mile

As mentioned before, data analytics has a logistics angle, since many players are involved, sometimes even hundreds or thousands. For illustration, let's look at an InsightBee use case in market intelligence, *The Last Mile*.

In this case, customized insights answering research requests get delivered to many decision makers at the right time in the right format via the right channel. This example also demonstrates that the logistics challenge can be far bigger than the actual analytic task. In fact, the vast majority of use cases are far less complex in terms of analytic depth, but far more demanding in terms of logistics.

From the InsightBee use case, we can see that the true challenges are (1) the collection of data, (2) the collection of analytics needs from the hundreds of decision makers, (3) the creation of Level 3 insights relevant to the individual end users, and (4) the handling of the workflow and the dissemination of the results. Figure I.5 shows the characteristics of the use case. We have thousands of data sources, some processing in the middle, and large numbers of decision makers and end users.

The term *Last Mile* applies here. It is widely used by telecommunications, cable television, and Internet service providers to refer to the part of the network chain that physically reaches the customer's house. We have borrowed this analogy for data analytics. Each decision maker has a certain bandwidth and protocol in which one can receive inputs (Level 3 insights). If a salesperson does not have the bandwidth to read a report, the insights do not even get the chance to create

InsightBee:
The Last Mile

Context

Organization
All organizations

Function(s)
All

Industry
All industries

Geography
Global

Business Challenge

- Facilitate exchange of information and transactions for knowledge-based services
- Provide research and analytics to thousands of end users directly via mobile devices
- Provide a foundation for research and analytics teams to launch complementary and value-added products and services

Solution

Thousands of end users: **Requests** ⬆⬇ **Last Mile delivery**

eCommerce Engine			
User interface	Request allocation	User management	Payment

Product Engine			
Manage standard reports	Configure new products	Enable human–data interaction	Generate reports

Knowledge Engine			
Knowledge model	Knowledge integration	Knowledge base	← External sources

Approach

Developed an agile cloud-based platform with:

- A simple interface to collect requests from thousands of users and deliver reports directly to their mobile devices
- A repository of standard products and use cases and flexible architecture to introduce new products
- A knowledge architecture that enables effective knowledge storage, reuse, and distribution

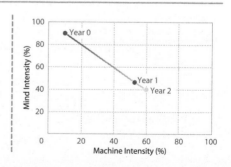

Analytics Challenges

- No standards for knowledge-intensive processes (e.g., research and analytics)
- Engaging on analytics projects on-demand involves significant administrative tasks
- Lack of building blocks for new analytics products
- Lack of AI solutions that can meaningfully address complex unstructured business questions

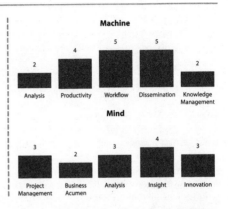

Benefits

Productivity	Time to Market	New Capabilities	Quality
• Over 90% reduction in time taken to conduct a transaction • Allows faster acquisition of customers by leveraging network effects	• Over 80% reduction in time taken to launch new product and services	• Ability to offer and administer a marketplace for new products • Ability to effectively reuse unstructured information and realize 'sharing economy'	• Significant improvement in user experience • Better quality insights from unstructured information through machine learning

Implementation

- Concept to minimum viable product (MVP): 6 months
- Initial cost: approx. USD 700 thousand
- Follow agile development methodology with a 3-week sprint schedule
- 3 additional development phases between Sept. 2014 and June 2016 costing an additional USD 4.1 million
- External partners included technology consulting firm, user experience designer, external development team, and experts in machine learning, text analytics and conversion optimization

The resulting platform provided:
- Possibility to rapidly build new features and test them with users
- Pay-as-you-go flexibility as clients only pay for reports that they order
- User-friendly mobile app interface

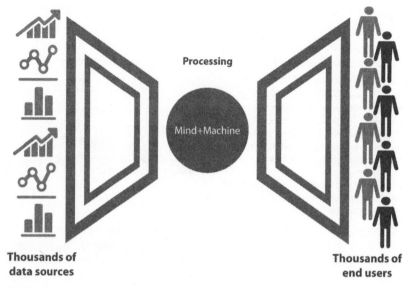

Figure I.5 The Last Mile

value. Similarly, if the reports are written in data scientist jargon, the service technicians won't understand, as they don't have the same protocol.

The Last Mile challenge is bidirectional, as it also applies to the analyst's ability to capture the context of the needs of the individual end user for specific analytics requests. Interviews with Evalueserve clients indicate that unless the end users' needs are met almost 100 percent, they are not going to be happy paying for the services delivered. In fact, the jump in terms of willingness to pay comes at about 90 percent customization or higher.

As an aside, this is a challenge currently faced by syndicated market research companies, as customized alternatives are available at a very reasonable cost. Analyst reports on certain industries or technologies are by definition targeted at the average customer, which in turn means that a large number of users won't have their needs met by these generic reports. If customers in such situations still want 100 percent of needs met, they have to buy expert consulting time at upwards of USD 3,000 per day.

The Last Mile is also highly relevant for the accounting and charging side of things. Companies have created very imaginative but very complex and expensive cross-charging mechanisms for the cost of centrally provided analytics services. This can become a major administrative trap. There is an energy company that bought a series of external services via a service division of the company, which in turn would cross-charge other divisions of the company for the services consumed. As this was a global company with lots of country organizations and lines of business, the accounting challenge became very complex. Guess what happened? This division started charging a premium surcharge to internal customers in order to become a profit center, and kept several people busy with the cross-charging activities—hardly the core business of an energy major!

The Last Mile concept is prevalent in many analytics use cases. The advent of Internet of Things and data analytics as a service (DAaaS) and the corresponding explosive growth in the number of use cases requires companies to come up with scalable and low-investment solutions to address their logistical challenges. There will be millions of use cases where the Last Mile applies at the beginning and/or the end of the analytics value chain. However, companies rarely have scalable platforms to distribute the Level 3 insights to the end user. Building point solutions for individual use cases will be too expensive in the future. However, running everything in the form of enterprise solutions requires scalable and easy-to-modify architectures that do not require IT projects for each change.

In addition, the needs of the Last Mile end user are changing rapidly. Decision makers and frontline employees are increasingly on the road and work in distributed teams. They want mobile solutions that are embedded in *their* workflow and save them time. They want Level 3 insights packaged in user-friendly ways, such as trigger-based alerting, and they want the logistics taken care of automatically (e.g., approval procedures, audit trails, or knowledge management). They don't want to sit down at workstations, go through log-in procedures, and work with multiple applications.

Fallacy #5

ANALYTICS IS JUST AN ANALYTICS CHALLENGE

Part II: The Organization

What are the various roles in the world of data analytics, and how do they interact?

Central data analytics and IT teams: Many companies have created strong central data analytics teams with various types of data scientists: the modelers and statisticians, who hold doctorates in financial mathematics, statistics, applied mathematics, operations research, and physics; the data stewards, who typically have master's degrees in computer science; the IT people in charge of the data architecture; the business analysts, who include MBA holders, financial risk managers, and chartered accountants; and the senior data analytics managers.

The primary issues with this whole population are their limited availability in the labor market and their annual costs, which (for an experienced team) can easily be USD 150,000 per head, or even up to USD 250,000. They must be able to prove their return on investment (ROI) in the medium term. We encountered a big industrial company that had created a central team with almost 100 full-time equivalents (FTEs), meaning somewhere around USD 20 million per year, and that's before counting any infrastructure costs. This group was cut significantly in a reorganization, which might indicate the perceived ROI.

I also know of a situation at a global bank that has a managing director of data analytics in wealth management. Managing directors usually cost the bank about USD 500,000 and upward on a fully loaded basis. This particular person told me that they were highly frustrated in their role, which involved "finding and implementing big data analytics in wealth management."

They said, "Marc, for the last 18 months I have been proposing use cases. So far, not even a single use case has made it beyond the PowerPoint stage. HQ Compliance shoots down every proposal at the end."

What a waste of resources—especially when you bear in mind that the USD 500,000 does not even include their team.

A McKinsey study predicts that by 2017, the United States will be short of individuals with deep big data and analytic skills by 140,000 to 190,000 people.[15] There is going to be a war for talent, and salaries are not going to decrease in such a situation.

Noncentral analytics teams: In many companies, there are also smaller noncentral teams of analysts. They generally consist of people who are closer to the business issue and further away from the central technology and IT functions.

Such units get created because the central teams are simply too far away from the business needs or because it is too complex to get anything done centrally due to the need to win the prioritization game. Or, as a business unit COO put it to me recently:

> "It takes a lot of effort to get the central teams to deliver exactly to our specs. I definitely do understand the position these guys are in. Every business unit fires requests at them. They need to prioritize. Moreover, IT isn't in their control, either. Getting an IT project under way usually means filing a request for capital expenditure, which needs to go the IT board for approval. Unfortunately, my business unit does not have the strongest of lobbies at the center. This means that we are getting things late, if at all. This is why I have decided to have a few business analysts near me, and get the rest outsourced to you."

The disadvantage is that noncentral teams usually don't have all the necessary skills and scale to run full analytics projects in the mind+machine mold end to end.

Business users: Ultimately, the business users are the end users of the analytics use case. This could be any function in the company. In international companies, the end users are usually spread out geographically, and increasingly cross-functional or cross–business unit. Of course, such dispersion adds complexity in several ways. The more different the user groups there are, the higher the likelihood that their objectives, needs, and organizational incentives will differ. Minds are minds and belong to imperfect humans with various agendas. It is surprising to see how much time it takes to align the decision makers' minds in many situations. Of course, the business users then report to the senior use case sponsor and budget holder either directly or indirectly. If you have a situation where there is only one budget holder, consider yourself lucky. In most companies, data analytics is an overlay function at multiple levels, which implies many decision makers and partial budget holders for any analytics use case.

Central risk and compliance team: In today's world of regulatory oversight and data protection laws, the risk and compliance folks have the power to bring down any project, and they do so frequently, mostly for very good reasons. Sometimes, though, internal compliance rules have been designed to create a safety buffer that regulators don't actually require. Nobody can judge whether such buffers are unnecessary or will be in the future, but the reality is that some of the rules remove a lot of the flexibility to execute analytics use cases, and correspondingly eliminate the potential for improvements—for example, enhanced productivity, shorter time to market, better quality, or new capabilities for the organization.

Here is an interesting example: a major universal banks cannot outsource any work containing client information. This sounds sensible given the current client confidentiality laws in many jurisdictions. However, one bank interprets these rules in exactly the same way for high-net-worth individuals and for normal B2B corporate clients. While the former is industry standard, the latter is not. This very strict interpretation creates an inability to conduct such work externally. As other banks do not follow this restriction, they might have a competitive advantage.

Business users should include their risk and compliance teams from the very beginning in order to avoid project failures due to unforeseen compliance issues down the line.

Here are two real-life examples. A US bank regularly conducts cross-selling campaigns where the idea is to sell new products to existing customers (e.g., student loans to credit card holders). When the data analytics team analyzed the data for student loans, they tried to find a proxy for someone being a student. What information about your client would you use? If you thought of age, you'd be wrong. Age is a data field that cannot be included in the search string for the search, as using the age field would expose the bank to the risk of discrimination on the basis of age. Any search string needs to be vetted by the legal team to make sure the bank does not get exposed to such risks. So now the team analyzes credit card transaction records to find out if the customers have bought academic books or materials. Personally, I would be much happier if the bank used my age rather than looking at my private purchase history!

In the second example, a very large wealth management firm looked at profiling high-net-worth prospects, analyzing their profiles, companies, and so on. Compliance stopped the project, because it would have involved giving the name of the prospect to an external party (even under a very strict nondisclosure agreement), which would violate the client confidentiality rules in spite of the prospects not even being clients yet. Since the client advisers needed the insights, they turned to Google to analyze their prospects. Interestingly, Google could in theory combine the firm's Internet protocol (IP) address and search terms to reconstruct the confidential information. This is an example of the relative immaturity of the data world and our understanding of it.

In both cases, it was essential to involve risk and compliance early.

Finance: The financial department is initially involved to set budgets for ongoing costs and up-front investments in the analytics functions. The corresponding budgeting is rarely done on a use case basis, but rather for an aggregate data analytics team, which makes it hard to show the ROI of individual use cases. Experienced sponsors of data analytics always make sure they have proof of the ROI. This is another topic that should be thought through early on and for each individual use case, as it can make the difference between having and not having a job in the future.

Orchestrating this multitude of players is complex even in the most positive of circumstances where everybody agrees with the objectives and the governance is clear. The complexity increases to an unsustainable level if all use cases are seen as a single blob of resources. BA Times lists some key areas where collaborations between these parties can go wrong, including incomplete stakeholder analysis, misunderstandings in terms of language used, rushing to design before the requirements are clear, approvals for fuzzy requirements, and late stakeholder involvement.[16]

Just counting the number of players and the potential for organizational conflicts shows that the business sponsor has to have the right leverage at headquarters to get things done centrally. This is probably more the exception than the rule. Company boards often embark on major spending sprees to set up large central teams because somebody has convinced the board that the future lies in big data. The central teams get endowed with a lot of authority to pull data, methodology, people, and use cases toward the center. After a few years, the CFO has started asking questions about ROI, but proof at the use case level has not been collected consistently and (more importantly) in formats approved by finance. There may not be even clear records of what the expected benefits should have been at the use case level. Then cost cutting begins. The losers are the end users, whose use cases remain unfulfilled.

Successful analytics approaches usually start in nimble ways, establish a solid use-case-based governance, think about the logistics issues, resist the temptation to go for large fixed costs and significant investments right away, and scale up from easy-to-communicate early wins.

Fallacy #6

REORGANIZATIONS WON'T HURT ANALYTICS

Reorganizations are increasingly frequent in today's global and dynamic economy. The drivers can be found in a variety of areas. Companies acquire other companies in classical mergers and acquisitions (M&A) or they adjust their internal structures because market conditions have changed, new technologies have been introduced, new markets are being explored, costs need to be cut, or sometimes simply for the sake of shaking up and reenergizing stale organizations. In addition to internal changes, the changing external environment brings along changing interfaces to a variety of external players such as suppliers, partners, channels, regulators, customers, interest groups, and many more. In a McKinsey study, 60 percent of surveyed managers said they had experienced a significant redesign in their organization during the previous two years.[17] Failure rates are well above 50 percent. The drivers for this increasing level of change are changing customer preferences, increased market dynamics, new competition emerging out of nowhere, new technologies, and generally higher levels of uncertainty and volatility.

You might ask what this has to do with mind+machine in data analytics. A great deal! This is probably the single most underestimated problem in data analytics, next to the compliance topic discussed before. As we will see, **built-in flexibility** has a lot of value!

In today's world, processes are highly interconnected, and the corresponding Level 1 data and Level 2 information flows and formats tend to become hardwired for obvious reasons. Automation requires programming of some kind. Once in place, code changes are only very reluctantly undertaken as this means additional spend. Systems such as enterprise resource planning (ERP), customer relationship management (CRM), data structures in databases, and reporting formats become rigid.

40

It is highly surprising to see how companies and managers believe that the most recent reorganization was the last one, at least for some time. It is certainly more hope than knowledge. Everyone seems to wish for stability, while the evidence suggests that the rate of change is accelerating.

My personal hypothesis after years of management consulting and research and analytics is that managers know that they are only going to be in their current positions for around three years. What happens afterward will no longer be their problem, but their successors'. (Are you also reminded of the attitude to the pension problem in many European countries or the way we treat the environment? Could this be a human characteristic?)

Because of this attitude, many analytic processes are not optimized for flexible change in the future, but to function for a fixed time frame. While it is fair to say that flexibility usually comes at a short-term cost, and information about what kind of flexibility will be required in the future isn't always available, if we want to build a sustainable mind+machine data analytics model with the flexibility to approach the coming huge number of use cases, we need to change.

As always, I would like to share an example. This is a small use case from the packaging industry. A leading supplier restructured three country organizations—Switzerland, Germany, and Austria—into a new, regional group with an integrated leadership and a unified marketing function. The newly designated regional marketing manager needed the consolidated Level 2 market share information for the region for all relevant package sizes. The underlying Level 1 data needed to be aggregated in a new way to reflect the new organizational structure. Unfortunately, the data provider's underlying Level 1 data structure was different for the three countries in terms of naming conventions and package sizes.

We were brought in to create a new overlay data framework that would deliver comparable market share data for the three countries and could be aggregated correctly into an overall regional market share. About two months and EUR 25,000 later, we had an Excel-based macro that could convert the basic Level 1 data from each country into consistent Level 2 information. The macro can be run with a single click and is flexible enough to be adjusted with very little effort to compensate for any future changes in the mapping table. It can be used even for any other region in the world at a fraction of the initial cost, provided that the mapping logic has been established. Moreover, the Level 4 knowledge of the logic is now properly stored for future reference, model audits, and reuse.

Why did it take so long to create this model? This aggregation level had never existed before, and there were quite a few discussions as to what was relevant. Some intermediate levels of packaging sizes needed to be dropped, as they simply did not exist in the other two countries. The main issue was the delay in decision making about the framework, not the actual working time by the analytics team, which is a very common issue in data analytics.

Market Intelligence Solution Suite:
Build for Flexibility

Context

Organization
Industrial conglomerate

Function(s)
Strategy

Industry
Capital goods & services

Geography
Global, HQ in Europe

Business Challenge

- Eliminate tendency to multiple versions of the information
- Manage large amount of quantitative and qualitative data of strategic interest
- Streamline knowledge sharing across globally spread decision makers

Solution

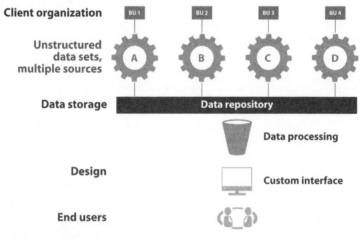

Client organization — BU 1, BU 2, BU 3, BU 4

Unstructured data sets, multiple sources — A, B, C, D

Data storage — Data repository

Data processing

Design — Custom interface

End users

Approach

- Designed a customized, modular, yet fully unified cloud-based tool that was standardized across business units (BUs).
- Set up a cross-functional team of technology experts, business analysts, and data analysts
- Established an efficient process for future upload and exchange of information, including automated classification of all transactions

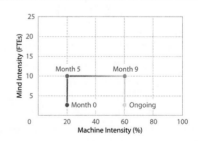

Analytics Challenges

- Structuring all the input and output cases, by establishing thousands of business rules using a high volume of unstructured data
- Standardization of data representation and terminology across all business divisions
- Designing solution allowing full flexibility of visualizations
- Standardization of tool without ignoring specific business unit needs

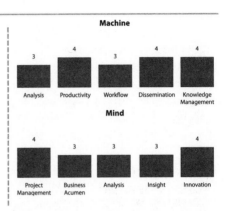

Benefits

Productivity	Time to Market	New Capabilities	Quality
• Centralized repository with unlimited capacity and global access for all business divisions	• Developed a solution suite hosting data of all business divisions and addressing needs of business users with varied profiles within 9 months	• New process for upload and exchange of information • Full flexibility for analyses, visualizations, and scenario building with high volume of data	• Standardized across business divisions • More than 90% first-time-right and on-time delivery

Implementation

- Integrated data for four business divisions in 9 months, with plan to integrate three more
- Established 1,000+ business rules to structure input and output cases
- Reduced manual effort for repetitive tasks by ~90%

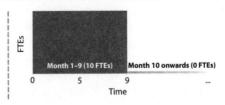

This was a very simple but very common use case. If such an easy problem could keep management busy for several months, you can imagine what must go on in more complex situations.

Another example comes from a yearlong integration project following an acquisition in the financial benchmarks industry. Earlier, a foresighted senior management team had already established clear governance rules for the integration of data-intensive acquisitions. They decided to take the acquired company's data and put it entirely on the acquirer's platform. The insight was that future acquisitions might happen and multiple production platforms would cause problems down the road. Sure enough, less than a year later, another acquisition was on the table. There was also an interesting learning in the area of data compliance, specifically intellectual property (IP) rights. An IP audit showed that a lot of attention needed to be given to the acquired data assets such that the integration did not cause any breaches of third-party IP rights. In general, the question of IP rights will gain a lot of importance in the future, as many companies' commercial models will contain the selling of pure data and information products.

In Part III we will propose a granular intellectual property architecture that will allow the creation of information products in a supply chain similar to the nested Tiers 1–3 automotive supply chain where companies like Toyota and BMW buy subsystems from their Tier 1 vendors, who in turn buy sub-subsystems from Tier 2 vendors, and so on.

These two examples had positive outcomes, but this is not always the case. As one of our clients put it recently:

> "I have given up. If I start the process for an IT adjustment to my analytics system now, it will be at least six months before I get the approval, if I get it at all considering the current cost-cutting environment. I have great ideas for lots of initiatives, but I will no longer be in this job by the time we get the approvals."

An implementation of a platform built for future flexibility is shown in *Marketing Intelligence Solution Suite,* where each division has its own modular setup. Future organizational changes require only changes to a module, while the overall platform remains unaffected.

As stability is an illusion or wishful thinking at best, there is a fundamental need for flexibility and protection of today's investments. We need **use case life cycle management** with built-in mechanisms to create the flexibility for the future knowing that things will change.

KNOWLEDGE MANAGEMENT IS EASY— WE JUST NEED SOME WIKIS

In this chapter we will take a closer look at knowledge management, which is an issue that will decide on the level of ROI for a whole class of use cases in the future. ROI is defined to include financial profitability, but also other benefits such as productivity, time to market, quality, or new capabilities, which are harder to quantify but still essential considerations.

Knowledge management is a tricky area in general. According to the Delphi Group, 7 to 20 percent of employees' working time is spent on reinventing the wheel, and 44 percent of employees are poor or very poor at transferring knowledge.[18]

Let's begin by categorizing the use cases according to whether they are already known and their level of return.

- **Known use case, known high return:** The low-hanging fruit of use cases (e.g., cross-selling in banking) have been around for quite a while. We could call them the "known no-brainers," but that would not do justice to the data scientists, as there is definitely a lot of brainpower involved in such use cases. As these use cases are highly profitable, companies can afford to reinvent them all the time.
- **Known use case, unknown return:** While we have not been able to collect solid statistics, I would estimate based on experience that about 80 percent of all known use cases fall into this category. Very few companies are geared up to analyze the profitability of individual use cases. They might know the overall costs of running analytics centrally, and possibly of some dedicated decentral analysts, but systematically capturing the benefits is

45

still something that very few companies do. Ideally, proper data governance should reveal the profitability of each use case and there should be clear Level 4 knowledge about successful and failed cases to ensure that failures are not repeated.

- **Known use case, negative return:** Companies with good governance kill failed use cases early on. However, many companies keep hanging on to them, because killing an analytic feed for someone else can turn out to be harder than it looks initially. We will see in Part III that the "fail fast" governance principle is critical in a world of increasing numbers of use cases and data sources.
- **Unknown use case, high return:** These are the gold nuggets everybody is trying to find. As we have seen in the big data chapter, small data use cases can be highly profitable, since they cost less. Big data use cases may or may not generate high returns. The question is how to find these golden nuggets. Are there patterns? Can we learn from other companies? Here clearly, knowledge management and reuse might have a major impact.
- **Unknown use case, marginal return:** This category could be transformed into high-return use cases if there was reuse. This group of use cases is very large and growing quickly. Companies that can adapt use cases quickly and flexibly have the chance to generate returns that their competitors might not be able to gain.

Everybody looking at use cases in this way would probably agree that reuse and knowledge management would make sense. However, what we see is a massive lack of knowledge management at many levels.

Remember the secondary use cases, the micro-variations of primary use cases? Senior managers often want the analysis done quickly. The employee who did it last time is likely to be chosen to do it again this time, so there is probably reuse and the knowledge management is done in the analyst's brain and Excel folder. But what happens when this employee rotates into a new position outside this department or even leaves the company?

We had experience with a global investment bank that lost 75 percent of its China front-office analysts in 2015, and with them all of the models and accumulated knowledge! Another bank lost 65 percent of its first-year analyst class in the United States in 2015. Granted, these examples of attrition are probably extreme cases. However, even in companies with lower overall attrition there is a big issue. Data scientists and smart business analysts are a very sought-after breed of professionals, not just by external companies or executive search firms, but also by internal competition.

Here is real-life example of internal poaching from a retail and commercial bank in the United States. According to the head of marketing analytics:

"Our risk department had just been told by the regulators to hire another 50+ risk analysts by the end of the year. Of course, there aren't 50+

experienced risk analysts in the job market, or only at prohibitive costs, so what does Risk do? They approach our marketing data scientists for internal job rotations for career development, and now I am losing some of my best people. How do I backfill? Well, I can't find enough people in the US anymore."

With primary use cases—the fundamental use cases addressing specific business issues—there are two levels of reuse and knowledge management: internally and between companies. To cut a long story short, we can say that knowledge management is still at an embryonic stage.

On the internal front, companies' central departments try to collect whatever knowledge they are responsible for. However, as soon as one goes to the frontline units (e.g., option pricing models on a bank's trading floor), it becomes increasingly rare. Even if some version of knowledge management is used, it usually collects the code for some specific tools (e.g., statistical packages or big data platforms), but hardly information pertaining to the ROI or the client benefits of the use cases.

Is this the organization's fault? Not really. Due to the lack of use–case-based thinking, there are simply no formats or tools to effectively store and manage vast numbers of use cases. In Part III we will discuss the methodology that can remedy this situation.

Sharing of knowledge between companies is even less common. Most of it happens between the heads of analytics at conferences or informally. Again, there are no commonly accepted formats for such exchanges, nor are there commercial models that work. Why should I give away my knowledge for no return? There is no currency for the exchange of use cases between companies.

Fortunately, some vendors have woken up to the issue and are offering exchanges: the Software AG marketplace, Teradata libraries, and Microsoft Azure. However, the problem in these instances is that they capture the knowledge management only for their own software, not for other components of the analytics value chain. Moreover, they capture neither information relating to the ROI of the use cases nor meta-level information about compliance, mappings, formats, IP ownership of data, and so on, unless specifically programmed to do so.

We should also consider the portfolio level of use cases: the complete set of all use cases a company runs. A European automotive manufacturer told us recently that the number of primary use cases in areas related to the Internet of Things (e.g., preventive maintenance) is going to grow from 50 to 500 from 2015 to 2017. This means that we are talking about some 25,000 secondary use cases that need to be managed—a truly daunting number. If the knowledge management already fails at the use case level, how can it work at the portfolio level?

Even if we had the tools and the formats, there is one more issue: use case governance. There needs to be an owner of the portfolio of use cases. Which CXO (the X stands for a whole zoo of different executives) should be this owner: the chief information officer (CIO), CFO, some kind of a chief data officer (CDO), or even the business or functional owners? Second, governance principles need to be signed off at the executive team level. These include rules such as "fail fast" or "kill unprofitable use cases." Third, there need to be the tools and processes to manage the use case portfolios. Part III of this book will look at governance in more detail.

Finally, risk and compliance functions have to be considered. As the CEO of a major European universal bank told the audience at a philanthropy event in 2013: "Last year we were hit with 88,000 regulatory changes across the globe." Even if the bank had the same number of employees and gave one change to every employee, they could not solve the problem, as many of these regulatory issues cannot be solved individually—they affect each other.

One investment bank has 6,500 different models (primary analytics use cases in our terminology) for pricing products or valuing assets. The challenge is that the bank found out that it has no systematic audit trail of who did what to these models at what time. Unfortunately, lots of products depend on such models either directly or indirectly.

The 2012 scandal involving manipulation of the London Interbank Offered Rate (LIBOR) shows very clearly what can happen when there is no audit trail and insufficient checks and balances on an underlying model or primary use case. Contracts worth USD 300 trillion were based on the LIBOR reference interest rate in 2012. Everybody using LIBOR *assumed* that it has been calculated correctly. When the probably criminal collusion to calculate LIBOR was revealed, the ticking time bomb exploded and the damage was incredible. Similarly, the 2015 Volkswagen scandal shows that a piece of test software can sneak into the product and be copied more than 10 million times with everybody *assuming* that it does the right calculations—until the time bomb explodes.

Ask yourself this: for how many analytics use cases are you the recipient, not the author? Imagine if one of the 10 most important inputs turned out to be flawed in major ways. Congratulations if you (1) know the risk already *and* (2) you have quantified the effects *and* (3) someone in your organization has the audit trail to prove to you that there is no ticking time bomb.

Use case governance should not just include ROI and benefits, but also assess the analytic risk, which needs to include all the downstream effects of any use case (e.g., product liability claims for truck manufacturers due to their preventive maintenance models built into their trucks). There is also a big limitation of being able to assess the downstream risks, as the author or owner of the use case might not even be aware that it has become embedded in downstream products or use cases. Nevertheless, there might be a liability arising from being the owner or author.

For now you should take away that there is currently a huge amount of waste and risk built into analytics in most companies, and given the coming growth in the number of use cases, this problem needs to be addressed urgently.

INTELLIGENT MACHINES CAN SOLVE ANY ANALYTIC PROBLEM

Artificial intelligence (AI) is making good progress, and the number of use cases for AI is growing. Clearly, use cases in the context of national security and academia have driven the development of "intelligent" algorithms analyzing massive text, voice, and video data feeds from telecommunications, payment networks, and the surveillance infrastructure. Several companies founded by former national security analysts apply these technologies to civilian use cases (e.g., email and chat surveillance of banking employees), which would clearly be impossible without such algorithms.

For very specific use cases, AI can do things more efficiently and quickly than even the brains of our super-smart data scientists. However, practical tests in real-life situations show that AI is helpful in very specific, narrow use cases for Level 1 data or Level 2 information, but hardly ever for Level 3 insight or Level 4 knowledge.

My objective here is to enable you to ask the right questions when confronted with hyped marketing collateral from vendors or pitches by super-enthusiastic data scientists among your staff. The main point is not that AI does not work but rather that it is limited to a certain level of use cases and to certain steps in the overall value chain of analytics. If used appropriately (i.e., with an understanding of its limitations and risks), it can be very valuable, enhancing human productivity as a part of the mind+machine approach.

Especially the domains of human creativity and interaction, the ability to spot and react to **new** patterns (as opposed to **known** patterns), to understand the broader business context, to differentiate between correlations and root-cause relationships, and to tell machines what to do will continue to be fundamentally human traits, at least for the foreseeable future. All of these traits are key ingredients for creating Level 3 insights or Level 4 knowledge. The main question is how to make this mind+machine collaboration work profitably in real life for a huge number of vastly different and dynamic use cases.

At Evalueserve, we use quite a bit of AI and machine learning to support our human analysts along the end-to-end use case journey. A nice little example is the machine-learning algorithm used for innovation scouting, where companies look for innovations they could use for their future products (see *Intellectual Property: Managing Value-Added IP Alerts*). Among other things, companies look at the competition's newly published patent applications to understand the potential impact they might have on their own in-market products or research and development (R&D) projects. An AI-based linguistic algorithm trained on patents automatically rates the relevance of each newly published patent for our respective clients' product and development portfolios and indicates a percentage of relevance to a human patent analyst, who then makes the final decision on whether it is relevant by clicking one of two buttons: Relevant or Not Relevant. This judgment is client-specific, as it includes the particular context of the client, as opposed to a model where we just look at the impact on a specific general technology. Each decision the human analyst makes gets then incorporated into the machine through machine-learning techniques, with the hope that the algorithm will get even better at deciding the level of relevance. Alerts for relevant patents will then be sent to the specific clients interested in that particular technology. The big advantage of this approach is the elimination of clutter. Our clients simply don't have the time to read reports of simplistic alerts from commercial databases. Note again: the AI algorithm is limited to a very specific part of the end-to-end creation of these alerts.

Many positive and very powerful uses of AI exist, but our experience testing AI engines for creating Level 2 information and Level 3 insights has been quite sobering, even for relatively simple problems. For Evalueserve's InsightBee Market Intelligence product, we needed a capability to semiautomatically search sources, select the most relevant facts, structure them, and feed them into a template that the human analyst could then work from. The objective was to improve the productivity of answering simple business questions or creating profiles of executives, companies, and industries.

We tested 25 commercially available AI engines in a global evaluation exercise. Only one of them, Squirro of Switzerland, was able to do a part of the job. The efficiency improvement was present, but still limited. The investment in this engine could be justified, but only because InsightBee has very significant volumes of work every year. Use cases with smaller volumes would probably not justify the significant investments yet.

The findings from these evaluations are probably representative of many AI use cases:

- The claims of the other 24 AI engines were strongly overstated.
- Even the Squirro engine needed quite a bit of training and fine-tuning for each individual primary use case and its variations.
- The productivity benefits of AI were limited to a relatively small scope in the overall workflow. Overall, the end-to-end cost of an InsightBee report is about half of the same report if produced by human analysts not using automation. However, the productivity gains come from several sources, of which the use of AI is only one. The most significant benefits come from the use of automated database interfaces (ADIs), a smart workflow system with optimized processes, specialized text editors and formatting tools, a semi-automated publishing engine, and a specialized knowledge-object-based knowledge management (KM) system called K-Hive that optimizes reuse. AI helped in collecting data from unstructured sources and presenting the most relevant findings to the human analyst for further evaluation and synthesis.
- AI helped with finding Level 1 data and with extracting relevant Level 2 information that could then be fed into the draft reports as raw materials. It did not derive any Level 3 insights or Level 4 knowledge by itself.
- The AI part was rather black-box and nontransparent, producing a lot of false positives, and the quality of the output needed to be fully reviewed by a human. Of course, it was clear that the engine would search the web and other sources, but the trials clearly demonstrated three fundamental issues with such approaches: (1) the lack of a transparent audit trail, (2) the false positives, and (3) the 80 percent quality issue (see later discussion for more details).
- Engineering the use cases took several weeks and very close collaboration. It was not something that we could afford for a one-off use case. This shows that AI is probably more applicable to very frequent and identical situations.
- It would not have been possible to come up with such engines in-house because of the complexity of building the engine. Squirro now acts like a Tier 2 supplier for our overall supply chain, and InsightBee acts like Toyota or Airbus (i.e., the integrator of multiple technologies needed to achieve the end-to-end benefits).
- The secondary use case was very specific. Even a minor deviation created an essentially new use case. The vision of having smart algorithms that can flexibly solve broad ranges of analytics use cases on their own is still a dream.

Let's now look at the three fundamental issues already mentioned: (1) the black-box nature of AI, (2) the false positives, and (3) the lack of proof of completeness.

Intellectual Property:
Managing Value-Added IP Alerts

Context

Organization
Global fast-moving consumer goods (FMCG) manufacturer

Industry
FMCG

Function(s)
Global IP & legal services

Geography
Global, HQ in Europe

Business Challenge

- Streamline and standardize the process of collecting, screening, tagging, and disseminating accurate IP and R&D information in a timely manner
- Reduce the amount of data that required screening and tagging by the client

Solution

Evalueserve analysts

Patents
Journals

Data searching   Screening

Client analysts

Review screening   Technology tagging

Client end users: R&D and legal teams

Repository of tagged documents   Receive alerts   Legal risk flagging

Approach

- Set up a dedicated team of business analysts with local market insight and data analysts for data-heavy initiatives
- Designed central data engine for storage and reuse of internal and external market information
- Developed over 15 market inventory reports covering key verticals and largest geographical markets
- Aggregated key market information in dashboards and set up a document repository platform

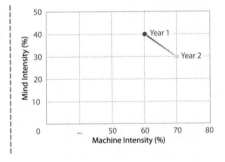

Analytics Challenges

- Creating a single integrated workflow accessible online by all individuals involved
- Providing a central dashboard to supervise the workflow status and manage the tasks
- Providing a dedicated environment for reviewing and tagging tasks in a protocolized and efficient manner
- Sending tailored alert notifications to client end users
- Automatically generating periodic trend and competitor reports using the repository data

Machine

Analysis	Productivity	Workflow	Dissemination	Knowledge Management
2	2	5	4	3

Mind

Project Management	Business Acumen	Analysis	Insight	Innovation
5	3	2	5	3

Benefits

Productivity	Time to Market	New Capabilities	Quality
• 14,000 patents analyzed per month • 40% productivity gain via automation • Serves 200 end users at client and Evalueserve	• Platform built in 4 months • New clients can be up and running within 1 month	• Single repository with latest updates and trend reports • Standardized configurable online workflow • Seamless collaboration across teams	• Machine reduces the amount of relevant documents that were missed by Mind by 10%

Implementation

- Secure cloud-based instance deployed within 48 hours
- Client-ready solution operational within 1 month
- 100 analyst hours per month for client workflow
- Opex of USD 0.14 million for solution for year 1

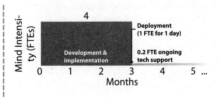

Being a black box is an inherent property of most AI methodologies due to proprietary technology and algorithms. But this creates a real issue. While black-box algorithms have been shown to produce useful results, they truly work only if everything is used correctly and the risks and limitations are fully understood. If a mistake is made due to an incorrect application or someone not understanding the limitations, the audit trail may fail—nobody will be able to reconstruct what happened in a black box.

Let me give you an example to illustrate the headaches and sleepless nights that might be caused. There is an AI methodology called a "deep belief network." How would you feel if you were a compliance officer of a bank and your 27-year-old executive director informed you that the bank is using a deep belief network to find patterns in the movements of commodity prices that the bank is betting USD 50 million on? Hearing the definition won't make you feel better: "A deep belief network is a probabilistic, generative model made up of multiple layers of **hidden units**."[19]

Such algorithms have been shown to produce useful results, and we can safely assume that some hedge funds made a lot of money using such models in algorithmic trading. The big issue is that everything is fine only if everything is used correctly and the risks and limitations are fully understood. However, as soon as one of the actors makes a mistake or hands over the model or code to someone who does not understand its limitations and risks, disaster is in the offing. The USD 50 million might suddenly be just USD 40 million and nobody would know why. There would be no audit trail of why the model did what it did, as per definition the units are hidden. The bank would simply be forced to write off USD 10 million. Under current financial regulations, the managing director who signed the declaration that risk management is fully implemented and working properly at the bank could even go to prison.

There are few specialists who really understand all these AI models and have the experience of dealing with them. At the minimum, independent human controls need to be in place to check what the AI is doing in your company, and you need to understand the risks involved.

False positives are the second issue. So-called intelligent search engines are supposed to deliver highly relevant search results. We all have everyday experiences with this reality: Google, Bing, or Baidu all seem to deliver accurate results. However, let's look a little more closely.

When you enter the search term "artificial intelligence" in the Google search bar, you get 68 million hits in about 0.6 seconds. How many do you really look at? Do you ever go beyond the first two or three pages? If you don't—and I believe most people don't—there are 67,999,970 unused hits. How many of these are really relevant, and how many aren't? Irrelevant results are called false positives (or type II errors = "failure to reject"), whereas relevant hits that are not seen are called false negatives (or type I errors = "incorrect rejection"). Everybody wants to minimize both the false positives and the false negatives. This creates an inherent trade-off. If the gold pan needs to capture every small golden nugget, it catches lots of unwanted rocks. If the gold pan has large holes, it will miss the small golden nuggets. What we would need are adaptive holes in our pan.

However, when we need to be absolutely sure that either we found all relevant search results or there are no unwanted hits, because the costs of making a mistake would be very high, we still need a human mind because it involves true judgment based on many factors that are not even contained in the data.

In a recent case, a bank was trying to build an internal search engine to search millions of pages of documents so that the bankers could find relevant pages in former pitches, saving them a lot of time by not having to re-create them from scratch. There needs to be a filter to ensure that no client-confidential materials, for example the ideas for a new M&A transaction, end up in a pitch for that client's competitor. This type of information is called material nonpublic information (MNPI). If MNPI leaks out into the market, the financial and reputational damage could be huge—in the billions of dollars. In this case example, the issue is that AI is currently not in a position to judge if a presentation slide contains MNPI unless the slide was tagged as MNPI. Even the tagging is problematic, as the status might change over time, and the effort to keep the tagging of millions of slides under control would be uneconomical.

False positives can create a lot of rework and risks in some situations. Minimizing them is the objective, but it has a cost attached. You need to be able to ask the right questions of your team members in order to judge the trade-offs.

The 80 percent quality issue shows up in cases where the quality of the product needs to be very high—100 percent or almost 100 percent according to some service-level agreements (SLAs). To illustrate the problem, let me present a case where Evalueserve wanted to create an information product called CXO Link with the help of AI. It should show the **shortest possible route** from a banker to the relevant executives or board members of a prospect. For example, the banker knows CEO A, who also sits on the board of Company B, where he served alongside CEO C, who is the banker's target person for the pitch. There was an existing product in the market called Relationship Science, but it was expensive, and our clients were trying to find cheaper alternatives. The only way to produce a cheaper alternative was to try out an AI-based approach that could sift through millions of documents (disclosures, annual reports, articles, etc.) looking for apparent (e.g., boards, charities) or hidden (e.g., golf clubs) relationships between such key decision makers. After a lot of testing, we could get the AI algorithm to produce a very nice quality of about 80 percent. The team was really proud of this achievement. Unfortunately for us, 80 percent correctness still implies 20 percent incorrectness, which was too much compared to the competition. And then we faced the fundamental problem of AI: how could we know which 20 percent were wrong? A data record does not usually look at you and tell you that it is wrong. You only find it out the hard way when the client tells you that

Investment Banking Analytics:
Logo Repository

Context

Organization
Investment banks

Function(s)
M&A advisory and capital markets

Industry
Financial services

Geography
Global

Business Challenge

- Make clean, high-resolution, background-free company logos readily available for investment banking pitch books

Solution

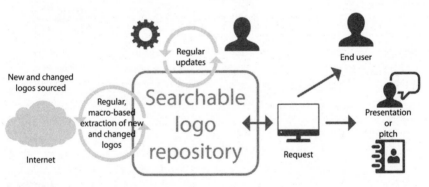

Analyst and design teams

Regular updates

End user

New and changed logos sourced

Regular, macro-based extraction of new and changed logos

Internet

Searchable logo repository

Request

Presentation or pitch

Approach

- Created a centralized project management office (PMO) to train teams to identify and analyze efficiency improvement opportunities
- Created a standard definition for the efficiency gains index, agnostic of the nature of the work being done by the various teams
- Established rules for efficiency gain sharing, hierarchical roll-up, and location indexes
- Created a live dashboard to summarize data along with multilayered analysis

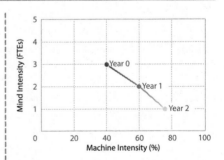

Analytics Challenges

- Lack of centralized logo repository
- Lack of availability of high-quality logos online
- Significant time spent on repetitive cleaning of the same logos
- Time to market of final document dependent on availability of specialized design personnel

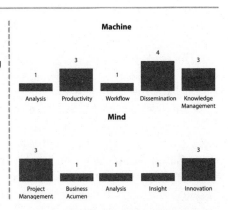

Machine

| Analysis | Productivity | Workflow | Dissemination | Knowledge Management |
| 1 | 3 | 1 | 4 | 3 |

Mind

| Project Management | Business Acumen | Analysis | Insight | Innovation |
| 3 | 1 | 1 | 1 | 3 |

Benefits

Productivity	Time to Market	New Capabilities	Quality
• Centralized repository benefiting multiple client teams • Up to 75% time saved in the overall process of using logos for pitch books	• Faster access to clean logos, leading to reduced overall cycle time while creating pitch book slides	• Form-based logo extraction interface developed on top of Microsoft suite of products	• Quick access to high-quality logos, increasing the quality of the final product

Implementation

- Set up of specialized design team to create logo bank in year 1
- Roll-out of tool to multiple client situations in year 2 along with strengthening of logo base
- Year 3 onward, minimal design support required to maintain and update logo database

the quality was insufficient. How to fix it? By way of human, manual rework. But here is the issue: You need to redo the work for 100 percent of all records, not just for the wrong 20 percent. This effect ultimately killed the product, since 100 percent human rework defeated the objective of creating a low-cost product.

Of course, a proponent of AI would now say that our AI programmers were simply not good enough, and that our AI algorithms could have been improved. Perhaps this is true, although we had quite a few super-smart data scientists on the job. However, the effort required would have been too big compared to the ultimate market of the product, which is why we abandoned the project. Had we known about this issue beforehand, we could have run some limited tests and saved a lot of time and money.

In another case, executives at a major commercial and investment bank told us about their compliance efforts in the areas of email, various online chat channels, and other electronic communication channels. The COO told us that they are investing double-digit millions of dollars into compliance software that tries to find suspicious patterns in written text. However, their finding was that such AI-based software still catches only the known and obvious cases, the so-called known unknowns. It cannot catch the unknown unknowns, as, per definition, the AI can check Level 1 data and possibly Level 2 information rules efficiently, but it does not act as the creative Sherlock Holmes who operated at Level 3 insight. Coded messages such as "The sun is green today" might convey insider information about a certain trade or company, but if this case has never been captured before, the software would not identify this as suspicious (yet). After realizing this deficiency of the AI-based approach, the bank implemented a human reviewing policy where every superior has to invite his or her team members at random intervals for a four-eye review of all email and chat sessions of the prior two business weeks. The COO said:

> "This has done more to the culture in our firm than any technical surveillance we could have ever achieved. To our surprise, a positive side effect of this measure was also that the interpersonal tone of the emails started improving dramatically. Of course, it is a huge investment in terms of working time, but it did the job—at all levels."

Another important dimension of looking at AI is its overall share in automation benefits. Of course, well-designed AI can contribute a lot in absolute terms, but it covers only a limited part of any end-to-end use case due to the characteristics mentioned earlier. In fact, our estimates show that AI contributes only about 20 percent of the overall automation benefits on average, while the other factors such as workflow platforms, productivity tools, analytics engines, formatting and dissemination engines, and knowledge management (KM) contribute the remaining 80 percent. Please also remember that AI really contributes close to zero percent at Level 3 insight.

Very few of the one billion use cases are high-AI-content use cases. For most of the more mundane, worldly use cases, the application of AI is far more restricted. This means that the one billion primary use cases have a far lower average applicability of AI, as either it is not economical or the use cases are too complex.

In order to understand the benefits of AI, we first need to define the dimensions of automation benefits. For this we introduce the **client benefits framework** (**productivity, time to market, quality, new capabilities**). Some experienced readers will know the classic cost-time-quality framework. We used it a lot at McKinsey & Co. However, at Evalueserve we had to come up with the expanded client benefits framework, since time to market expresses the time dimension more clearly, and the new capabilities dimension was missing altogether. All use cases displayed in this book give an overview of the client benefits according to these four dimensions:

1. **Productivity:** The automation productivity benefit is defined as the number of human working hours saved by applying automation divided by the number of human working hours *not* applying any automation for the same end-to-end use case. In pitch book production for investment banks, we see up to 30 to 40 percent productivity benefit from automation for some clients. This means that for every 10 analysts, automation reduces the need to six or seven analysts.

2. **Time to market:** Time to market is about being faster than the competition. Consulting firms invest heavily in processes that allow them to hand in their proposals more quickly, which requires a series of fundamental process changes. Similarly, the asset management industry has also understood that their pitches to pension funds and other institutional investors need to become more streamlined. We are seeing reductions in throughput time of up to 33 percent.

3. **New capabilities:** This has become the dominant dimension in many of my discussions with clients these days as they request new ways to increase competitiveness. It includes things like building complete data assets from scratch, such as an environmental, social, and governance (ESG) index requiring the analysis of well over 1,800 companies, or enabling completely new ways to present content where the slides are dynamically linked to the data, which allows for a far more interactive discussion due to the live drill-down capabilities.

4. **Quality:** Increasingly, quality refers not just to low error rates, but also to audit trails and model checks. Two examples of current approaches are financial models that include automated checks for allowed parameter ranges, and reducing the likelihood of simplistic human errors such as factor-of-10 errors due to wrong placement of the decimal point. Creating audit trails for changes to models helps improve the accountability, since the records show clearly who made what change at what point in time.

These four factors are the underlying drivers for the ROI of any use case, so planning, execution, and assessment should always apply this framework.

Where do the automation benefits stem from in each factor? There are five sources of productivity benefits: analytics tools including AI, productivity enhancements (processes and tools), workflow platforms (processes and tools), publishing and dissemination engines, and knowledge management (processes and tools). For the vast majority of use cases, smarter processes supported by some pretty straightforward tools get you 80 percent there. AI is the 20 percent icing on the cake.

The use case *Investment Banking Analytics: Logo Repository* is one of my favorites. It is such a trivial idea that it is almost embarrassing presenting it to clients. It involves a central, multiple-client library of 40,000 clean logos and a PowerPoint plug-in that places the right logos at the right places in pitches. This process change saves about 12,000 working hours per year for the average investment bank, meaning the bankers can focus on more exciting activities—like going after clients. The only AI in this use case is some limited machine learning around the size and the position of the logos after placing them—smart, but not really driving more than 20 percent of the benefits. The 80 percent was from using a smarter process, a library that can be used across clients, a fairly simple plug-in, and some deep understanding of desktop publishing (DTP) processes.

Another good example is *Intellectual Property: Managing Value-Added IP Alerts* discussed earlier, in which smart machine learning is applied to a relevance rating of recently published patents. While that's really useful and helpful, 90 percent of the automation benefits come from a smart workflow, automated formatting of the alerts, automated dissemination, and KM, as with an increasing number of customers there is significant reuse of work already performed. There are many more use cases like these. But again, helpful as it is, AI contributes only a part of the value.

For all the reasons mentioned, there has to be mind+machine playing together in a well-orchestrated manner for the vast majority of use cases. I hope I have also shown you that the term Machine is much broader than AI and includes many other elements, such as ADIs and tools for workflow, productivity, dissemination, and knowledge management.

EVERYTHING MUST BE DONE IN-HOUSE!

The risk and compliance functions of banks and corporations have become bigger and more powerful since the financial crisis of 2008 and other recent scandals. The culture in companies seems to have shifted from an attitude of trusting the employee to one of distrust and surveillance affecting even the most loyal employees. Compliance has gained a level of unassailable institutional power and authority. Granted, there was a need for increased compliance—the financial crisis and other events were real. However, it does not generate revenues and is not a source of competitive advantage. Compliance is a high direct and indirect cost to the business with a fundamental perspective of "No, we cannot" rather than "Yes, we can." To be fair, this attitude reflects the role of the compliance functions—they are paid to be risk averse.

Compliance affects analytics in multiple ways. Depending on the use case, various angles need to be analyzed. For example, in marketing-related cross-selling analytics, client confidentiality and discrimination laws matter. For calculations of indexes, the key topics are the correctness of the calculations and potential conflicts of interest by banks holding positions of assets based on such indexes. Therefore, each use case has a compliance profile with varying degrees of priority for each dimension. This complexity doesn't make anybody's life easier.

Now comes the crucial part. There are certainly layers of compliance that are simply prescribed by the regulators or are needed to avoid risks. However, there are layers of compliance that are self-imposed by the organization, either knowingly or unknowingly, limiting the company's freedom to do business and to compete. Granted, not everything is black and white. The regulators' rules have to be interpreted. Sometimes regulators in different geographies have different views and priorities on the same issues. Global companies are certainly caught in this dynamic web of rules, as some regulations are in the pipeline and it is not clear how they will turn out at the end after all lobbying is said and done.

This leads to situations where compliance functions need to decide if they go for maximum anticipatory compliance—even if it is not necessary in certain jurisdictions—or for a very precise approach, carving out each niche of the multidimensional compliance space, fighting on behalf of the company, defending every bit of freedom to do business. The jury is still out on which approach will ultimately prevail.

From a vendor's perspective, it is interesting to see the differences across our client base. Sometimes the interpretations and corresponding actions are starkly different across companies in the same industry. For example, some banks have decided to sell off their index businesses, since they feel they will not be able to address the inherent conflict-of-interest issues, while others have decided to keep theirs but create separate compliance functions controlling the quality of the calculations and potential conflicts of interest.

Another area where there are many differences is data security. Of course, analytics needs lots of data. This is why data compliance rules directly affect what can be analyzed and what can't, who gets access and who doesn't, and whether the company can partner externally for certain use cases. Again, there are huge differences between companies. For example, one European universal bank considers all client information to be "internal only," even unproblematic B2B company data. Of course, everybody understands that the name of a high-net-worth individual might be subject to such privacy laws and the data cannot leave the bank's premises. Similar rules would apply to law firms and accounting firms. However, is the name of a corporate customer really something that needs the same level of protection? Most other banks don't consider this type of data to be "internal only," which allows them to outsource a lot of work and to get access to very efficient specialist vendors. Even if such names are protected, masking techniques could be applied, substituting the truly confidential information with an identifier that can be replaced by the real information once the work has been performed externally.

Data compliance and other types of compliance are often used to justify all work being performed in-house. This can lead to significant inefficiencies and additional costs to the business—both cash and opportunity costs. What are the reasons for such stringent interpretations? Well, these are slightly muddy waters where I need to tread very carefully. We know from some off-the-record conversations that there are two reasons: genuine risk aversion by compliance, and fiefdom building in operations. Combining the two creates the perfect storm, killing potential outsourcing.

The winners are typically the so-called captives. A captive is an internal operations department owned by the company, frequently in a lower-cost location, such as Poland or India, or in second-tier cities in the United Kingdom or the United States, such as Manchester or Salt Lake City. Of course, more work means more people means more power for the corresponding managers. Here are the questions you should be asking if confronted with this:

- Does the regulator drive this explicitly in the relevant jurisdiction, or is this part of a self-imposed layer of compliance?
- Are there any technological measures such as masking that could address the compliance issue?
- Who wins from keeping the work in-house? Could there be a conflict of interest between individual objectives of the captive's manager? And what is best for the company?

There is certainly one area of information and insight that should be kept in-house at all times. It is the so-called material nonpublic information (MNPI), such as inside information about an impending merger or acquisition. If leaked, such facts can move stock markets and share prices, causing billions of dollars of damage. These are the nuclear devices in the information space. Smart vendors would not even touch this information. However, for about 90 percent of all use cases, suitable solutions can be found relatively easily.

An interesting subfallacy is the idea put about by internal IT departments: "Internal security is better than external security," which I refer to as the "Cloud is bad!" syndrome. Data might actually be safer in the hands of Amazon Web Services, which has a whole business model built on hosting and protecting data, than under the protection of a team of generalist IT administrators.

You do not have to become a specialist in compliance-related matters, but you do need to be able to ask the right questions for your own use cases, and challenge boilerplate answers by internal IT and compliance. A little digging might save you millions and get you better benefits faster.

Managing Indirect Procurement Market Intelligence:
Efficient Procurement

Context

Organization
Oil and gas super major

Function(s)
Indirect procurement
market intelligence

Industry
Energy

Geography
Global

Business Challenge

- Develop timely insights on market, supplier, and competitor procurement
- Ensure compliance and business continuity and mitigate supplier/procurement risk

Solution

Type of Solution	Solution	Impact
Accelerators	⚙ Spend intelligence studies ⚙ Cost model	Innovation in procurement function Fact-based and effective sourcing decisions Helping drive business growth
Process Optimization	⚙ Commodity code structuring	Ensuring compliance across supply chain Enhanced reporting and ROI
Enablers	Category intelligence Supplier identification and profiling Supplier risk assessments	Analysis-driven decisions Empowering category managers with actionable insights Minimizing risk across supplier base

⚙ Process- or framework-based component
⚙ Tool- or dashboard-based component

Approach

- Created a framework to assess and monitor the financial risk of suppliers, and short-listed distressed suppliers
- Created a deep-dive financial model for in-depth analysis of distressed suppliers
- Identified cost-saving opportunities by conducting cost analysis, identifying category trends, and assessing supplier bargaining power
- Identified and profiled set of suppliers for RFP/sourcing
- Provided regular updates on supplier and category key events

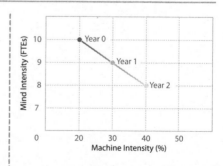

Analytics Challenges

- Identifying and implementing a scalable mechanism for regular monitoring of category and supplier news
- Creating an automated framework for scanning large number of noncritical suppliers
- Identifying suitable suppliers while leveraging historical information efficiently
- Comparing supplier price quotes with "should cost" estimates and assessing rationale

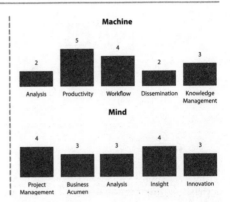

Benefits

Productivity	Time to Market	New Capabilities	Quality
• A total of 2,620 hours saved annually thanks to suite of automations • Gained 25% productivity in cost model creation	• Supplier score card tool allows category managers to reduce time spent on collecting necessary information	• New "should cost" models that estimate the cost of sourcing end-to-end e-discovery services • Financial model to assess future financial stability of distressed suppliers	• Consistency in templates • More precise and insightful financial risk analysis template

Implementation

- Total development time for all tools came to 290 hours:
    - Stage-gate approach: 100 hours
    - Financial health check tool: 50 hours
    - Smart Newsletter Automation Platform (SNAP): 100 hours
    - Proofing tool and add-in: 40 hours
- Total implementation time for all tools came to 50 hours
- Ongoing quarterly maintenance time is 30 hours
    - SNAP: 20 hours per quarter
    - Proofing tool and add-in: 10 hours per quarter

Fallacy #10

WE NEED MORE, LARGER, AND FANCIER REPORTS

It is puzzling how stubbornly long-lived and sticky recurring reports are—I see them as bacteria that have become resistant to all types of antibiotics, with their growing population and ability to reach almost every cell in the organism. William Heitman, managing director of Lab Consulting, writes that 85 percent of the 200 Fortune 500 companies surveyed did not have anyone in their finance department keeping track of the number and use of reports produced on a regular basis.[20]

There are seven fundamental drivers for this worsening situation:

1. **Programming:** Many reports are auto-generated (e.g., in CRM or ERP systems), and this can mean they take on a life of their own. Some simply run along on a schedule, even if the original need for them has long since expired. The ones that are actually useful occasionally require changes in the data structures, generating maintenance work. Some might turn into inputs to other reports, creating some nested structures and making it harder to alter upstream reports.
2. **Psychology:** People want to be on all the distribution lists because they are afraid of being left out. It feels good to be important, and often people mistake being present on distribution lists for being important.
3. **New data types:** The advent of social media and the Internet of Things has created a whole new world of use cases for which reports can be produced— a "land of milk and honey" for reporting nerds.
4. **New reporting standards:** The financial crisis of 2008 probably caused more growth in the global number of reports than any other single event has done. *Disclosure Overload and Complexity: Hidden in Plain Sight*, a study by KPMG, lists 200 new documents issued by the US regulators and

accounting standards bodies, such as the Securities and Exchange Commission (SEC) and the Financial Accounting Standards Board (FASB) with its Accounting Standards Updates (ASUs).[21] Of course, companies have to comply with all these new reporting requirements. Worldwide, national, and international bodies have done the same thing.

5. **Temporary needs:** The world is becoming increasingly dynamic and volatile, as evidenced by the fact that many CFOs we are in touch with are talking about the living nightmare of rolling quarterly budgets. Some temporary needs often lead to permanent reports, since people do not know whether these reports are still required. Somebody having the big picture would immediately realize that a report should be killed. However, reports that cut across departments or geographies rarely have an integrated owner with the big picture. Everyone *assumes* that someone still needs the report and sees the cost of running it as effectively zero, but it is entirely possible that the report is deleted or ignored by those receiving it, as we've seen.

6. **Attrition:** Many reports continue to be generated even after their owners have moved on.

7. **Supporting every decision with facts:** It seems that decision making has morphed into a process where each and every decision needs to be documented and supported by tons of facts. Some people think that Sarbanes-Oxley (SOX) regulation is the driver, but I would argue that SOX is only the expression of a renewed propensity toward a modern type of witch-hunt mentality and finger-pointing.

Entrepreneurs in the nineteenth and twentieth centuries still led based on gut feeling. Then, at the turn of the millennium, we had the big scandals, like Enron and WorldCom. Nowadays, every decision needs to be documented and supported by facts so that future generations will be able to figure out who made which mistake at what point in time and why. Of course, there are some benefits of better documentation and more facts, but many managers say that the pendulum has swung too far from gut feeling to the other extreme.

For all these reasons, the number of reports is going up, not down. Thanks to big data tools that can run thousands of models within seconds, we get inundated with more reports. One Fortune 200 manufacturing company produces 10,000 regular management reports in the finance department alone, one for every 25 employees.[22]

Since powerful computers generate reports effortlessly, many people come to think that such reports are free—which is far from true, as we will see. The main issue is not even the cost of generating a report (estimate range from a few hundred dollars to several thousand per year). It is the opportunity cost of the time spent to consume a product without insight. Moreover, who hasn't spent time trying to reconcile different numbers in various reports to create the absolute truth? The time spent on such conflicting reports can take tens of working hours for the involved parties and last for several weeks, requiring multiple meetings.

Especially when sensitive decisions such as bonuses or promotions are based on such reports, emotions can run very high, as a construction material company experienced in unpleasant ways. Multiple versions of market share reports were being used by three different hierarchical levels in the company: the country organizations, the regional headquarters, and the global business units and marketing functions. The market shares in each country were among the top three key performance indicators (KPIs) of the local country managers for their respective annual performance assessments. As they could not agree on the absolute truth, the work was given to an external agency, which discovered that definitions for the term *market share* were different across the reports. The numbers could never align.

There is a significant lack of real Level 3 insight. Most reports just produce tables of Level 1 data or Level 2 information, but hardly any insight, and almost no knowledge. Think of your past 90 business days: we can safely assume that you had three sets of monthly and one quarterly reporting cycle. How many reports did you receive, and what were they about? How many of these reports actually delivered some actionable Level 3 insight? In a few conversations with managers, I heard 5 to 10 percent, and this was only after studying the tables for quite some time.

In a BusinessIntelligence.com report, CEOs and CXOs also complained about the format of reports delivered to them.[23] While more than 50 percent want them to be delivered in the form of actionable dashboards, only 15 percent use dashboards regularly as primary sources of insight. Moreover, 72 percent of business leaders say they cannot pull their business information via mobile devices, let alone such key insights being pushed on mobiles in the form of action-oriented alerts. The same group also complained about the reports not being customizable or allowing them to drill down on specific issues.

Ultimately, we keep hearing that managers would like to get **short, relevant alerts in time**. *Short* means a few lines of text maximum, possibly with a link to the relevant underlying information. *Relevant* means that they do not want the clutter that is irrelevant to their personal context. *Alert* means something that pops up on their phone on their way to work, not an alert on an intranet website. And *in time* means something that comes as and when it happens, not at the end of the monthly or quarterly reporting cycle. This finding is highly relevant for the future of the report generation industry and for analytics in general. Our example is *InsightBee Procurement Intelligence: Efficient Management of Procurement Risks*. Decision makers in indirect procurement organizations are alerted when their suppliers are suddenly at risk or some events potentially threaten the supply chain.

The opportunity costs of spending all this time on reports rather than receiving targeted and relevant alerts can be very high. Look at the population of salespeople and sales managers. They are supposed to spend their time in client meetings. If they can spend 10 to 20 percent more time on the road rather than at their desks bogged down in administrative tasks, this can translate into many more sales meetings. But salespeople are expected to take time to enter data into some reporting processes, and they receive a lot of reports to read.

Of course, some reports are useful, necessary, or both. However, there are certainly reports that do not provide Level 3 insights and could simply be cut and others that could be delivered in more suitable format: two or three relevant points as text messages or in an app would be far more mobile device friendly than newsletters full of hyperlinks to documents.

From these points, it should be clear that many analytics use cases should simply be subject to economic Darwinism; that is, they should be eliminated on the basis of lack of ROI. Others containing hidden insights should be converted into proactive, action-oriented alerts: the right insight at the right place in the right format at the right time!

InsightBee Procurement Intelligence:
Efficient Management of Procurement Risks

Context

Organization	Function(s)
Medium-sized and larger companies	Category managers, procurement, market intelligence, CPOs
Industry	Geography
Indirect procurement, all industries	Global

Business Challenge

- Manage procurement risk
- Track suppliers and supplier categories for risks and events
- Provide analyses and insights to drive decisions

Solution

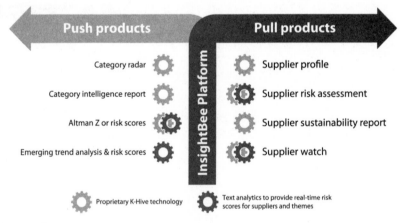

Approach

- Send alerts and weekly summaries to clients based on their customized profile
- Provide deeper analyses on selected risk events
- Support a straightforward custom query service with custom reports to drive actions (supplier profiles, supplier risk assessments, supplier sustainability reports, supplier watch)
- Provide a customizable interactive dashboard

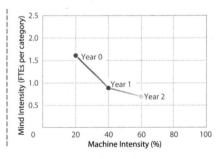

Analytics Challenges

- Integrating information from large number of data providers (>1,000) on a daily basis
- Analyzing significant amounts of daily news to identify category and supplier risks and events
- Quantifying the risk associated with more than 1,000 suppliers
- Creating a cost-effective platform to analyze financial risk associated with all suppliers of a client in a category
- Ease of access to news based on client's supplier portfolio and risk categorization

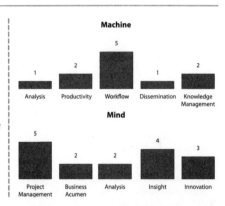

Machine

Analysis	Productivity	Workflow	Dissemination	Knowledge Management
1	2	5	1	2

Mind

Project Management	Business Acumen	Analysis	Insight	Innovation
5	2	2	4	3

Benefits

Productivity	Time to Market	New Capabilities	Quality
• Proprietary knowledge management technology improves productivity by more than 50%	• Delivery of custom reports 50% faster • Category intelligence report continually updated • Functionality to deliver risk alerts on a real-time basis	• Proactive risk monitoring of categories and key suppliers • Real-time quantified risk alerts • Access to new data through dynamic dashboard	• Insight-driven category and supplier decisions

Implementation

- Covers all indirect procurement categories and expands to selected direct procurement categories
- Serves the needs of thousands of clients efficiently
- Pay-as-you-go model provides flexibility to clients
- Scalable platform with possibility to expand to other clients and services

- Tool based on the InsightBee platform technology
- Concept to minimum viable product: 4 months
- Cost: USD 200 thousand
- External partners include user experience and user interface designer, external development team, text analytics expert

ANALYTICS INVESTMENT MEANS GREAT ROI

L et me paint a scenario we have observed in some cases. Do you recognize any of this?

In recent years, the boards of directors have been bombarded with marketing collateral on big data and artificial intelligence (AI). The standard question to the CEO and the executive team in board meetings has become "What are you guys doing about big data? There seems to be huge value."

Such statements tend to lead to some gung-ho initiatives. Step 1 is usually to hire a chief data officer (CDO) and a team of expensive data scientists who in turn ask for extensive infrastructure such as data lakes, big data tools and licenses, and the authority to copy any data in the company into the central data lake. Moreover, they also get the mandate to be the central authority in the company for anything that has to do with data analytics.

However, the objectives of these central initiatives are rarely thought through. For example, within one year a large industrial manufacturer builds a team with an annual run rate of over USD 20 million—and these are the internal costs only. After a while the detailed study of the use cases shows that additional skills and software are needed, which can easily add up to another 50 percent of the internal costs. Of course, after about 12 months, there are some early wins of some good use cases, the low-hanging fruit, which are usually the self-contained use cases that do not need the interaction with lots of departments (e.g., forecasting of stock levels). The early wins are then demonstrated to the whole company as proof of the data scientists' advanced analytics capabilities.

After a certain honeymoon period of 12 to 24 months, the low-hanging, self-contained use cases have been cracked. Suddenly, cross-functional and cross-geography use cases show up on the radar, or even use cases that involve networks of external partners (e.g., distributors, dealerships, suppliers, and regulators). HQ Compliance has also started homing in on the new data world. That is when things become messy. Such use cases are more about organizational change than about data analytics. Suddenly, the data scientists meet a lot of passive or active resistance across the organization. At that point business consulting starts becoming more relevant. More IT investments are required. Compliance also starts shooting down potentially interesting use cases, mostly for good reasons. Then some feedback from the line functions starts trickling in. Statements such as "HQ analytics does not understand our business" or "I don't know what they did to my data—I don't accept the results" will be strategically spread when the business heads visit the local units.

Of course, in the spirit of analytics supremacy and the corresponding rush of adrenaline, people did not make sure that they had proper systems to track the ROI and the benefits of individual use cases, nor is there proper governance on how to deal with the portfolio of use cases. Typically, central analytics calculates some benefits for some use cases, but more often than not finance or controlling have not bought into these frameworks. Then the CFO starts asking questions, and discovers no proof that the USD 30 million created the required business impact. In the next downturn for the company, 50 percent of the central analytics team gets laid off.

If you feel this is too gloomy a picture, I'm afraid it can get even worse. One industrial player and one financial services player even invested in data analytics companies. While the valuations of the deals were not made public, it can be safely assumed that the 2014 and 2015 valuations for data analytics companies were strongly hyped—they could easily have been up to 20 to 30 times revenue! This means that a company with revenues of USD 20 million would be valued at USD 400–600 million. Just for comparison: normal services companies are valued at about 1.5 to 3.5 times revenue, and 12 to 14 times earnings before interest, taxes, depreciation, and amortization (EBITDA).

Now here is how the game works: such analytics companies look for large corporations with a well-known brand name and a lot of data. Then they offer a small percentage of the company for acquisition, say 3 to 5 percent per acquirer and up to 30 percent of equity in aggregate, on the basis that the analytics revenue generated from the acquiring company will by itself drive up the value of the analytics company and will attract other strategic investors at higher valuations who will again give revenues to the analytics company, driving up the value even further, and so on, until the company will be listed and everybody gets huge returns on their initial investments. The promise is essentially that the early-stage investors get all the analytics services and the corresponding benefits for free. Isn't that wonderful? This is a great model, if everything works out. However, if things go sour, then it starts looking more like a Ponzi scheme that can collapse at any time, which it has in at least one case.

During a panel discussion at the Gartner Business Intelligence and Analytics Summit in early 2013 in Barcelona, vendors estimated that 70 percent of analytics projects fail to meet expectations.[24] The reasons were quoted as analytics being performed before fully understanding the business issue at hand, and half-baked implementation. In a way, the 1980s were great. You had almost no data to work with, and getting it was very expensive. Big budgets were out of the question at the time, so the first step was the creation of the old-fashioned issue tree to understand the structure of the business issue and the objectives. Then you tried to figure out a way to answer the subissues. Guess what that required? Thinking. These days there is so much data that people do not spend the up-front time on thinking anymore.

Brand Perception Analytics: Assessing Opinions in the Digital Realm is a good example of where the precise definition of the analytics question avoided a ridiculous excess of work with little impact. New data sources such as social media are especially prone to attractive but extensive effort that does not yield impactful insights if not structured very well up front.

Contrast this example with a more modest model where the company that needs the analytics puts in place the right governance and financial controls right away, requires each use case to be clearly defined in terms of scope and objectives, and manages the portfolio of use cases ruthlessly, eliminating unprofitable use cases and using a balanced mix of central and noncentral resources. The company could have a strategy to create interesting businesses staffed with intrapreneurs—entrepreneurial managers who get to run such initiatives centered around specific use cases. Granted, such a model doesn't look as glamorous and the board members have to be slightly more patient, but if sustainable development is an objective, this is the way to proceed.

It seems that people focus a lot on the analytics but less on the aspects surrounding them in order to create an impactful end-to-end solution for the end user. Neither the Mind nor the Machine parts are about analytics only.

- **Mind:** In addition to the data scientists, cross-functional program managers, business analysts, and IT, representatives of the end users and external partners need to be part of the project teams. Links into financial controlling and risk and compliance need to be established early on. Of course, not every use case requires all of the components, but certainly the most important families of use cases do.
- **Machine:** End-to-end solutions need many more components, not just the analytics. Productivity tools, workflow platforms, dissemination or Last Mile engines, and knowledge management are essential for the success of any use case. Moreover, capturing the benefits systematically in ways agreeable to finance is critical.
- **Governance and life cycle management:** Initial analytics excitement lets many people forget to establish proper governance for each use case and

for the overall portfolio of use cases. Also, thinking through the likely life cycle of any use case can make things much easier for everyone, especially in case of frequently changing environments.

The ultimate recommendation is to resist the idea that analytics is supreme, and not to jump into analyzing data without thinking about the elements just mentioned.

Brand Perception Analytics:
Assessing Opinions in the Digital Realm

Context

Organization
Pharmaceutical division of a life
science company

Function(s)
Marketing

Industry
Life science and healthcare

Geography
Global

Business Challenge

- Build an information tracking and management solution to actively implement digital strategy
- Send instant qualified alerts to brand owners

Solution

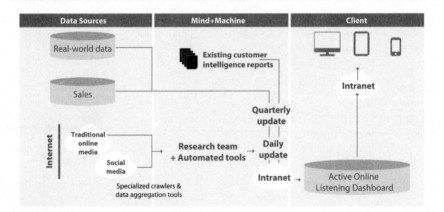

Approach

- Designed individualized data tracking
  protocols for each brand and its
  challenges in key markets
- Set up multilingual analyst team for data
  treatment and insight generation
- Developed cloud-based user interface for
  viewing of analysis, trends, and insights

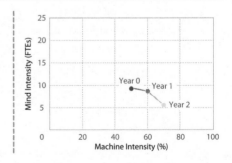

Analytics Challenges

- Setting up a solution with a dynamically evolving set of design principles and specifications
- Accommodating the business priorities of each brand with a standardized data gathering process and analytical framework for a unified visualization experience
- Automating research and analysis to process large amounts of data and keep information solution refreshed and updated

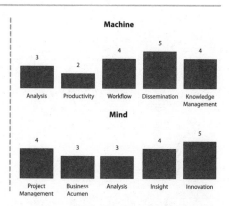

Benefits

Productivity	Time to Market	New Capabilities	Quality
• 15% efficiency gains in research process thanks to automated data processing	• Proof of concept within two months; full solution in two more	• New brand monitoring and management tool (new to client) • An early warning signal detection system	• Carefully curated contextual information with insights • Multilingual coverage

Implementation

- Full solution tested and implemented within four months with a staggered approach (2–3 brands per month)
- Usage statistics and feedback collection mechanism implemented in the steady state
- Steady-state research and user experience maintenance team of 6 FTEs 3 global centers, multilingual

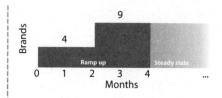

Fallacy #12

ANALYTICS IS A RATIONAL PROCESS

The psychology of analytics is probably its most underestimated and least understood dimension. This regularly leads to situations that simply eliminate the ROI that could have otherwise been achieved. The psychology of analytics has multiple areas that can affect the outcome of any analytics projects in nine major ways:

1. Nerd–antinerd interaction
2. Data power trip
3. "Not invented here" syndrome
4. Misalignment of incentives and priorities
5. Irrational enthusiasm for or distrust of analytics and machines
6. "Let's delegate this to the CDO" failure
7. Functional and geographic silos
8. Lack of colocation
9. Short-term thinking

Everybody thinks that analytics is a rational process. We think of mathematics as the rational and logical subject, but this is a fallacy. There are strong emotions related to it. Some high school students fall in love with it. Others get bad grades and will hate it for the rest of their lives. Some students might even project their hate back onto the people who were good at it, who in turn will resent this. These kids who love math and science—often called nerds or geeks—form their own social circles and develop their own way of communicating with like-minded kids they encounter in classes such as physics, statistics, computer science, and engineering. I myself am an electrical engineer and definitely part of the nerd population, and I remember learning this nerd language!

Let's imagine one such individual. After successfully earning an MSc or even a PhD in something like probability and stochastic analysis, the person hits the workforce, now called a data scientist, and starts in a corporation, where the new hire meets all the antinerds, who have become marketing specialists, salespeople, project managers, general managers, human resources (HR) managers, or compliance specialists after studying liberal arts subjects, largely freed from nerd language. With their different mind-sets and personality profiles, speaking different languages, these two groups clash again in the workplace, reviving the high school feelings.

Let's also study the angle of personality profiles. Are you familiar with the Myers–Briggs Type Indicator (MBTI) test? If you haven't taken it, it's well worth your time. The underlying data set is really robust. It is one of the few HR frameworks that have really worked for me in my career and my personal life. It helped me understand some of the aspects of my own personality, but more importantly, it helped me understand others and how I need to communicate with them. The MBTI test slots you into one of 16 boxes determined by four dimensions: introvert–extrovert (I–E), intuitive–sensing (N–S), thinking–feeling (T–F), judging–perceiving (J–P). I am an INTJ, which represents about 2 percent of the overall population—but about 30 to 40 percent of McKinsey consultants, interestingly enough! I am an intuitive introvert, a thinker, and a forward-looking planner: it's a typical nerd profile. My wife, who is a psychotherapist, is an ESFP, representing about 8.5 percent of the general population. She is a sensing, feeling extrovert, and likes to live in the day: it's actually the typical antinerd profile. We've developed a communication protocol that has served us well through 24 years of marriage.

Why is this important to mind+machine? We all need to understand and be understood. People don't exist in just a simple binary of nerd and antinerd: we have various levels of awareness of our communication requirements and ourselves. When we can't find a common language and means of communicating, we may clash around the handling of various processes, including analytics. We haven't done any research with precise percentages for the relative sizes of these groups, but based on 25 years of experience in this field, I would venture to say that communication clashes happen in about 25 to 50 percent of cases, depending on the culture of the company. If companies spent more time on training everyone on frameworks like Myers–Briggs, the ROI of many analytics use cases could be higher.

Next, let's look at the data power trip. People tend to consider their data to be a valuable asset, so they want to trade rather than just give. Usually, such data is really only Level 1 data, not even Level 2 information. Nevertheless, the data owners behave as if they owned Level 3 insights and want to price it this way. This leads to unnecessary ego-driven delays on analytics projects.

The "not invented here" syndrome can also be seen quite frequently, even with vendors. Data scientists feel that they should be the only ones to analyze the data and only using their methodology—which of course remains secret. The black-box character of certain use cases becomes a source of organizational monopoly, a power guaranteeing jobs and high salaries. Things like audit trails or knowledge management might endanger this, so there is a rejection of external processes, including oversight.

With shared, central resources—be they data scientists, IT specialists, vendors, or assets and infrastructure—the battle for priorities of one's own use cases can be a struggle. The biggest challenge to overcome is the attitude that the incentives might be misaligned. "Why should I invest, if someone else is getting the benefit?"

A large European manufacturing conglomerate wanted to implement a competitive intelligence dashboard with the help of an external vendor. This included the design and testing of the software. However, the IT policies did not allow the remote access that is state-of-the-art in most analytics vendor relationships these days (e.g., via Citrix or leased lines). It was permitted only under remote sessions that an IT person had to supervise one-to-one. That individual did not have much of an understanding of the project or the underlying use case. During the holiday season at the end of December, the IT department simply shut down such types of support, which caused a massive project risk, as proper testing was not possible.

Enthusiasm for analytics and machines is often met by rational or irrational distrust. Data scientists can become completely convinced of their power to forecast through the use of advanced algorithms and engines. Enthusiasm can get things done. However, if the enthusiasm goes overboard it can be dangerous, for example, when crazy valuations are being paid or when counterarguments are being ignored. Constructive distrust is healthy in such situations. On the other side of the spectrum, there are also the irrational distrusters, the people who have something against machines. The optimum situation is as always somewhere in the middle.

Hiring a CDO reporting to the chief information officer (CIO) is common practice because senior executives want to put analytics into the hands of someone, similarly to finance being delegated to the CFO. When asked why, a response might be that few of the business unit heads understand data or machines. However, they underestimate the fundamental and transformative character of mind+machine for the business. Of course, CDOs are necessary and can add a lot of value, but should they be in charge of the actual use cases? Analytics is changing how business is being done. End-to-end use cases ultimately require line managers to be in charge of the use case, not a central staff function one or two levels removed from the business.

Organizational silos are another important impediment to end-to-end use cases. Businesses need to be focused, so silos are necessary by definition, whether by business unit or by geography. The practical implication is that there are hardly any cross-silo management processes that allow for efficient decision making in case of cross-silo analytics use cases. Any problem between two business units needs to be escalated to the CEO of the company if proper organization procedures are to be followed. While this sounds good in theory, it is very bad in reality. The bad news is that successful analytics use cases require lots of micro-decisions involving the parties. Issues get stuck, not because people don't want to resolve the issues, but because they don't have the time in the day to understand and decide them.

Another human trait is inertia. Project members sit in their own offices, even if they could be colocated. Such physical distance removes lots of quick and informal opportunities to resolve design issues of analytics use cases. Colocating the data scientists, use case owners, business analysts, and IT people can speed up projects very significantly, or make the difference between success and failure.

Only when we forced our business analysts, data scientists, and IT people to physically colocate for the duration of the aforementioned competitive intelligence dashboard project did things start working. The reasons were very simple. None of the three types of people really understood the other groups' challenges in enough detail. Once together and able to gather whenever a problem came up, things improved. They were not distracted by other topics, they could share their screens informally and comment very easily, and they generally started interacting much more frequently instead of just every second day on a planned conference call. This collaboration is a key factor for success for any analytics use case. Electronic collaboration platforms simply have not reached the level of ease of use required to allow for this level of interaction to happen in virtual ways.

The final psychological aspect is short-term thinking. On average, employees rotate into new positions about every three years, either internally as part of career development or across companies. This means that there is limited interest in issues that are likely to surface after their next move. Therefore, topics such as use case life cycle management and knowledge management are typically undermanaged.

We have looked at several dimensions of the psychology of analytics. I am not suggesting that there are easy answers to all of them. However, you should now be in a position to spot dysfunctional behavior in your organization that might affect the success of your mind+machine efforts.

PART I: CONCLUSION

There are one billion analytics use cases out there in the world. mind+machine is the answer to garner their ROI. You are not alone in the quest to achieve this ROI, and you don't have to be a specialist in data science to navigate this maze. Understanding the top 12 fallacies should already equip you with a first set of intelligent questions allowing you to challenge some of the conventional wisdoms used by vendors and internal functions. I have introduced several important concepts that we will use throughout the book. The main ideas are:

- The massive analytics use case set is still growing rapidly with the advent of new data sources (Internet of Things, social media) and business challenges. Only 5 percent of these use cases are about truly big data; 95 percent follow the concept of "Small data is beautiful, too." This opens the door to a large world of opportunities with a lot of potential to create value.
- Use cases are supposed to provide actionable Level 3 insights (not just Level 1 data or Level 2 information) to the right end users at the right time in the right format. This includes solving the Last Mile problem of capturing the end users' individual needs and delivering the insights in user-friendly ways.
- Use cases should be managed individually and as portfolios on the basis of ROI and the four categories of client benefits: productivity, time to market, quality, and new capabilities for organizations.
- Machines are highly useful and provide capabilities that the human mind can leverage, helping to get the right ROI from use cases and turn use cases into positive ROI. However, for most of today's use cases, artificial intelligence, while certainly useful, is not the main driver of client benefits. Workflow platforms, productivity tools, visualization and dissemination engines, and knowledge management tools account for more than 80 percent of the benefits.
- Reuse and knowledge management are at a nascent stage at best. New approaches are needed to harness their potential.
- The psychology of analytics and organizational limitations can make the difference between the success and failure of mind+machine use cases. Understanding and addressing the underlying drivers are critical. Enthusiasm

for mind+machine is certainly welcome, but it should not replace robust thinking about ROI and client benefits.

Let's now focus our attention on some important trends in mind+machine that are enabling new models. It's time to equip you with a set of intelligent questions that will help you to make your mind+machine efforts more future proof.

PART II

13 TRENDS CREATING MASSIVE OPPORTUNITIES FOR MIND+MACHINE

The underlying drivers for the mind+machine approach are fundamentally changing how use cases are conceived, designed, implemented, and maintained over their life cycles. They are opening new dimensions in mind+machine, and broadening the solution space for achieving business objectives. New technologies have brought down the cost of production and distribution so much that access to leading-edge analytics is now possible even for companies without the massive budgets of the Fortune 500 companies. We have entered the era of democratization of mind+machine analytics.

If you recall the demographics model in Part I, there are about 1.2 million companies on Earth with more than 50 employees, of which only 180,000 have more than 250 employees. Previously, perhaps only the top 5,000 of these companies had the budgets to hire internal teams and buy data warehouses and software licenses. Driven by the mind+machine trend, even small companies can now use data analytics to become disruptors in a matter of a few years. Analytics are a must for any company's survival, regardless of their size—especially in this ever more volatile environment with quickly changing customer needs that can destroy once powerful companies such as Nokia in less than five years.

The restaurant delivery start-up Deliveroo is a good example of how a small company can use analytics efficiently and effectively to drive its growth. Deliveroo replaces the server with an app and a delivery person, increasing the reach of any restaurant by multiple factors over the number of seats available to any given dining establishment, thereby changing the economic equation dramatically. No wonder it has grown to 5,000 delivery people within three years. Its data scientists really understand the business, permanently analyzing the available internal and external data in order to improve the routing of its deliveries and better understand the end customers' and restaurants' needs and preferences. Deliveroo wins the game by being faster, more reliable, and more user-friendly. All it needed was its app, the Internet, and some commercially available computers—and some great unconventional and innovative minds. The business was said to be valued at USD 600 million at the end of 2015.

I am not just going to wax lyrical about how wonderful new technology is and what opportunities it brings. My focus is helping you understand the underlying drivers that shape the demand. The end user and the decision maker who receive the analytics output decide if the decision support was valuable, not the central data scientist team or software used. The use case methodology is based on the specific business needs of the end user. Any use case should first be defined as a business problem to be solved, not as an analytics problem. The analysis simply follows the business problem—and that is something that companies and the people responsible for central analytics occasionally forget.

THE ASTEROID IMPACT OF CLOUD AND MOBILE

A round 66 million years ago, the Cretaceous–Tertiary extinction event occurred, causing the disappearance of an estimated 75 percent of plant and animal species, including most dinosaurs. The generally accepted theory is that an asteroid hit Earth, with a catastrophic effect on the global environment. Through adaptive radiations (i.e., jumps in biological diversification), a huge variety of new species emerged and the era of the mammals began.

What the asteroid did to the species of our planet is what cloud and mobile technologies have done to the corporate world. The new species of companies emerged within 15 years rather than taking a few million years. Although it's hard to say where the first impact site for cloud and mobile was—Silicon Valley, the Boston tech belt, Austin, Beijing, Geneva, Oxbridge, Munich, Stockholm, Singapore, Tokyo, or Zurich—it does not really matter. The advent of cloud and mobile is real, it is global, and it is here to stay.

The point of this chapter is not to sing the praises of cloud and mobile. There is enough of that in the world already. But while artificial intelligence (AI) and big data are overly hyped, the impact of cloud and mobile is real and affects the applications of mind+machine in analytics. So let us focus on the benefits of leveraging cloud and mobile along the Ring of Knowledge. As we will see, the Last Mile is a major driver for why cloud and mobile are essential.

Cloud and mobile is transforming the IT landscape at a truly breakneck speed. Forrester forecasts the public cloud market to reach USD 191 billion by 2020 with growth rates between 20 percent and 30 percent per year. This is over six times larger than the market in 2013.[1] Most importantly, cloud applications will take two-thirds of this market, with cloud platforms and services taking the balance.

Wealth Management:
InsightBee for Independent Financial Advisers

Context

Organization
Global financial services provider

Function(s)
Independent financial advisers (IFAs)

Industry
Wealth management

Geography
Global

Business Challenge

- Generate insight into HNWI (high net worth individuals) to maximize the quality of advisory services and revenues through targeted wealth management proposals
- Provide high-quality insights at low cost with a quick turnaround and without baseline commitment

Solution

InsightBee

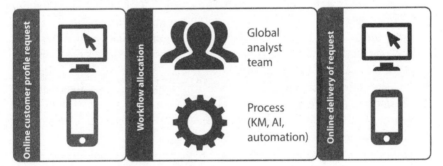

Online customer profile request

Workflow allocation

Global analyst team

Process (KM, AI, automation)

Online delivery of request

Approach

- Create on-demand HNWI profiles and enrich them with actionable insights in quick turnaround time
- Apply critical thinking to convert information into insights for the IFA
- Facilitate ordering and delivery using the InsightBee digital marketplace
- Simplify payment via online pay-as-you-go engagement with no baseline cost

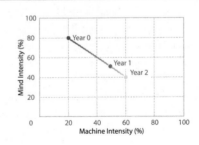

Analytics Challenges

- Large amount of noise obscuring information relevant for analyses
- Requirement to combine personal and professional data on the customer
- Small budget but a need for on-demand reports with short deadlines
- Avoidance of duplication of work in sourcing, aggregating, and processing of information

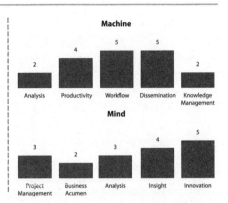

Benefits

Productivity	Time to Market	New Capabilities	Quality
• Focused automated alerts & follow-ups • Higher ROI from meetings • Efficient use of financial advisers' time • Access to relevant insights on demand	• Total turnaround time reduced	• Single source of data lending itself to multiple end uses • On-demand recent insights about end clients • Increased opportunities for interaction and business	• Next-generation architecture to pull data from reliable sources • Technology enhances data cleaning and enrichment • Data validation checks

Implementation

- The solution is based on the InsightBee platform technology and no further development was required
- Creation of report templates during consultation with the IFA
- Administrators and users can order reports immediately
- Analysts call IFA after receiving an order to ensure 100% alignment before the report is created
- Technology used to gather data on the customer
- Analyst cleans, ensures relevance, and adds actionable insights on the HNWI

These estimates do not even include so-called private clouds. These exist within closed company environments where all data and services need to be stored and delivered from a company's internal systems and dedicated hardware, for example because regulators or company policies require all sensitive data to be stored in-house. The public cloud uses a shared infrastructure outside the customer's environment, and hybrid clouds use the two models in parallel.

You are certainly already using cloud-based services, such as LinkedIn and Facebook in the individual B2C market and Salesforce.com and HubSpot in the B2B market. There are not many areas that cloud applications, platforms, and services that have not touched in B2C or B2B. Compliance functions eye cloud models very carefully because of the data being outside of their control, especially when regulators are looking over their shoulders or when legislation specifies location (e.g., on which continent data can be stored).

Why do people choose cloud applications over classic enterprise solutions? There are nine reasons:

1. Cost savings due to flexible scalability and shared resources
2. Enablement of increasingly mobile workforces
3. Better interaction with customers and partners
4. Better use of data to gain insights
5. Enablement of new products and services
6. Facilitation of new business models
7. Enablement of global shared services
8. Better agility and faster time to market
9. Improved interaction and alignment with employees

HubSpot is a good example of how pervasive and enabling such models have become. We have no relationship with HubSpot beyond being a happy customer of the product, so this is not a sales pitch!

A prime example of a democratic cloud model for inbound marketing and sales, HubSpot charges customers by the number of contacts hosted, identified uniquely by their email addresses, and allows small companies to scale up affordably without any major IT investment or additional IT complexity. The Marketing suite allows the setup of inbound landing pages and outbound campaign emails and effectively facilitates the running of campaigns. A task that earlier locked up internal IT resources for days can be accomplished in a few hours.

HubSpot delivers all the interesting information about the prospects, such as how they navigated on the pages or how far down they scrolled in a campaign email. Using HubSpot allowed us to identify that the average partner at a law firm or other professional services firm does not scroll down at all, either because they still use BlackBerrys or because they simply don't have the time. This helped us readjust our content to ensure that we reach the point within the first 10 lines.

The beauty of HubSpot is that it fully connects customer relationship management (CRM) capability with the marketing engine, unlike more sales-oriented CRM platforms. As it is cloud-based, it allows our teams to collaborate seamlessly—a major asset for a global and virtual insights business. Of course, the marketing and sales organizations of Evalueserve still had to do the hard Mind work of figuring out the necessary processes, but no platform can do that work.

HubSpot is a great example of a completely new capability enabled by cloud technology, packaged into a new commercial pricing model of plug-and-play, pay-as-you-go. It checks almost every one of the nine benefits listed earlier.

The second megatrend affecting mind+machine is mobile technology. On October 7, 2014, the number of mobile devices and gadgets surpassed the number of humans living on this planet for the first time: 7.19 billion devices, of which 1.5 billion were smartphones, were registered, and this does not even include machine-to-machine connections.[2] As we will see in the next chapter, the Internet of Things is going to endow the world with an explosion of machine-to-machine connections. By 2019, the number of smartphones alone is forecasted to reach 2.6 billion.[3] We have seen so much change in the B2C market. Who doesn't use their smartphones in their daily lives?

Companies using mobile are looking for three benefits:

1. Increases in employee productivity and satisfaction
2. Improvements in the efficiency of field operations
3. More business and a competitive edge

However, when it comes to B2B or companies' internal applications, research shows that there is still considerable room for improvement. In the previously referenced BusinessIntelligence.com survey, 72 percent of senior executives said that they could not easily access their data on mobile devices; 74 percent said that they needed to access their data from multiple unconnected sources, and that there was a very big gap in terms of how they would like information to be displayed versus what they were actually getting.[4]

Unfortunately, emails and spreadsheets are still the reality for most business leaders. Does this sound familiar? You are trying to join a conference call from an airport lounge or a hotel room. A few minutes before the call you get an email from one of the participants with some enormous Excel attachments that are impossible to properly see and manipulate on your mobile device.

What senior leaders want is focused content that is easy to understand and that can be seen easily on mobile devices. It almost seems that the underlying evolution of technology and the penetration of the individual consumer markets have left the B2B world behind by about a decade. Are there improvements? Of course, but think through your own experience. How much has really changed in your daily business life? Bankers are still complaining to me that their compliance-driven mobile environment does not allow them to use the phones they prefer. Moreover, business information and the corresponding analytics are still being presented in archaic ways: largely uncondensed reports that don't highlight the issues and insights, aren't based on push alerts, and have old-fashioned visualization.

What a waste it is to have 90 percent of the impact of great mind+machine work lost on the Last Mile stretch. Mind–machine interfaces will be far more critical in the future, as only modern approaches will allow the delivery of the right insights in the right form at the right time.

Cloud and mobile feed each other. Companies such as Microsoft have made very specific choices to combine the two. In May 2015, Satya Nadella and other Microsoft executives announced upcoming capabilities for Office and Windows designed to reflect the company's focus on "mobile first, cloud first."[5] They claim that these will deliver consistent user experiences across devices. New products such as Office 365 and Azure cater to all the new fundamental needs of mobile customers in partly or fully virtual organizations. A big advantage of such cloud applications is that upgrades happen automatically without massive upgrade programs.

Unfortunately, such upgrades are still far away for some companies. Just recently I met a very senior banking client who told me that the bank is now thinking about upgrading to Office 2013, possibly as early as 2016! Office 2013 is not built for the cloud, and the user manuals for the integration of any cloud storage or other functionalities are impenetrable to nontechies.

Democratization of cloud models is benefiting small- and medium-sized companies, as they can be more agile and much faster at much lower fixed costs and significantly lower internal IT complexity than was previously possible. Let's now study the impact that cloud and mobile have on the Ring of Knowledge, our analytics value chain.

Step 1: Data gathering. As discussed in Part I, the Last Mile works in two directions, with insight requesters and data generators. Cloud and mobile can facilitate several tasks in very elegant ways.

Requesters log their needs via an Internet-based interface rather than clumsy emails. Of course, the definition of *data* needs to be widened to include customer requests, which can be categorized rather as Level 3 insights than just Level 1 data or Level 2 information. The data generators are people or devices sending their data into the cloud, where the data will be stored and analyzed. Of course, they have to opt-in to become data generators, but in return they also get significant benefits, such as improved service. Such a model would have been next to impossible in the era before cloud and mobile.

Access to publicly available data via the Internet is easy by definition. Sharing data across company boundaries has suddenly become much easier as well. The InsightBee Sales Intelligence platform uses massive amounts of external data from hundreds of sources, and smart algorithms that can search for Level 1 data and Level 2 information very effectively and efficiently.

Step 2: Data cleansing and structuring. Access to certain cloud-based services that help in data cleansing and structuring is now very easy. Evalueserve's InsightBee platforms work with external partners such as Squirro and Rage Frameworks and with internal technology such as our natural language processing platform for patent information, KMX. Together, they sift through massive amounts of structured and unstructured data to return a more digestible set of structured Level 1 data and Level 2 information in a live environment.

Of course, all this information will still need to be put into context and further analyzed by Minds to create value-adding insights, such as qualified sales opportunities, supplier risk alerts, or relevant new patents filed by our clients' competitors, but the cloud-based machines support our Minds in a seamless fashion for the Level 1/2 work, not exactly a job a 27-year-old would want to do all day long.

Steps 3 and 4: Creation of insights. While these steps are largely about Mind, cloud and mobile still have a role to play—mainly because the correct term should be Minds, not just Mind. Increasingly, no individual can derive wonderful Level 3 insights or even Level 4 knowledge on their own. Especially in analytics-heavy environments, teams of analysts and decision makers with different skill sets are needed to solve a given problem. Remember the demographic analysis in Part I: 90 percent of analytics use cases are driven by high-analytic-intensity companies, most of which are internationally or nationally dispersed.

Let's have a look at a patent landscape for insulin pumps for diabetes control. Patent landscapes depict technology spaces and are like geographic maps that reveal new patents relevant to specific products or technologies. They help heads of R&D define what their research focus should be and identify intellectual property risks—nobody wants to get sued for a few tens of millions of dollars just because they missed a competitive patent.

The output is elegant, but the work that can go into a patent landscape can be incredibly complex. In this example, the analyses of patents require multiple disciplines: molecular biology, medicine and surgery, electrical engineering, mechanical engineering, software engineering, and micro-manufacturing technologies. Multiple patent analysts have to work together, and they are unlikely to be in one office. To efficiently and effectively collaborate on generating insights, a cloud workflow platform is ideal.

Steps 5 and 6: End user delivery and decision making. The Last Mile is probably the part of the Ring of Knowledge where the impact of cloud and mobile is highest. As we've established, all of the good work done is rendered pointless if insights don't reach the decision maker in the right format, at the right time. Managers are increasingly mobile. The majority of salespeople have always been mobile. Other functions increasingly have several work sites, even if this just means working in the office and from home.

Fortunately, the potential to deliver insights via the cloud to mobile devices is there. At Evalueserve, we've embraced this potential. I'm including an example here to show the possibilities. The type of patent landscape mentioned earlier can be generated and viewed through our IPR+D "Clarity" Dashboard, which uses cloud hosting and is compatible with a number of mobile devices. Thanks to proper tagging of the underlying data, the user can click to drill down on areas of interest. Whenever the landscape updates due to changes in the underlying data, all users can immediately access the new view.

Steps 7 and 8: Creating and sharing knowledge. This is another area where cloud and mobile are very strong. Possibilities include adding commentary to insights from mobile devices and being able to see that commentary automatically elsewhere, having been informed about it via an alert—expanding the Level 3 insights and adding and disseminating Level 4 knowledge. Cloud and mobile allow us to push relevant content to the people who need it, while unused content can face its ultimate fate: the archive.

Just to illustrate this point a little better: the data security officer of a major bank told me about two years ago that the bank had 100,000 internal network drives where data and documents resided passively. The bank estimated that well over 90 percent of the data was outdated and would never be used again. Raw data is probably outdated within a few days, information in a few weeks or months, insights in about a year, and knowledge within five years. Should we really keep all this data and clog up wikis and SharePoint repositories? Probably not.

One argument often used against the cloud is data security. But is it really safer in-house? Let us compare the proficiency of data security departments of big cloud players, such as Microsoft, Amazon, Google, and Salesforce.com, which are bombarded with all sorts of attacks every day, and those of small and medium-sized companies and professional services firms, and even large firms. The answer is fairly simple according to the head of a specialized data security firm: there is always a residual risk, but the firm's practice shows that in-house IT departments are significantly less experienced than the big cloud players when it comes to data security.

In fact, the majority of data breaches never get published in the first place, because it is in nobody's interest. Imagine: even the banks who pride themselves on high data security are losing data and need to buy it back on the black markets of the deep Internet. There is even a specialist consulting firm that runs a trading division to buy back stolen customer data and credit card records on behalf of banking clients. In a case in Switzerland, an ex-employee was able to burn a CD with thousands of German clients, which he then sold to the German tax authorities.

Do internal IT people openly admit that they are vulnerable? Sure. They say things like "There is always a residual risk, but we will still keep the data in-house." Why? Compliance!

While some industrial companies can transform, as demonstrated by the likes of General Electric, large banks that are subject to stifling regulation should be really worried about a new breed of agile competitors: FinTech (financial technology). Slow industrial conglomerates like the steel and manufacturing company mentioned in Part I should also be concerned.

Here is a small test you can use: if your IT department thinks that collaboration with external parties should be made as difficult as possible by not allowing cloud-based processes, something is fundamentally flawed at your company.

Cloud and mobile is having a very profound and highly positive impact on the Ring of Knowledge, and this goes well beyond cost savings. It has democratized competition to the point where the balance of power has shifted away from large, slow companies to dynamic small- and medium-sized companies for the first time in economic history.

Trend #2

THE YIN AND YANG OF THE
INTERNET OF THINGS

The Internet of Things offers huge opportunities, but there are still some perils to be avoided. As in the previous chapter, we will not even try to write an exhaustive overview of the Internet of Things, but focus on how it will affect mind+machine analytics.

First, what is the Internet of Things? The interconnectedness of the universe is a good analogy. Einstein's general theory of relativity showed that space and time are glued together in a space–time warp connected by gravity. Every star is connected to every other star by way of gravity. The distance between the stars determines how strong the glue is, but even stars that are very, very far away still attract each other and influence each other's paths in space. This is an unbelievably big web of bilateral relationships. Galaxies and stars tend to cluster, establishing a kind of a loose hierarchy. The Internet of Things is very similar. Replace gravity with the Internet, the stars with the billions of connected or connectable devices, and the clusters of galaxies, the centers of galaxies, and the suns at the center of solar systems with network nodes.

The light that is exchanged between the stars could be likened to the data flowing directly between these connected devices—for example, a smart fridge talking to British online supermarket Ocado to order supplies that a drone will deliver to a robot butler, which will stash them in the fridge. Early adopters are not far from having this in their lives!

Now, we should address the dark side of things. Stars explode in massive supernovas sending shock waves of matter through the universe, leaving behind black holes that absorb almost everything that comes their way. We also deal with the elusive dark matter and dark energy. Current models of cosmology estimate that we cannot see 95 percent of all matter or energy in the universe—we only know it must be there, because we can measure its gravitational pull.

The Internet of Things is again very similar. Just replace the explosions and the corresponding shock waves with risks that have turned into real disasters, and replace dark matter with the invisible part of the Internet, the Dark Web, where all sorts of criminals enjoy their hidden life. People deploying the Internet of Things need to be aware of what can happen when a virtual supernova explodes.

The definition of the Internet of Things in simple terms is:

A network of devices that contain embedded technology to communicate, sense, and interact with other devices.

In short, the Internet of Things is a way for everyday objects to talk to each other and to talk to you, such as when a refrigerator alerts a mobile phone that the milk has run out. There are already plenty of impactful use cases around the Internet of Things. *Analytics in Internet of Things: Benchmarking Machines Using Sensor Data* details a proof of concept we conducted with a global equipment manufacturer where we used our analytical approach to extract use cases from the data from the sensors embedded in their machines.

Let us be absolutely clear: the Internet of Things and big data are not the same thing, whatever media and marketers might claim. By way of clarification, consider this: a European engineering firm designed and implemented an Internet of Things use case for a European railway operator. Using a low-bandwidth channel, the locomotives running on diesel would regularly send just one number representing the diesel level in the tank. Even assuming a few hundred trains operating on the network, this does not amount to more data than 10 kilobytes of data per hour. It is a beautiful example of a small data Internet of Things with very simple analytics but very high ROI, as the owners of the trains can collect the information and use that in negotiations with the operators, who are leasing the trains from them. The data helps the owners understand how often the trains are idle or out of service.

Most of the data going between devices comes in the form of simple sensor readings, such as: locations; temperatures; levels of some liquids; indications of the presence or absence of some object; mechanical factors such as forces, speeds, accelerations, tensions, vibrations, and pressures; and electrical factors such as currents, voltages, magnetic fields, and light. Such simple data still needs a lot of processing to make sense of it. Just collecting it does not help.

Higher-level data is already preprocessed locally inside the device. For example, an electricity meter could send meter readings, the state of health of some machines, or some simple diagnostics analyzed by software. Noncentral processing has the advantage of the raw data getting compressed into a useful finding that another machine can use. The drawback is that local electronics become more expensive. For example, a sensor in a tire is pretty dumb, as it cannot cost too much and the physical forces inside a tire are very demanding for normal

Analytics in Internet of Things: Benchmarking Machines Using Sensor Data

Context

Organization
Global equipment manufacturer

Function(s)
Technical services

Industry
Manufacturing

Geography
HQ in Europe

Business Challenge

- Use sensor data to segment a large base of installed machines into performance clusters
- Use findings to improve uptime of machines

Solution

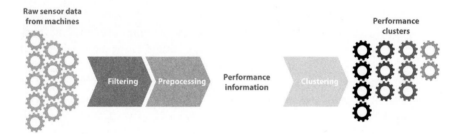

Raw sensor data from machines

Filtering

Prepocessing

Performance information

Clustering

Performance clusters

Approach

- Put data scientists, product engineers, and software specialists working as one team
- Use data dictionary and technology expertise to understand and process raw data
- Join data sources to create master data set
- Harmonize and filter master data to standardize formats
- Calculate KPIs and preprocess data for later analysis
- Cluster machines based on performance, and define segments

Analytics Challenges

- Processing and understanding large volumes of sensor data detailing all aspects of machine operations
- Reading around 100 GB of raw data and transforming it into relevant machine KPIs
- Applying state-of-the-art algorithms to identify performance segments

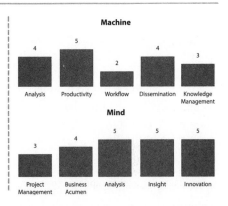

Benefits

Productivity	Time to Market	New Capabilities	Quality
• Enabled very efficient analysis and testing of multiple clustering scenarios • Automated for future runs	• Only one month from initial data pull to insight delivery • Fail-fast methodology: much faster learning and quicker iterations	• Constant monitoring allowed quick trend and risk identification in the installed base • Data-driven leads generated for the sales team	• Final model was accurate and actionable • Audit trail available

Implementation

- Project team: 2 data scientists, 2 data engineers and 1 project manager
- Workshop: Project and client teams spent 2 days on business question feasibility, ease of implementation, and potential value and cost before selecting use cases
- Data preparation: Project team spent 2 weeks collecting data sources to support selected use cases
- Analytical modeling: preprocessing and clustering were implemented as a sprint over the course of one week

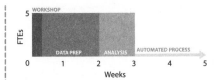

electronics, but a smart meter might already contain some significant amount of local processing power.

If you would like to get some hands-on experience with the world of Internet of Things, buy a Lego Mindstorm and program some simple use cases, such as making the Mindstorm robot follow a carpet line in your living room. You will quickly understand the programming of the sensors and actors. Lego Mindstorm can teach you the fundamentals of the Internet of Things in less than a week.

The forecasted numbers of devices are staggering. The GSMA estimates 24 billion connected devices by 2020, half of which will be mobile.[6] Cisco, the largest networking provider in the world, estimates the number of connected devices to reach even 50 billion by 2020, implying that there will be more than six connected devices per human.[7] If we further know that the combined population of Organization for Economic Cooperation and Development (OECD) countries is only about 15 to 18 percent of the global population and that most connected devices are going to be in the OECD countries in the medium term, the average number of connected devices per OECD inhabitant will be more like 30 to 40. Just think of your own home: refrigerator and deep freezer, phones, tablets, laptops, music and entertainment systems, climate control, garage, car and garage doors, lights and shutters, mailbox, security systems, pet feeders, and drones… I am sure I missed a few. Any fully connected home can easily have more than 100 sensors and connected devices. Do we need all of this? That is probably more of a philosophical question! But this is the world we have.

What are the application areas for the Internet of Things? As much as I feel that marketers overuse the word *smart*—since many of the devices don't actually learn or do more than basic data cleansing—it does apply to the potential of this technological concept in four areas:

1. **Smart life:** Making our lives simpler and safer. This includes services in our homes, personal healthcare, food and nonfood retailing, banking, insurance, and private and public services.
2. **Smart mobility:** Making transport faster, more enjoyable, and more reliable. This includes the connected car, urban and multicity traffic management, payment solutions, distribution and logistics, and fleet management of trucks, cars, trains, airplanes, drones, and so on.
3. **Smart cities:** Managing city infrastructure more efficiently by connecting the inhabitants to make them safer, running grid management and smart metering to provide more efficient utilities, and improving facilities management and waste management to make cities cleaner.
4. **Smart factories and supply chains:** Improving manufacturing and supply chain processes to lower cost and improve uptime and quality. This includes preventive maintenance, better process control and compliance, better planning through decision support, faster time to market for manufactured devices, and better integration of whole supply chains

and market demands. Industry 4.0 promises depend a lot on the Internet of Things.

The Internet of Things is still in its infancy in general, but some companies are pushing ahead as the leaders in the field—namely General Electric (GE), Google, and Cisco—trying to create whole ecosystems around themselves involving technology platforms and services companies. Before all the promises of the Internet of Things can be realized, a few fundamental issues need to be addressed.

Standards: Interoperability in the Internet of Things is still an unsettled and unsettling matter. At a minimum, this is slowing down the evolution. What language should all these 50 billion devices speak with each other? Unlike humans, who appreciate the richness of culture, machines don't like dialects and different languages unless the languages have been taught to them (i.e., programmed into the machines).

The standardization landscape in the Internet of Things and machine-to-machine (M2M) communication is still fragmented and domain-specific. As it affects so many industries with totally different requirements and existing regulations, standardization is complex by nature, but the race is on. Not-for-profit standardization bodies in various domains and consortia set up by vendor communities are trying to address the issue. Here are a few examples, as just describing the standardization bodies and their efforts would be a big data project by itself. In 2014, Google's Nest, a company that provides smart thermometers for home heating, announced the Thread standard together with Samsung, ARM Holdings, and others. Thread is a standard for better connectivity for household devices. Open source standardization efforts such as the Open Interconnect Consortium are under way. The Industrial Internet Consortium of Intel, Cisco, GE, AT&T, and IBM is trying to standardize the Internet of Things for manufacturing and industrial applications.

Standardization is not enough, though. A certification and testing ecosystem enforcing any new standards is also needed, very much like the communications industry has achieved with the Global Certification Forum. This topic is going to keep lots of people busy for a very long time to come. Leading industrial players will continue to drive their influence and their business in various industries by setting de facto standards for their particular areas of interest. Will all of this work out in the long run? Of course. Will there be a lot of duplication, lack of interoperability, and reduced numbers of choices for customers, and therefore higher costs? In the medium term, absolutely.

Privacy: Another major, completely unresolved, and worsening issue with the current Internet of Things is the complex topic of data privacy. What information needs to be protected, why, for how long, by whom, and where? Even fundamental agreements thought to be robust are now being called into question. For example, in 2015 the European Court of Justice declared invalid the Safe

Harbour Decision from the year 2000, which had made it possible to transmit personal data of individuals resident in the European Union to the United States. This decision has put on hold several other agreements with the United States, even for countries that are not part of the European Union, such as Switzerland. Legal concerns abound in Europe regarding the US Patriot Act, which allows US authorities to access not just any data stored in the United States, but also data stored on any US-headquartered company's servers. This might call into question the legality of storing any European personal data on any company's servers where the destination of the data might lie outside the European Union.

In addition to all these fundamental differences in policy between countries, there are also fundamental technical and information-related issues in guaranteeing the privacy of the data passed between machines. How does Machine B know whether the data transmitted by Machine A might be subject to a specific privacy agreement between an individual and a service provider? Imagine you have diabetes and use an insulin pump. You are certainly fine with your blood sugar levels being measured by the pump so that it can dispense the insulin. Are you also fine with this data being provided directly or indirectly to your current or future health insurers? Since this might affect your health insurance premiums, the answer is probably not.

Privacy is an issue because fundamentally different interests and powerful agendas are at play, not relatively simple technical issues. You need to know that any Internet of Things initiatives you are taking will have to be very carefully protected legally, as legal liabilities can accumulate quickly and massively if a violation (that is judged to be a violation by a court even a few years later) has been committed a few million times in the meantime—something that happens rather easily when machines repeat tasks day in and day out.

Intellectual property rights (IPR): This topic gets completely overshadowed by the hype and by the standards, privacy, and safety issues. The Internet of Things will need a very clear and easy-to-implement economic model for owning, pricing, selling, and using various types of Levels 1–4 data, information, insights, and knowledge if participants want to get their proper returns for their ownership rights.

Here is very simple question: why are you giving away your personal data to players such as Google, Facebook, and LinkedIn for free? Because they provide a service to you that you think is useful. But think of the photovoltaic cells on your roof that pump unused electrical energy into the grid. Would you give away this energy for free? So why is it different to "pump" personal data into Facebook or search histories into Google? Why do these companies get all the economic benefits?

Many analytics products are based on assembly lines of prior enhancements. You might agree to give your personal data to a chain of players, but you would like to get your fair share of the profits. The current models are not able to cope with anything more sophisticated than some general umbrella terms and conditions that nobody really understands or even reads. There are no low-cost payment mechanisms, either, such as micro-payment engines that might enable such a flow of value back to you, the originator.

We will propose a consistent framework for IPR in Part III. At this stage you should know that you or your company might be creators of valuable data. Why not charge for it? On the flip side, there are also very significant legal risks in creating chains of data, information, and insights. Such products might become quite complex and based on the variety of sources and intermediate value addition. How can you prove that you are allowed to use the data and that you are using it in compliance with the license? You may have contracts with all your vendors, but what happens when these vendors aren't obvious database vendors with proper licensing agreements?

Security: We need to be aware that every connection in the Internet of Things is a potential opportunity for unauthorized access, especially when the data flows through the open Internet. Statements such as "a multi-faceted, defense-in-depth approach is required to ensure the overall security of the smart metering system [...] against known and unknown attacks" sound great, but how many companies are really on top of this in every aspect of the Internet of Things?[8]

Internet of Things security is best compared to home security. You can try to protect a house with a lot of expensive equipment, which certainly raises the bar for the thieves. However, if the prize inside the house looks sufficiently valuable, they will still make the attempt. The best defense against theft is not to have something in the house that looks worth the risk of stealing it. As the decision maker, you need to understand the worst-case scenarios for each use case assuming that there *will* be a breach.

Liabilities and accountabilities: What are our liabilities, and who is accountable for what? These are the two questions companies deploying Internet of Things solutions and their insurance companies must ask. Let's assume you are in the field of preventive maintenance and you have guaranteed machine uptime. Then your sensors or your algorithms fail to detect a problem. Since the machine fails, a whole host of manufacturing processes further down the chain has to be halted. Indirect damages are being claimed. If just a sensor failed, the problem would be limited to one machine. If the algorithm failed, hundreds of machines could be affected simultaneously, and the claims could easily add up to very large amounts—in the double-digit millions. The insurance industry will have to develop entirely new models to deal with such distributed and nested accountabilities.

Audit trails: Failure to monitor will be a risk in itself. Internet of Things solutions will need lots of audit trails, not just for the outcomes of the use cases, but also for the algorithms used. Who did what to the software or the hardware at what time? Which players were involved how? What were the audit procedures in the first place? And if you are a data provider, how was the data used downstream and by whom? There is currently no adequate infrastructure for monitoring what is going on, but the liability question and the regulators will definitely put more emphasis on such topics in the future.

Most effects discussed in the chapter on cloud and mobile apply to the Internet of Things because it is largely built on cloud and mobile, but there are three new dimensions specific to it: the explosion of use cases, the data explosion, and how the Mind will be involved.

Explosion of use cases: Fifty billion connected devices will open up opportunities for millions of new analytics use cases. A global truck manufacturer recently told us that between 2015 and 2017 the firm expects the number of primary use cases in preventive maintenance to go up from 50 to 500. A food packaging manufacturer told us that their volume of analytics use cases driven by the Internet of Things is already hard to manage and will only increase. Of course, this means that there will be thousands of secondary use cases linked to these primary use cases. This will put a strain on resources, and require completely new approaches in knowledge management and reuse of existing analytics use cases. We will discuss this further in Part III.

Data explosion: Streamed sensor data will increase data volumes multiple-fold. If several hundred sensors send temperature or pressure data every few milliseconds or cameras send video feeds, the data could easily go into gigabytes of data every hour, even for relatively simple systems. Streamed data adds a totally new quality to data analytics and its use cases, as humans won't be involved in the actual digestion of the data at the level of the data flow.

It won't be just the primary data that will pose a challenge. There will be a lot of overhead or metadata to deal with. Metadata is data that provides information about other data (e.g., an audit trail). How are we supposed to make sense of it and transform it from Level 1 data to Level 2 information or Level 3 insights? Dealing with such data requires tools that can both flexibly handle and analyze streamed data and set in motion event-specific sequences of actions. Caberra, which is a cognitive connector, is an example of such a flexible engine. It enables users to connect devices and sources, detect relevant events, and trigger actions. With such an explosion of data and analytics use cases, portfolio management will become essential.

Role of the Mind: Humans are too slow to get involved at the streaming level, full stop. We must focus on the development of the analytics use cases, their governance, and the usage of any Level 3 insights generated. Use case engineering might become a new function, with people working on useful Internet of Things opportunities, creating prototypes, fine-tuning the prototypes that work and discarding the ones that don't, and then building production versions that run semiautonomously, supervised by humans that are assisted by machines.

The Ring of Knowledge will play an essential role in the age of the Internet of Things. Very few individuals will have all the skills required to run such complexity in a single (human) brain. The level of knowledge management required to keep all of this somewhat under control simply does not exist yet.

ONE-TO-ONE MARKETING

Don Peppers and Martha Rogers advanced the concept of one-to-one marketing as a customer relationship management (CRM) approach in their 1994 book *The One to One Future* (Crown Business). One-to-one marketing uses personalized interactions with customers to generate better customer loyalty and higher ROI. Companies such as Amazon, Alibaba, and Zalando, and food retailers such as Ocado have been using the principles of personalized marketing since their inception. In its most refined form, it can be thought of not just as what customers want, but as what *each individual* customer wants.

These entities store all data from interactions with you, combine them with other types of information, and then create personalized offerings for you. Non-refined forms of such personalized offerings have shown up in our in-boxes for years as emails from Amazon and similar sites.

But one-to-one marketing is evolving. More advanced approaches now embed mobile devices, triggers, social media, and point-of-sale data to make the experience even more immediate. For example, if you allowed your e-commerce apps to use your mobile phone's location, you could receive offerings specific to where you are. The trigger is generated because you are close to a location relevant to the marketer's focus. Location-based services are on the rise, as companies such as Uber and Kabbee demonstrate.

While e-commerce has been demonstrating for years how one-to-one marketing works, analytics and decision support are still in their infancy when it comes to affordable customized analytics and service levels. This creates a latent frustration in any manager's mind. Customized mind+machine service does not seem to have arrived in the B2B or internal company environments.

There is a whole industry that produces syndicated, pull-only market research or analyst reports on a huge variety of topics. By definition, a syndicated report cannot be customized to a segment of one. Instead, it addresses the average customer, and as such can meet maybe 40 to 70 percent of your needs. To get the remaining 30 to 60 percent from the same industry means accepting an offer for very expensive analyst time. Very similar mechanisms are at work on the internal front. Unless you are really high up in the hierarchy and have a direct say over how the reports look, you'll have to accept what you're served.

Analysis and report service levels have not improved much over the past two decades.

- **Customization:** Limited or no possibilities to request customization for a segment of one
- **Triggers and alerts:** Pull-only or regular rather than responsive reports. Many clients have told me that they receive reports on a monthly or quarterly basis, but that the interesting events happen at random intervals between these planned reporting dates. For example, a monthly utilization report might miss a drop in utilization by three to four weeks.
- **So what:** Lack of clearly defined use cases leading to a lack of "so what" insight
- **Time to market:** Internal and external analytics being subject to lengthy processes
- **Formats, visualization, and delivery:** Lack of understanding of the right format

As mentioned before, reports often come as document attachments to emails and are hard to read on mobile devices. Most are still static and don't allow the recipient to drill down.

While people want one-to-one analytics for decision support, are they willing to pay for it? The market for generic but insightful reports still exists, but it is stagnant or shrinking in many areas. There is another market for monopolistic or oligopolistic data assets, but this does not provide Level 3 insights without further analytics work. Companies typically buy expensive umbrella subscriptions to Gartner, Forrester, Gerson Lehrman Group, IMS Health, Bloomberg, or Thomson Reuters. However, companies are increasingly reviewing such subscriptions due to their high cost.

In our *six million* hours of customized research and analytics every year, we realized that clients are willing to pay only if the end product meets at least 95 percent of their exact needs in terms of content, visualization, and time and pathway of delivery. Between the "hill of syndication" and the "mountain of customization," there is the "valley of disinterest," where customers are not willing to pay for something that won't meet their needs exactly (see Figure II.1). In a way, this is a very binary market, and companies need to be specialized in either service.

The transaction costs are simply too high for this to have happened in most areas. Even creating a simple competitor profile usually takes several iterations on

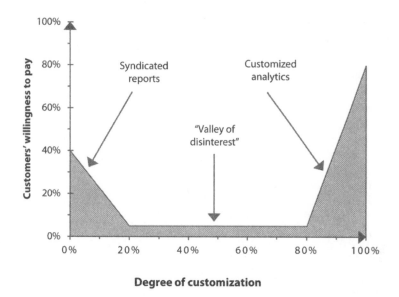

Figure II.1 Willingness to Pay

phone calls and via emails. Such efforts are viable only if the ultimate objective is a recurring stream of such profiles in the future.

There must be easier ways to do this with much lower transaction costs, especially given that we will be hit with several million additional primary use cases in the near future. We will discuss such platform approaches in Part III, but here are some teasers.

The cloud-based InsightBee Market Intelligence solution allows clients to order profiles on companies, executives, and industries and submit general research questions in seconds. The available options allow for a 95+ percent customization in a few more seconds, and there is an option to add some text so that the analyst will be able to spin the final product to address 100 percent of the customer's need. InsightBee's more advanced versions for Sales and Procurement Intelligence will also send you customized alerts in response to defined triggers. Thanks to the best-practice templates, there is no need to have lengthy debates to invent various options from scratch every time. This is a good example of knowledge management and reuse at the template level.

SurveyMonkey is another great example of how the old-style market research industry has been shaken up by one use case being cracked in a very elegant cloud platform that dramatically reduces interaction costs. If you have access to the people you want to survey, there is no need to hire an expensive agency that might not give you access to the underlying interview data. Moreover, by providing more than 15 types of survey templates, the customer always has access to the best available templates.

InsightBee:
Market Intelligence via Pay-as-You-Go

Context

Organization
Companies of all sizes

Function(s)
Marketing and sales, strategy, R&D,
management consulting teams, etc.

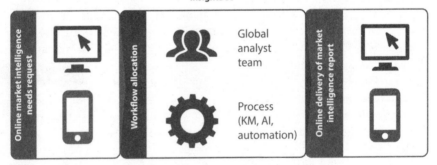

Industry
B2B corporate verticals,
professional services, financial
services, etc.

Geography
Global

Business Challenge

- Enhance end users' ability to close more deals with superior intelligence on customers and markets
- Be able to manage peaks and troughs in the demand for tailor-made insights without having to invest in significant infrastructure

Solution

InsightBee

Online market intelligence needs request

Workflow allocation

Global analyst team

Process (KM, AI, automation)

Online delivery of market intelligence report

Approach

- Online pay-as-you-go engagement using a credit or debit card or through a corporate plan with lifetime validity credits against invoice payments
- Tailor-made reports on companies, executives, sectors, or business questions
- Up-front estimate of price and estimated time of arrival through a global workflow tool
- Delivery of reports via an easy-to-use online platform

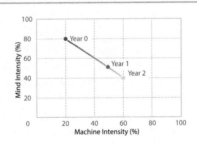

Analytics Challenges

- Make the process of getting tailor-made market intelligence as effortless as possible
- Deliver high-quality customized reports twice as fast at half the price of comparable solutions
- Build a robust workflow across global delivery centers to give a seamless experience
- Leverage industry experience from the various pockets of the parent firm within a short response time

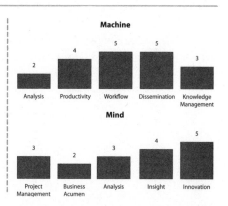

Benefits

Productivity	Time to Market	New Capabilities	Quality
• 100% more productive than any current approach • Cloud-based interface • Automation and artificial intelligence improve research efficiency	• 50% faster than any comparable approach • Quicker scope specification thanks to a web-based, mobile-enabled ordering interface and live chat	• Pay-as-you-go commercial model, no up-front investment in infrastructure • Last Mile capability • High degree of reuse of existing knowledge	• Specialized teams and processes enable better quality of insights • Substantially enhanced user experience • Average feedback score of 4.6 out of 5

Implementation

- Concept to minimum viable product (MVP): 6 months
- Initial cost: approx. USD 700 thousand
- Followed agile development methodology with a 3-week sprint schedule
- Consistent request growth of 30% per month in the first year (2015)
- Team growth from 15 to 70 FTEs in the first year
- Reference customers include Shell, NetApp, JLL, and SKF
- Pay-as-you-go model provides flexibility as clients only pay for reports they order

The key is to capture the end user's needs in a way that allows for low-cost solutions. Being able to cover 95 percent of any use case in such well-prepared ways will lower the costs in the system dramatically, and will drive up customer happiness manyfold.

However, this all comes back to a very basic point that I have made repeatedly: the analytics use case needs to be thought through *beforehand*. We cannot expect to create a data lake, buy some very expensive tools at headquarters, and give Tableau and Qlikview licenses to everyone, and then think that things will happen miraculously. The key to success for modern analytics platforms will be the user experience of one-to-one marketing, not the smartest big data tool.

REGULATORY FLOODING OF THE RING OF KNOWLEDGE

In the aftermath of the 2008 financial crisis and the earlier scandals around WorldCom and Enron, as well as the 2012 London Interbank Offered Rate (LIBOR) manipulation, we are faced with a potentially ruinous level of regulatory rules flooding every industry. Governance broke down in those instances, and regulatory bodies are trying to prevent any recurrence. The risk and compliance functions in companies have undergone unprecedented growth, even in a world of shrinking budgets and cost controls. The complexities are huge, and while the regulators might agree on the fundamental objectives of the additional regulation, they take very different approaches around the globe. This regulatory flood creates big opportunities for mind+machine, but it also makes things harder and more expensive.

To demonstrate how complex relatively simple analytics use cases can become in this environment, let us look at financial benchmarks regulation. Prior to 2012, several banks manipulated LIBOR in their own interest. This was possible because LIBOR was calculated in a surprisingly simple and ungoverned way: a simple survey of 18 global banks. With no real governance to check if the survey answers were in line with actual market transactions by the submitting banks, the responses could be manipulated relatively easily.

The analytics involved in the LIBOR calculation could be performed by any smart fourth-grader: addition and division with 18 numbers. This is another good example of analytics actually being the smallest part of the analytics use case. What matters is the stuff around it.

When the scandal broke, an independent review was called and the UK Financial Conduct Authority (FCA) introduced sweeping reforms. Then the other regulators started homing in on this topic in totally different ways. For example, the European Commission proposed an EU-wide regulation of financial benchmarks, the details of which are still being fought over. This shows that even when everybody agrees on the objectives, the responses can be very different.

However, global banks operate globally by definition. So, how should they behave in this maze? There are three fundamental forces at work. First, people have very different responses to the same issue. Aligning everybody's interests is hugely complex and time-consuming, especially when multiple countries and regulators are involved. Second, the changes are not independent of each other. In the worst case, some might even be conflicting. Third, the regulation is fuzzy on the details in some areas and still open to interpretation.

The point of this chapter is not to describe all these regulatory changes in detail, which would be both boring and impossible. We can, however, categorize the regulatory efforts and describe their impact on mind+machine (see Figure II.2).

Financial Services		Healthcare		Other Industries
Global:	Basel III BCBS 239	US:	HIPAA HITECH	Industry- and/or country-specific regulations & standards
EU:	Solvency II CRD IV PSD MiFID II EMIR Financial Benchmarks	EU: APAC:	Mainly national Mainly national	
US:	GLBA Dodd-Frank			
APAC:	Local regulations			

Privacy:	EU:	GDPR, EU–US Privacy Shield Revoking safe harbour
	US:	National, but industry-specific (HIPAA, GLBA) State-level (MA Data Security Protection Act, CA Online Protection Act)
	APAC:	Less stringent, but rapid development in privacy law (Personal Data Protection Act 2012, Singapore)

Governance:	US:	Sarbanes-Oxley Act

Sustainability:	US:	Rules set by EPA/FDA
	EU:	Rules set by European Commission

Figure II.2 Regulatory Map

While an increasing regulatory zeal can be seen in many industries, functional areas, and geographies, there are certainly some hot spots of activity, some of which have global impact and generate thousands of new primary use cases around the world. Clearly, there are two industries that stand out: financial services and healthcare. However, there are four functional areas of regulation that are affecting companies globally: privacy, governance, discrimination, and sustainability. Nobody has the resources to run all these analytics manually, which creates a lot of demand for mind+machine. Let's look briefly at each area, but only from the perspective of mind+machine, not the underlying regulatory issues and discussions.

Financial services are clearly the front-runners in the race for who can create more regulatory oversight. Figure II.2 shows the most important areas, including topics such as capital adequacy, payments, financial benchmarks, risk and compliance, and all sorts of financial instruments in banking, asset management, and insurance. Each and every one of these regulations comes hand in hand with huge reporting needs that generate very significant analytics needs with large, rapidly changing data sets. Interestingly, regulators required the hiring of additional risk analysts in 2015, not an easy task in an already dried-up market for risk analysts. With tough deadlines and high penalties, managers simply have no choice but to comply with all regulations, even hiring expensive full-time equivalents (FTEs) with less experience than one would expect, given the salaries. The COO of a Swiss asset manager told me that he paid CHF 200,000 in base salary (approximately USD 208,000 in March 2016) for a risk and compliance manager with a combined *two* years' experience in business. Economists use the term *inelastic market* for this effect. These regulatory changes are driving analytics use cases in risk, compliance, and fraud, and a whole industry of tool and service providers has grown in this market.

Compared to financial services, the regulations in healthcare are surprisingly stable with respect to mind+machine, with the exception of how they apply to new topics. For example, should smart watches that send personal health information (PHI) to apps run by corporations be considered regulated by the Health Insurance Portability and Accountability Act (HIPAA) of 1996?

The functional topics that drive analytics are another aspect. New regulations for governance and compliance—for example, the MiFID II (Markets in Financial Instruments Directive), BCBS 239 (Basel Committee for Banking Supervision regulation for risk aggregation and risk reporting), or the 2002 Sarbanes-Oxley (SOX) Act—drive new levels of oversight and compliance. While MiFID II and BCBS 239 are focused on banking, SOX is ubiquitous for all companies listed in the United States. These rules create a lot of analytics use cases.

Another functional area of new reporting needs is sustainability. Companies are now asked to track and report their activities, and agencies such as the US Environmental Protection Agency or Food and Drug Administration or the European Commission continue to set their own rules.

All of the preceding areas require a huge amount of activities along the Ring of Knowledge, stretching it to the point of breaking. In particular, regulations that require companies to aggregate their risks centrally force them to collect, analyze, and report data from across their organizations. In addition, there is a big need for audit trails, spotting strange patterns, errors, or suspected improper behavior. The twenty-first century is likely to become the Century of Reporting and Audit Trails, as all people want to cover themselves. A simple back-of-the-envelope calculation shows that there is new demand for 5,000 to 10,000 new professionals in risk and compliance globally.

THE EUROPEAN UNION AND PRIVACY RULES: THE GENERAL DATA PROTECTION REGULATION AND THE EU–US PRIVACY SHIELD

Vicious and often stealthy attacks on our privacy and personal identity have emerged as a truly dangerous threat, because whatever personal data is out there will remain out there—as many hopeful applicants who would have liked to be hired now realize. We are not in full control of what is shared by us—certainly, we can share our own photos from the wild party we attended and that's our responsibility, but we can also appear in other people's posts.

Fifteen years of very liberal default settings on a ton of social media channels combined with a surprising amount of exhibitionism have created the largest set of public personal data ever in the history of this planet. Only now are the regulators waking up to the topic. These new rule sets make the data scientist's life more difficult, but better protect the consumer on privacy issues and who should own, process, or sell personal information.

The European Commission is the leading regulator in this field with its General Data Protection Regulation (GDPR), which will go into effect in 2018.[9] It will affect the Ring of Knowledge in a major way, so it is worth understanding in more detail. Here are some key excerpts:[10]

The rapid pace of technological change and globalization have profoundly transformed the way in which an ever-increasing volume of personal data is collected, accessed, used and transferred. New ways of sharing information through social networks and storing large amounts of data remotely have become part of life for many of Europe's 250 million Internet users. At the same time, personal data has become an asset for many businesses. Collecting, aggregating and analyzing the data of potential customers is often an important part of their economic activities. In this new digital environment, individuals have the right to enjoy effective control over their personal information. Data protection is a fundamental right in Europe, enshrined in Article 8 of the Charter of Fundamental Rights of the European Union, as well as in Article 16(1) of the Treaty on the Functioning of the European Union (TFEU), and needs to be protected accordingly. Lack of confidence makes consumers hesitant to buy online and accept new services. Therefore, a high level of data protection is also crucial to enhance trust in online services and to fulfill the potential of the digital economy, thereby encouraging economic growth and the competitiveness of EU industries.

Modern, coherent rules across the EU are needed for data to flow freely from one Member State to another. Businesses need clear and uniform rules that provide legal certainty and minimize the administrative burden. This is essential if the Single Market is to function and to stimulate economic growth, create new jobs and foster innovation. A modernization of the EU's data protection rules, which strengthens their internal market dimension, ensures a high level of data protection for individuals, and promotes legal certainty, clarity and consistency, therefore plays a central role in the European Commission's Stockholm Action Plan, in the Digital Agenda for Europe and, more broadly, for the EU's growth strategy Europe 2020.

THE TEETH OF THE GENERAL DATA PROTECTION REGULATION

Putting individuals in control of their personal data: Users are often not fully aware that their data is being collected. "Although many Europeans consider that disclosure of personal data is increasingly a part of modern life, 72 percent of Internet users in Europe still worry that they are being asked for too much personal data online. They feel they are not in control of their data. They are not properly informed of what happens to their personal information, to whom it is transmitted and for what purposes. Often, they do not know how to exercise their rights online."

- **Respect the "right to be forgotten."** This will include provisions such as "an explicit requirement that obliges online social networking services (and all other data controllers) to minimize the volume of users' personal data that they collect and process; a requirement that the default settings ensure that data is not made public; an explicit obligation for data controllers to delete an individual's personal data if that person explicitly requests deletion and where there is no other legitimate reason to retain it."
- **Give data breach notifications.** Companies will be required "to strengthen their security measures to prevent and avoid breaches; and to notify data breaches to both the national data protection authority—within 24 hours of the breach being discovered, where feasible—and the individuals concerned without undue delay."
- **Improve individuals' ability to control their data.** "Ensuring that, when their consent is required, it is given explicitly, meaning that it is based either

Virtual Analyst:
Intelligent Pricing & Dynamic Discounting

Context

Organization
Global mobile network operator

Industry
Telecommunications

Function(s)
Corporate marketing

Geography
India

Business Challenge

- Monitor the performance of an intelligent pricing and dynamic discounting solution
- Develop a strategy to drive its growth across 10 regions in India
- Make the solution scalable for efficient future growth

Solution

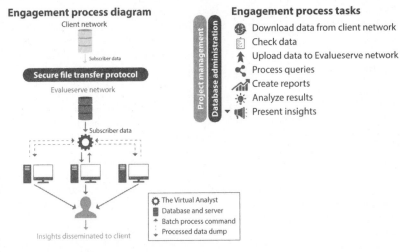

Engagement process diagram
Client network
Subscriber data
Secure file transfer protocol
Evalueserve network
Subscriber data
Insights disseminated to client

Project management
Database administration

Engagement process tasks
- Download data from client network
- Check data
- Upload data to Evalueserve network
- Process queries
- Create reports
- Analyze results
- Present insights

The Virtual Analyst
Database and server
Batch process command
Processed data dump

Approach

- Prioritized process tasks into three distinct stages:
  Stage 1: Created the Virtual Analyst to automate core **data-processing** tasks
  Stage 2: Enhanced the Virtual Analyst by automating **presentation-related** tasks
  Stage 3: Enhanced the Virtual Analyst to include **project management** tasks

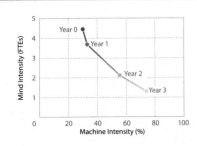

Analytics Challenges

- Inconsistent volume, velocity, and structure of subscriber data from different regions
- High manual effort: repetitive interventions, which made the output error-prone
- Complexity of designing algorithms by identifying trigger events and interfacing different stages
- Sensitive subscriber data
- High dependence on IT infrastructure for the creation of a simulated environment and to replicate user load

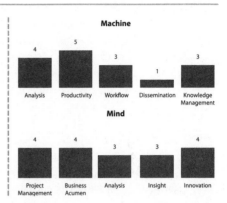

Benefits

Productivity	Time to Market	New Capabilities	Quality
• Achieved 70% efficiency gains over 15 months • Increased efficiency of project management and governance	• Reduced the deliverable turnaround time • Improved reporting performance by achieving efficiency gains in Stage 2	• Introduced triggers to improve reaction efficiency • Freed up analysts' time so that they could focus on providing valuable insights	• Reduced error probability to less than 1% • Improved attrition management by documenting processes • Enhanced visualization through effective trend analysis

Implementation

- **Design:** 180 hours
- **Implementation:** 400 hours
  Stage 1: 220 hours
  Stage 2: 110 hours
  Stage 3: 70 hours
- **Testing:** 150 hours
  Stage 1: 90 hours
  Stage 2: 30 hours
  Stage 3: 30 hours
- **Maintenance:** 40 hours per annum
- Annual savings of 4,500 hours

on a statement or on a clear affirmative action by the person concerned and is freely given; equipping Internet users with an effective right to be forgotten in the online environment: the right to have their data deleted if they withdraw their consent and if there are no other legitimate grounds for retaining the data; guaranteeing easy access to one's own data and a right to data portability: a right to obtain a copy of the stored data from the controller and the freedom to move it from one service provider to another, without hindrance; reinforcing the right to information so that individuals fully understand how their personal data is handled, particularly when the processing activities concern children."

- **Improve the means for individuals to exercise their rights.** "Strengthening national data protection authorities' independence and powers, so that they are properly equipped to deal effectively with complaints, with powers to carry out effective investigations, take binding decisions and impose effective and dissuasive sanctions; enhancing administrative and judicial remedies when data protection rights are violated. In particular, qualified associations will be able to bring actions to court on behalf of the individual."

Reinforcing data security: "Encouraging the use of privacy-enhancing technologies (technologies which protect the privacy of information by minimizing the storage of personal data), privacy-friendly default settings and privacy certification schemes; introducing a general obligation for data controllers to notify data breaches without undue delay to both data protection authorities (which, where feasible, should be within 24 hours) and the individuals concerned."

Enhancing the accountability of those processing data: "Requiring data controllers to designate a Data Protection Officer in companies with more than 250 employees and in firms which are involved in processing operations which, by virtue of their nature, their scope or their purposes, present specific risks to the rights and freedoms of individuals ('risky processing'); introducing the 'Privacy by Design' principle to make sure that data protection safeguards are taken into account at the planning stage of procedures and systems; introducing the obligation to carry out Data Protection Impact Assessments for organizations involved in risky processing."

Protecting data in a globalized world: "Individuals' rights must continue to be ensured when personal data is transferred from the EU to third countries, and whenever individuals in Member States are targeted and their data is used or analyzed by third country service providers. This means that EU data protection standards have to apply regardless of the geographical location of a company or its processing facility. In today's globalized world, personal data is being transferred across an increasing number of virtual and geographical borders and stored on servers in multiple countries. More companies are offering cloud-computing services, which allow customers to access and store data on remote servers. These factors call for an improvement in current mechanisms for transferring data to third countries. This includes adequacy decisions—i.e., decisions certifying 'adequate' data protection standards in third countries—and appropriate safeguards such as standard contractual clauses or Binding Corporate Rules, so as to secure a high level of data protection in international processing operations and facilitate data flows across borders."

These rules will have a very significant impact on the relationships with other countries, as already experienced through the termination of the Safe Harbour agreement with the United States, which obviously came as a shock to the 5,000 US companies that had registered their activities under it. A replacement needed to be found rapidly. On February 2, 2016, the European Union and the United States agreed on a new framework called the EU–US Privacy Shield, which essentially ensures the protection of EU consumers equivalent to the GDPR. "The new arrangement will provide stronger obligations on companies in the US to protect the personal data of Europeans and stronger monitoring and enforcement by the US Department of Commerce and Federal Trade Commission (FTC), including through increased cooperation with European Data Protection Authorities."[11] The key provisions in this framework agreement are:

- Strong obligations on companies handling Europeans' personal data and robust enforcement: US companies wishing to import personal data from Europe will need to commit to robust obligations on how personal data is processed and individual rights are guaranteed. The Department of Commerce will monitor that companies publish their commitments, which makes them enforceable under US law by the US Federal Trade Commission. In addition, any company handling human resources data from Europe has to commit to comply with decisions by European data protection authorities (DPAs).
- Clear safeguards and transparency obligations on US government access: For the first time, the United States has given the EU written assurances that the access of public authorities for law enforcement and national security will be subject to clear limitations, safeguards, and oversight mechanisms. These exceptions must be used only to the extent necessary and proportionate. The United States has ruled out indiscriminate mass surveillance on the personal data transferred to the United States under the new arrangement. To regularly monitor the functioning of the arrangement there will be an annual joint review, which will also include the issue of national security access. The European Commission and the US Department of Commerce will conduct the review and invite national intelligence experts from the US and European data protection authorities to it.
- Effective protection of EU citizens' rights with several redress possibilities: Any citizens who consider that their data has been misused under the new arrangement will have several redress possibilities. Companies have

deadlines to reply to complaints. European DPAs can refer complaints to the Department of Commerce and the Federal Trade Commission. In addition, alternative dispute resolution will be free of charge. For complaints on possible access by national intelligence authorities, a new ombudsperson will be created.

Without any doubt, the EU–US Privacy Shield will have a strong model character for all other countries trying to do business in the European Union or with EU consumers.

PRIVACY IMPACTING THE RING OF KNOWLEDGE

How will this affect the Ring of Knowledge? Massively. Any mind+machine effort, specifically the ones using personal information, will have to put safeguards in place that automatically comply with the GDPR and the EU–US Privacy Shield. Essentially, all Minds and all Machines will have to be trained on what this means for them.

The definition of *personal data* is the real crux of the matter. Is it just data that identifies an individual either directly or through combination with some other information, or are pseudonyms or unique identifiers enough (i.e., without some other information that allows reidentification)? This is a critical question for all data scientists operating in the field. Currently, in the European Union, only data that directly identifies an individual and data that identifies an individual when combined with other information held by the data controller, which is the company that decides how personal data is to be used, is considered personal data. So stand-alone pseudonyms or unique reference numbers were not considered personal data, unless the data controller could combine them with other information to identify the individual. GDPR *will change this*. All data that identifies an individual, whether directly or indirectly, will be personal data. There is no longer a requirement for the company to personally hold another data set that would allow the reidentification. So any pseudonym or unique identifier is likely to be considered personal data. This broader definition of personal data will affect lots of analytics use cases, and you must be on top of this in order to avoid ticking time bombs in your operations. More importantly, due to the EU–US Privacy Shield, US companies also need to take this very seriously. The only question is how the regulator will treat pseudonymous data and how stringent the detailed rules will be. There is still a lot of lobbying going on from both sides, and only time will tell. Prudent businesses will certainly prepare their systems to cope with any outcome.

The area of profiling is also hotly contested, which has been broadly defined as "any form of automated processing of personal data intended to evaluate certain personal aspects relating to a natural person or to analyze or predict in particular that natural person's performance at work, economic situation, location, health, personal preferences, reliability or behavior." This is a very broad definition, and could capture any big data analytics use case of any data-driven business. Your smart watch might already be producing a lot of this data, and your daily activity levels and your heart rate might be very interesting for life insurance companies. GDPR will require your *explicit* consent for this data to be collected *and used for personal profiling and for any repurposing of the data*. For example, Google ads would require your consent to use your past search history. More importantly, the regulation will require the default settings to be for opting out, which means that Google will not be able to use your past search history unless you give your consent by actively hitting a button or checking a box. Gone will be the days where you spend an hour trying to find and figure out the settings on Facebook, scratching your head, having to switch at least 20 settings to "me only." And if companies want to sell or repurpose the data, they need to tell you and get your consent. Good luck with this one!

THE NINE QUESTIONS YOU NEED TO ASK YOUR CIO REGARDING PERSONAL DATA

So, here are the nine questions you need to ask your chief information officer (CIO) in order avoid fines of up to EUR 1 million or 2 percent of annual world-wide revenues:

1. Do we have all the right data protection policies in place? The national regulators might ask for them.
2. Do we have a governance group managed by a senior executive, and if we have more than 250 employees, do we have a data protection officer? Can we properly report our activities regarding data protection?
3. Do we have an updated data register telling us what data we have where and why? Can we prove that we *minimize* the collection and storage of personal data, and that we store it for only a "justifiable duration"? This might be harder than it looks. A bank's personal data project officer told me that the bank was going through 2,500 software applications and more than 100,000 share drives to find out where it had stored personal data. The project took more than three years and several million Swiss francs.
4. Did we get the explicit consent for data storage and profiling from our customers, and can we prove it? What do we do with pre-GDPR data sets? Are our profiling activities limited to customers who have given consent, or are our data scientists *unknowingly* still using personal data without consent somewhere deep down there in the often *undocumented* code?
5. Do we have a breach notification process in place?
6. Are we ready for the rights to be forgotten, of erasure, and of data portability? Can the customers see their own data online and easily request its deletion online?

7. Are we ready to provide transparency to the customer on repurposing of the data? Are we sure that nobody creates a hidden profit center selling data to third parties?
8. Are we in control of data transfers to other geographies or to third parties? Can we guarantee that the right intracompany and intercompany agreements are in place, effectively ensuring that GDPR applies?
9. Are our systems designed using "privacy by design," and can we prove it, independently of whether we bought or built the systems? Are our vendors and partners on top of GDPR?

Any analytics use case using personal data needs to be compliant with this framework. This means that the issue of personal data needs to be documented and knowledge-managed along the whole Ring of Knowledge *and by each individual use case*, not just for the general portfolio of use cases. How to do this? We will address this topic in Part III.

It is not likely that more than 1 percent of the readers of this book will be even remotely in a position to judge all of the preceding questions, but the likelihood is high that you will have a few great questions to ask if someone is trying you to bluff you with talk of AI, big data, and the Internet of Things, but the person has not yet thought through the implications of these data privacy issues. I hope that this thought compensates you somewhat for the headache you got from reading this chapter!

THE SEISMIC SHIFT TO PAY-AS-YOU-GO OR OUTPUT-BASED COMMERCIAL MODELS

In restaurants, in sporting events, in space missions, and in business, success is entirely dependent on the *outcome*. If the result is not what people want, then there will be no applause or satisfaction. Analytics use cases are no different. Decision makers in sales, marketing, R&D, licensing, supply chain, and general management are willing to pay to get the ultimate insights, not just to get data scientists, big data tools, and AI algorithms.

Why is it then that 99 percent of all analytics delivered by mind+machine or Mind alone is still dependent on input-based pricing? Why are people still paying for teams of data scientists, expensive licenses for data and tools, and the opportunity costs of other people in the organization to make sense of tables and reports regardless of whether the ultimate insight can be generated? It might be because the decision makers are not even experiencing the cost directly (e.g., if they are paying via nontransparent allocations from corporate headquarters). They will be told that this is the cost of doing business.

Recently, a division head told me that he had received a multi-million-dollar allocation from corporate for something called "central analytics services." At the same time his sales and marketing people gave him some lukewarm feedback on the central output with no independent ability to prove any positive ROI for the division. Does this sound familiar? The same manager told me: "Actually, the overhead cost allocation itself is a big data analytics use case! It keeps everybody busy for about three months during the budgeting season. But

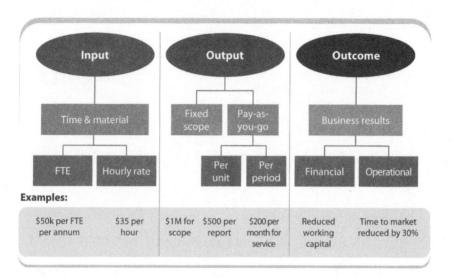

Figure II.3   Input versus Output versus Outcome Based

who should do this analysis? The data scientists themselves? No way. Finance? Hmmm. Then who? So, every year we end up with some top-down decision making nobody really understands. Whatever we pay for, it is certainly not output-based."

Clearly output-based mind+machine services models will gain a lot of traction in the future. But before we dive into the pros and cons of such models, we need to clarify the terminology. As with big data and AI, there is already a certain confusion creeping in. Figure II.3 tries to give some structure to this discussion.

There is a big difference between output-based and outcome-based delivery models. In our restaurant analogy, the menu defines the exact outputs (i.e., the dishes) at very specific prices. You are not interested in how many chefs or servers there are in the restaurant. All you want is a great, tasty meal for a known price. Outcome-based, in contrast, would correspond to your feeling after having consumed the dishes and the beverages. You might feel happy, elated, disappointed, or simply full. This analogy also works quite nicely, because it shows the restaurant's lack of ability to influence everything.

In business it is very similar. Output is defined as a product delivered, for example a qualified early-stage sales opportunity, a pitch book in investment banking, an updated valuation model for a medium-complexity company, or a patent landscape. Outcome-based models are defined in terms of a business outcome, for example a 5 percent reduction in accounts receivable. Both models have about as many flavors as there are species and cultivars of roses in Queen Mary's Gardens in the Regent's Park in London. There are specialist consulting firms such as TPI Consulting or Alsbridge that specialize in this field, but the basics are quite simple. It always comes down to a continuum of allocation of scope, responsibilities, and economic risk between the client and the provider. At one extreme there is a simple staff augmentation (i.e., you hire a team of, say, five highly trained professionals and tell them exactly what to do), whereas the opposite extreme is managed services, where the service provider takes over the full responsibility for the process or the use case, and the output will be measured according to cost, time, and quality. Very often it is very difficult to describe and measure the exact scope of activities, though, which makes managed services a little tricky. Since the early days of IT outsourcing in the 1990s, the industry has evolved a lot. The capabilities of the vendor community significantly outstrip the skills of some functions inside the companies, which is why there is a trend toward more outsourcing and more specialization. Cloud services are a new wave of specialized services that are starting to emerge. In analytics, the same trends are visible, likely to be called DAaaS (data analytics as a service), as these days anything that is not dubbed "aaS" ("as a service") won't engender the feeling of great value. A friend jokingly remarked to me recently that restaurants might soon be called FaaS!

It all started with GE Capital International Services (GECIS; now Genpact) and American Express's Travel Related Services Company (TRS) unit in India in the late 1990s, where advanced analytics became possible in a remote service provisioning model, called knowledge process outsourcing (KPO). Since then an increasingly mature vendor community has emerged globally.

It is clear, of course, that outcome-based relationships must be far broader in scope, as the vendor delivering such outcomes must be able to make decisions on behalf of the client. Such engagements are still small in number and are fraught with risks for both parties for obvious reasons, as the service provider will hardly ever, and should not, control all aspects of decision making. But how can they then be responsible for the business results and be paid on performance? There are certain areas where such deals work reasonably well, as the processes are straightforward and clearly defined without too many interfaces (e.g., for accounts receivable management, payroll, or some specific areas in the supply chain). Other areas such as sales, marketing, or innovation are much harder to insulate in terms of measuring outcomes or allocating clear responsibilities.

In mind+machine analytics, the big push is not happening in outcome-based models, but in output-based models, where units and the corresponding prices can be clearly defined. The share of such models is likely to increase from less than 2 percent in 2016 to about 20 percent by 2021. Why? A favorable combination of specialization leading to lower per-unit costs, faster delivery, better quality, new capabilities, and the need for more flexibility adjusting to the uncertainties of today's volatile markets.

Now here comes a very important but usually badly understood point, which is highly relevant for mind+machine analytics. Everybody seems to focus on external service providers, neglecting the fact that there should not really be any difference between internal and external service providers in how they are being measured and managed. Why should companies' internal central big data scientist teams or Indian, Latin American, or Eastern European captives (i.e., subsidiaries of global companies in low-cost locations) be measured differently in any way compared to external service providers? There are no reasons. But why is it that captives usually have far less performance pressure than external providers? Why aren't there clearly defined service-level agreements (SLAs) in place with the actual end users in the line? Why do captives rarely develop leading-edge technology for mind+machine use cases? We are back to the topic of psychology in analytics, compliance, and the lack of thinking in analytics use cases.

Captives are blocks of cost, usually paid for by the center. As an example: a major bank set up a captive unit in India. In order to push volume into the unit, the center prefinanced all investments and the businesses were loaded with only the variable costs (i.e., the salaries of the employees). In the due diligence process for selling off the captive, we learned that several components (e.g., a special type of telecom equipment) cost about *three times* what we had paid for exactly the same type of equipment just a few months prior. Of course, such mechanics lead to a distortion of the economic realities, as the businesses can buy the services on a variable-cost basis only, which is probably about 30 percent lower than the actual, fully loaded cost. Inevitably, such misguided economics will come to light once the first and possibly second generation of managers who built the captive have gone and the true picture is allowed to emerge.

Of course, there are also good reasons (e.g., truly required compliance rules) to have captives, and many of them are tightly run and managed, for example the large-scale captives of some of the major consulting firms, banks, or industrial players. The point is not to say that captives or central data scientist teams should not exist—far from it. The point is that the line unit managers paying for the service should be able to insist on transparency for their own analytics use case. Part III will discuss how the Use Case Methodology can be used to force transparency.

Increasingly, Evalueserve's clients are asking for output-based pricing for analytics use cases, something that did not exist even in 2012 or 2013. Where does this trend come from? Clearly, cloud-based offerings in various domains have created demand for such offerings in analytics as well. Microsoft Office is now being sold via the web in monthly installments, pay-as-you-go (PAYG). Autodesk's 3D CAD/CAM platform Fusion 360 is cloud-based and PAYG. The mobile operator Lebara sells monthly bundles of mobile minutes and data packages, as do many other mobile virtual network operators (MVNOs)—companies that own their own brands but use a classical operator's network. Cloud-based models such as CRM on HubSpot are also PAYG. Applying such generic models to the world of analytics is only a small, logical step. What are the drivers for output-based PAYG models, in cloud or enterprise mode, and what are their benefits for the customers? Here are eight possibilities:

1. **Low up-front costs and investments:** Getting started is easy and quick. For example, a company profile costs USD 200 to 1,000 depending on

the complexity and depth. A patent landscape costs USD 1,500 to 2,500. Most companies have threshold levels for investments that need to be approved by a central investment committee. This can take ages. PAYG helps in transforming capital expenditures (capex) into normal operating costs (opex). This can mean the difference between a painful three- to six-month approval process at very senior levels and a quick business-oriented decision at the business owner's level.

2. **Reduced risks and increased managerial flexibility:** Due to the smaller commitments, the risks involved are much smaller as well. The client can switch on and off according to its own demand, matching the user's market volatility with shorter time commitments at the back end. If business is bad, costs can be taken out quickly. Your CFO will like this.

3. **Specialization:** If units of output can be defined and if there is enough scale, the potential of mind+machine can flourish to its fullest degree. The provider of the use case can come up with best-practice automations that improve the product significantly, way beyond what captives would be able to do. In fact, a company profile generated by InsightBee is only half of the cost of a fully manual profile, since it uses specialized software and processes to create the product. Similarly, Google can invest billions in making its searches better. Nobody would get their own internal IT function to build the next search engine. This is an area that is a strategic issue for captives and internal data analytics units, which will become a major problem with an increasing level of Machine coming in. Captives and internal teams have only a single client by definition: their own company. They do not get the broad exposure to a wide global market with very different customer needs. Moreover, they usually don't have the millions of dollars to invest and later amortize the technology over large volumes of work.

4. **Increased agility:** Being agile is becoming increasingly important. When companies use agile as their development methodology for new products (e.g., three weekly sprints for software development), PAYG can make a huge difference, as a solution can be tried out and launched within a few days.

5. **Improved transparency:** Cost allocation becomes much more immediate and can be linked to the user in a far more transparent way, avoiding complex and nontransparent cost allocations altogether. Of course, a small downside is that volume swings can create cost swings as well, which may make things harder to plan.

6. **The right incentives for everyone involved:** Would you saw off the branch of the tree you are sitting on? Probably not. So then why would an internal function or a vendor who charges you for inputs (i.e., data scientists, data and software licenses) want to reduce the per-unit costs? Right, they won't, unless they have an incentive to do so. Per-unit pricing achieves this, since a vendor will be able to improve its profitability by becoming more

efficient. Ultimately, such benefits will be passed on at least partly to the clients as well. Here is a quote from a meeting with a COO of the asset management division of a major bank: "mind+machine for pitches? We have not heard this from our captive or graphics vendors so far. Everything is still manual. You can really take out 30 percent of the cost by automating? But then again, why would they want to reduce their head count? I get it."

7. **Plug-and-play in combination with the cloud:** When you combine PAYG with cloud solutions, it becomes almost plug-and-play. Such solutions need far less solution engineering than the current enterprise solutions. Granted, some data interfaces that can exchange data with other machines automatically (e.g., application programming interfaces and ADIs) are required for a seamless interaction between two machines, but especially in analytics this is rather straightforward.

8. **Always up-to-date:** PAYG allows instant upgrades, as by definition the contract period is so short that it allows instant renewal. In this way, the business will be up-to-date at all times. Of course, application programming interfaces might need to be adjusted, but this is still much better than having to wait for the expiry of the current licenses that have been paid for up front or contracted for one to three years.

As you will see in Part III, the Use Case Methodology is ideally suited to the PAYG model. Of course, there is also the vendor's perspective, be it an internal vendor like a central data analytics team or an external vendor like InsightBee. There are advantages and disadvantages. Let's analyze three advantages first:

1. **Huge addressable market:** Innovative attackers can easily overtake sleepy incumbents, but some of them have grabbed the PAYG opportunity. What would have happened if Microsoft had not switched to its cloud and mobile strategy? Microsoft's share price has doubled since April 2013. Assigning the full gain to its PAYG strategy in the cloud would certainly not be justified, but the commercial cloud offering is growing quickly and has already surpassed USD 9.4 billion in Q4 2015. A lot of it is PAYG of some kind. Adobe's share price has more than doubled since April 2013. Adobe has also gone completely cloud and mobile and largely PAYG. Its three key areas, Creative Cloud, Document Cloud, and Marketing Cloud, are both expanding existing markets and addressing new customer segments. In fact, Adobe estimates its 2018 market opportunity to be around USD 27 billion.[12]

2. **Attackers love it:** Where sleepy incumbents have been slow to adapt, the attackers are having field days. Companies like HubSpot in CRM and marketing or players in human resources, such as Zoho, Workable, or SnapHRM, are growing aggressively in a field formerly dominated by the

heavyweight enterprise resource planning (ERP) system providers. Clearly, some incumbents have not switched their strategies as aggressively as Microsoft and Adobe, and are therefore going to be subject to the onslaught by such agile attackers.

3. **Shorter sales cycles and lower cost of sales:** Services provided in the classical enterprise model have extremely long sales cycles, from at least a few months to several years. Due to the much lower barriers to entry, the sales cycle can be minutes in some cases. Due to the cloud nature of most of the PAYG models, the costs of sales are much lower than the costs of the classical enterprise sales. Granted, there are hybrid models and the classical key account managers are still very valuable, but addressing the small and medium-sized companies market is now possible.

So far, this model has worked extremely well for software providers. In the mind+machine market the first few models are becoming available now—for example, InsightBee for sales intelligence or the Banker's Studio for investment banking pitch books and models. However, it is clear that the same software market drivers are also going to provide large opportunities for service providers in the analytics market. Evalueserve expects to multiply its user base from about 50,000 people to about 1 million users on the basis of its cloud-based platform InsightBee. The Market, Sales, and Procurement Intelligence versions of InsightBee (see use cases) were the first cloud-based mind+machine output-based models in market, sales, and procurement intelligence. They provide very clearly defined products on a PAYG basis supported heavily by machines.

Of course, there are also a couple of disadvantages:

1. **Volume swings:** What is an advantage for the customer can turn into a planning nightmare for the provider, especially in a mind+machine model. In a pure software model, scaling up and down is easy. A few servers will get a little more or a little less work. In a mind+machine world, utilization is critical for profitability. While there is certainly underlying growth, volume swings during low-demand times such as the end-of-year holiday season can be as much as 50 percent.

2. **Lower stickiness and increased, global competition:** Very short contract or subscription periods or fully variable PAYG models reduce the stickiness of the client relationship. Such models can easily turn into the winner-takes-all situations for the market leader. Followers must have the better product in order to win. This will certainly create much tougher competition, as hiding behind sticky enterprise contracts will no longer be possible.

Of course, not all services will ultimately be output-based. However, the philosophy of analytics use cases forces everyone to focus on the output rather than the reallocation of the costs of the inputs. With the predicted explosion of

InsightBee Sales Intelligence: Proactive Identification of New Sales Opportunities

Context

Organization
Companies of all sizes

Function(s)
Sales and business development

Industry
B2B companies only

Geography
Global

Business Challenge

- Proactively identify qualified sales leads and deliver them to salespeople via mobile devices
- Help target opportunities faster
- Set account strategies

Solution

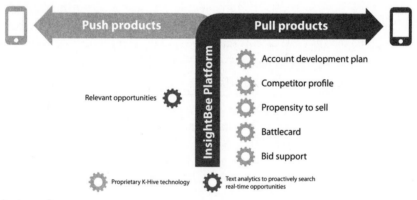

Push products

- Relevant opportunities

Pull products

- Account development plan
- Competitor profile
- Propensity to sell
- Battlecard
- Bid support

InsightBee Platform

Proprietary K-Hive technology

Text analytics to proactively search real-time opportunities

Approach

- Assess client's sales strategies, products, and target accounts
- Set up a mind map and algorithms for the Opportunity Engine
- Commence daily monitoring data sources for sales opportunities via the Opportunity Engine
- Qualify leads and send alerts to the client
- Integrate with CRM systems to improve workflow and tracking of leads

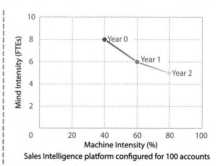

Sales Intelligence platform configured for 100 accounts

Analytics Challenges

- Understanding the events and development triggers in the B2B sales scenario to create a mind map of events
- Identifying and prioritizing the sales triggers that define the search algorithm within the Sales Intelligence platform
- Customize platform for particular clients and their target accounts
- Analyzing information from thousands of structured and unstructured data sources to identify a potential opportunity

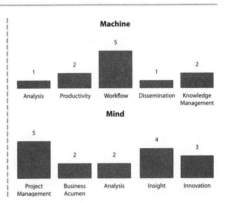

Benefits

Productivity	Time to Market	New Capabilities	Quality
• Knowledge management technology improves productivity by at least 50% • APIs integrate with the client CRM to improve workflow	• Custom reports delivered 50% faster	• Proactive monitoring of key prospects or sectors • Cloud-based platform for easy access • Scalable to the needed number of accounts & industries	• Customized to filter out unimportant news • Accept/reject option for each alert (continual learning)

Implementation

- Revenue of USD 6 million for a telecommunications client in less than a year
- Increased its sales pipeline from USD 25 million to USD 61 million in less than a year for a leading data storage system
- Identified opportunities worth €150 million for a manufacturing company
- Tool based on the InsightBee platform technology
- Concept to minimum viable product: 6 months
- Cost: USD 350 thousand
- External partners include user experience and user interface designer, external development team, text analytics expert

analytics use cases (e.g., through Internet of Things, risk and compliance, and big data), output-based thinking will be essential if you want to keep costs from going through the roof.

This chapter has shown how new economic models are emerging. The big behemoths of software have already based their entire strategies on them. mind+machine analytics will follow suit, albeit with an offset of 5 to 10 years.

THE HIDDEN TREASURES OF MULTIPLE-CLIENT UTILITIES

Here comes a chapter that shows that there is a huge savings potential left in many processes if smarter and better architectures were applied. As a bonus, there is the potential for additional efficiency gains from applying machines.

Let's start with a small example to illustrate the point. Think of the country you live in. Now think of the cities in your country and the roads connecting them. Would it make sense to build a direct road without any intersections for every possible city-to-city combination? The electorate would certainly vote politicians out of office for suggesting something as nonsensical as this, of course assuming some form of direct democracy!

Then why is it that there are so few multiple-client utilities (i.e., joint data assets serving a whole industry)? Let's look at the famous example of "know your customer" (KYC) in banking. There are about 20,000 retail and commercial banks in the world, many of which want to do business with a varying subset of the other 19,999 banks. To do so, they need to satisfy the so-called KYC requirement; that is, they need to know that the correspondent bank isn't some money-laundering outfit. So they need to collect some information about that bank according to a standard form. Currently all banks do KYC on every other bank they are trading with, even though they all collect almost the same information. In mathematical terms, this is like a chessboard, just with 20,000 rows and columns instead of eight each. If every bank were to do KYC on every other bank, this would lead to about 400 million KYC documents being created and kept up to date in the world. Fortunately, not every bank trades with every other bank. So let's assume that we are talking about only 10 percent of this number (i.e., 40 million documents). Now, let's further assume that creating and maintaining

133

each document takes a few hours per year—say five hours. This corresponds to an average of five people for every bank doing this work, or a total of 100,000 employees. Of course, big banks would have many more, whereas small banks would probably have only one or two.

Now think of a central collection point that could store such records and be accessible to banks that need the KYC information. In such a situation, 20,000 banks would provide the documentation and the global need for KYC personnel would be only 50 full-time equivalents. What huge savings! The banks have tried to agree to a common standard. Companies such as KYC Exchange Net AG have developed very nice technology. So why is it not happening? Nobody knows. Banks are not really competing on the basis of KYC, or at least we hope they are not. And ultimately, you are paying for this inefficiency. It is amazing to see that everybody seems to reinvent the wheel, and not just one wheel: many slightly different wheels all doing the same job.

Over the years we have seen lots of such unnecessary duplications. Here are a few further examples. Every competitive intelligence department in the world seems to feel that its template is better and needs to be different. Every equities analyst seems to believe that his or her valuation models need to be unique. How could it otherwise be possible that during a model audit we found 12 different definitions for the "number of shares" in a single equities research department? Definitions included shares at the beginning or end of the month or quarter, with or without warrants, and so on. This is not only artistic freedom—it is simply risky. Sometimes such differences are simply differences in taste or interpretation, but not fundamentally flawed. However, sometimes they are simply wrong.

Why do companies not reuse thinking other people have done before them? We are probably back to the psychology of analytics, the not-invented-here syndrome. There would be a huge potential for shared utilities and reuse if there were a way to certify best practices and to share them with other users for all the use cases where companies do not directly compete.

In client meetings, I use an example of a very simple utility everybody understands immediately: the clean logos use case we discussed in Part I. Have you ever had to cut and paste a company logo from a company's website onto a PowerPoint page? From the highly engaged and emotional reactions I get when I ask this question, I estimate that there are very few people who have never done this during their careers; maybe they are as rare as planets with some kind of life form on them. If you belong to this population, you belong to a very lucky species not to have wasted your time. This is a classic example of an embarrassingly simple multiple-client utility that generates huge savings. The asset has to be built and updated only once. The macros go and fetch the clean logos in milliseconds. We calculated the time saved to be about 12,000 hours per large investment bank and probably even more for consulting firms. According to Wikipedia, there are about 120 large or independent investment banks and financial conglomerates doing mergers and acquisitions (M&A) work, and about 100 largish consulting and accounting firms. Collectively, they would therefore save more than a staggering *one million hours* if everybody used the same utility. How's that for savings? Imagine what the bankers and consultants could do with all that time.

Let's go back to the demographics of mind+machine analytics use cases. Even with very conservative estimates, a truly huge amount of work could be saved, probably in the billions of hours. Of course, not every use case is as simple. Many of them have to be slightly different for very specific reasons. However, many of them can be parameterized while still maintaining the same underlying logic. Smart engineering using mind+machine can still realize a large percentage of these savings.

Why hasn't it happened so far? There is no efficient mechanism to allow sharing and reuse. It happens only when vendors see the potential across their client base and come up with products that make sense. In Part III, we will discuss how the Use Case Methodology can make this process far more efficient.

Trend #7

THE RACE FOR DATA ASSETS, ALTERNATIVE DATA, AND SMART DATA

There is a fuzzy idea that having proprietary data assets is worth a lot of money: the more data assets, the better. People gather, grow, and buy data assets at a rapid pace, even though for many of them the intended use is not even clear yet. What people should be looking for is competitive differentiation, new revenue streams, and better efficiency by way of reuse.

Let's look at acquisition first. Facebook's USD 19 billion acquisition of WhatsApp in 2014 is widely seen as the acquisition of the world's largest mobile phone directory and collection of mobile human-to-human relationships. It is a growing data asset of gigantic proportions, an infrastructure play. What kind of services and commercialization opportunities it will provide in the future are probably not even known to the founders of WhatsApp yet, even though they probably have pretty advanced plans for it already. The point is that there is a huge option value in this data asset—something that might have some value in the future, but we are not sure yet what it could all be.

Similarly, Google's acquisition of Nest could be seen as access to a huge amount of household data. Again, this is an infrastructure play. What services can we dream of if we know what people are doing inside their homes? Targeted ads for cereals when the sleepy-eyed kids come into the kitchen to have their breakfast in the morning? Of course, the ad engine knows what brand of cereal the fridge had been told to order the week before, so a competitor brand can communicate why it is better than the brand that the kids like. Of course, the parents will receive a different ad from the same brand after the kids have left for school, focused more on the nutritional value of the cereal.

Or why do you think there are all these wonderful wearables these days (e.g., the wristbands such as Jawbone's UP3 or Fitbit Surge or the Lenovo Vibe Band VB10)? I actually like the naming of the Pivotal Tracker 1 best. It says exactly what it does: track you and store the data. It is another infrastructure play for health and personal data. What will be the services here? Better-priced life insurance offers as a function of your healthy activity? Automatic shipping of vitamin D in case you don't exercise enough?

All these infrastructure data assets have option value for the future, and thousands of use cases will be built on top of them. Clearly, all these infrastructure plays are going to be impacted massively by the EU–US Privacy Shield, as they are certainly storing more than a "minimum amount of data necessary for the business purpose." The jury is out on whether the regulators are going to be fast, smart, and rigorous enough to even remotely control this landscape. What used to be a great job market for former financial regulators is soon going to be a great job market for former privacy regulators and lobbyists.

Relatively few companies can play in the infrastructure field, while others will focus on specific use cases. Let's look at a few examples. Consulting firms have also started acquiring data assets for very specific use cases. Figure II.4 shows how professional services (PS) firms in management consulting, accounting, IT services, and data provisioning have increased the momentum in acquiring data assets and/or companies owning them.

For professional services firms, the objectives are clear as well. They want proprietary data sets they can use for proposals, for benchmarking, and for project delivery that nobody else has. With the consulting space having

Management Consulting	• Industry-specific insights • Visualization • Quicker decision delivery	• Booz (Epidemico) • McKinsey (QuantumBlack, 4tree, Risk Dynamics, VisualDoD)
Big 4 Audit	• Regional niche players • Internet of Things	• EY (Bluestone, C3 Business Solutions, Entegreat) • KPMG (Label Insight, Bottlenose) • PwC (GeoTraceability, cundus AG, Kusiri)
IT Services	• Business intelligence suites • Industry-specific capabilities	• IBM (Truven, Explorys) • Accenture (i4C Analytics, Gapso) • Hitachi Data Systems (Pentaho)
Other PS	• Functional expertise • Industry-specific capabilities	• Millward Brown (InsightExpress) • Thomson Reuters (Tamr) • D&B (NetProspex)

Figure II.4 Data Assets Acquired by Consulting Firms

grown by factors in the 1990s and lots of alumni consultants now being in CXO positions in the corporate world, there is overcapacity in the market. Unless the consulting firms can differentiate, they will be squeezed out or need to merge, as can be seen in the midsize segment of the management consulting space where Booz has been acquired by PwC or where Roland Berger was just an inch from being acquired by one of the big accounting firms. But the consulting firms are also creating their own data assets and proprietary use cases, as experienced by McKinsey Solutions with its 22 data solutions, led by the flagship Periscope offering improved pricing capabilities, among other things.

Are such opportunities left only to the big online businesses or the big consulting firms? Not at all. There will be millions of opportunities for companies to build use cases based on such assets. Of course, few of them are going to be as big as the ones discussed before, but there are going to be lots of them. Any company in the world should think about its opportunities to build small and medium-sized data assets that are going to differentiate it in the marketplace. For example, at a micro scale, the 40,000 clean logos were such an asset. Similarly, InsightBee is creating a reusable asset as well, as all research that has been done is stored in the form of patent-pending knowledge objects (e.g., text boxes, little graphs or charts, or tables). All of these can be reused if still relevant. The point is that several million hours of work that has been done once already can be made available for other uses.

So, the message is simple. As if you were settling land on a new frontier, grab a few stakes, mount your horse, and get out there to put your stakes in the ground for your own use cases.

Customer Analytics: Aiding Go-to-Market Strategy shows how we helped an online retailer use its data to gain a better understanding of its customer base.

In the race for alternative data, there are a few good examples to illustrate the wide range of new use cases. The first concerns how equities research divisions of banks are tapping into new data streams in the hope of giving their clients deeper insights into the stock market. They are setting up dedicated data labs to come up with new, proprietary insights based on alternative data: for example, they are using satellite images to track traffic in the parking lots of fast food chains in the United States with a view to making more accurate revenue predictions for those businesses.

Another alternative data stream comes from the analysis of social media data in a range of languages. For global product managers of luxury brands, it used to be challenging to gain insight into brand perception in major markets that have very little English coverage, such as China, South Korea, and Japan. Now, it is possible to apply natural language processing (NLP) to social media feeds that are in local languages (Chinese, South Korean, Japanese, etc.) and gain sentiment insights.

Internet of Things data is also going to be a rich source of alternative data. It is no exaggeration to say that it will allow the creation of millions of completely new use cases.

However, alternative data sources do not always have to be new or previously unexplored. Smart combinations of existing data sets are already providing very valuable insights. Combining data across internal silos can be an efficient and effective way to leverage existing data, as in the 800-bits use case, where human resources data combined with information about database licensing saved the company millions.

Moreover, internal and external data together can provide powerful new insights, such as when wealth managers look at the total "wallet" or wealth of their high net worth customers rather than only the share of assets managed already.

Finally, we need to consider smart data and the related infrastructure, which also enable whole classes of new use cases. As an example, Germany is investing heavily in a smart data strategic infrastructure (http://www.digitale-technologien .de/DT/Navigation/DE/Foerderprogramme/Smart_Data/Projekte/projekte. html) in these five areas:

1. Cross-company data ecosystems allowing efficient flow and exchange of data and knowledge between companies, e.g., in interlinked production and delivery systems
2. Cross-process ecosystems where different "process silos" are learning to interact, e.g., in Industry 4.0 factories
3. Mobility platforms spanning multiple industries, e.g., in logistics systems
4. Regional data infrastructure to spot regional trends or enable local catastrophe management
5. Health data platforms for better integration of health services
6. Platforms that handle different data types automatically and in more flexible ways

The increased use of machines to support creative minds is a common characteristic of many alternative and smart data use cases, serving as further illustration of the growing importance of balanced mind+machine analytics.

Customer Analytics:
Aiding Go-to-Market Strategy

Context

Organization
Online drinks retailer

Function(s)
Online retail strategists

Industry
E-commerce of alcoholic
beverages

Geography
US, UK, Australia

Business Challenge

- Improve understanding of the customer base
- Customize go-to-market strategy and reduce customer churn
- Develop a reusable framework for monthly segment refresh

Solution

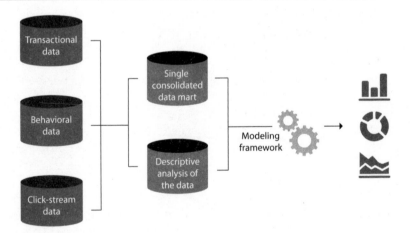

Approach

- Conducted on-site workshop to better understand the client's business and data architecture
- Mapped data from multiple sources to highlight a single truth version of the customers
- Created customer segments
- Ran multiple algorithms to map the best operating business segment
- Classified the insights into customized views to create interactive dashboards

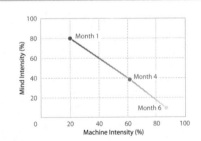

Analytics Challenges

- Creating a single data mart from over 40 data sources with multiple dimensions and 20+ million records
- Coordinating with multiple teams located in different geographies
- Iterative approach to select the best machine learning algorithm for dimensionality reduction

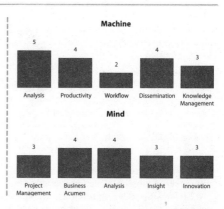

Benefits

Productivity	Time to Market	New Capabilities	Quality
• 95% productivity gain via automation	• By standardizing and automating the solution framework, the time to market was reduced significantly	• Optimized customer segments based on business rules & statistical significance in B2C market scenarios.	• Test–control framework evidenced high-quality insights from different marketing campaigns.

Implementation

- 3 FTEs for 3 months for model development
- 1 FTE for 1 month for visualization
- 1 FTE for 2 weeks every quarter to refresh the solution
- Achieved 95% productivity gains during the refresh phase

Social Insights:
Asian Language Social Media Insights

Context

Organization
Large fast-moving consumer goods
(FMCG) company

Function(s)
Marketing, branding, advertising

Industry
FMCG

Geography
China, Japan, South Korea,
HQ in the United States

Business Challenge

- Subpar quality of Asian language data from social media listening platforms
- Build client-subscribed platforms offering high-level reporting and analysis of social data
  in Chinese (Mandarin and Cantonese), Japanese, and Korean
- Address specific business questions using social data

Solution

MACHINE: Automated data extraction, basic processing, reporting of social data

Quantitative data
(sales data from e-commerce portals, etc.)

Qualitative data
(Asian-language customer reactions, views of KOLs,
etc. obtained via NLP
platform for those languages)

Further data processing

Use case-driven frameworks for data collation and processing

MIND: Insights as per business and research questions

Analysis by industry experts

Final insights in English

Approach

- Created flexible use case-based platform
  for collating and analyzing Asian
  language social data
  Note: 100s of use cases possible;
  use defined by client's specific
  business questions
- Implemented a number of micro-
  innovations for deeper data processing,
  reporting, and analysis
- Set up a team of analysts speaking
  target languages, with strong local
  market insights

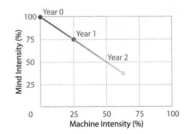

Analytics Challenges

- Producing meaningful insights for business and research questions as opposed to just capturing high-level buzz
- Enabling hundreds of use cases based on social data, depending on business functions of corporates and/or data set
- Data quality control for each country
- Deeper processing of data requiring extensive use of micro-innovations and automations

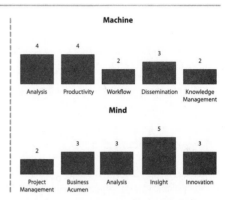

Machine

| Analysis | Productivity | Workflow | Dissemination | Knowledge Management |
| 4 | 4 | 2 | 3 | 2 |

Mind

| Project Management | Business Acumen | Analysis | Insight | Innovation |
| 2 | 3 | 3 | 5 | 3 |

Benefits

Productivity	Time to Market	New Capabilities	Quality
• Human effort reduced by 35% • Gains via automation, micro-innovation, & standardization	• Considerably faster delivery of actionable insights to digital marketing, branding, advertising, and sales teams	• New source of in-depth customer intelligence • Solutions meeting business and research needs	• Better quality, more meaningful insights • Better ROI on social listening

Implementation

- Initial setup done in 4 weeks, including team creation (dedicated analysts speaking required languages) and initial set of processes, tools, etc.
- Client receives standard, semi-standard, and custom insights on an ongoing basis
- As use of social insights continues to be exploratory, evolution of use cases and frameworks continues

- Budget of USD 100K in the first year
- Dedicated team of 2 analysts
- Additional developer working on automations (0.25 FTE)
- Automation benefits of 40% within the first 2 years

Trend #8

MARKETPLACES AND THE SHARING ECONOMY FINALLY ARRIVING IN DATA AND ANALYTICS

"Marketplaces" and the "sharing economy" have been around for 3,000 years. What is really new is the online character of these marketplaces and sharing models, which was simply not possible before because of the high transaction costs involved. You have certainly heard of or used online market-places and the sharing economy in one way or another by now. Of course, the Amazons and Ubers of this world are the most prominent models, but similar models have started mushrooming in many areas. In hospitality, players such as CouchSurfing, Airbnb, Feastly, and LeftoverSwap are growing rapidly. In the work space it would be companies such as Mylittlejob, TaskRabbit, Mechanical-Turk, crowdSPRING, DeskNearMe, and many more. In transportation, in addi-tion to Uber, it includes Zipcar, AirDonkey, Lyft, and Getaround; in retail and consumer goods you have Neighborgoods, SnapGoods, Poshmark, and Tradesy; and in media there is Amazon Family Library, Wix, Spotify, and Soundcloud. Even flea markets have found their way into the peer-to-peer sharing world (e.g., the Japanese Fril). And there are certainly many more on the way to launch.

In its online report *The Sharing Economy—Sizing the Revenue Opportunity*, PwC predicts that the size of the sharing economy will be equal to the size of the normal rental economy by 2025, reaching USD 335 billion in revenue.[13] The drivers are straightforward: (1) lower cost, because assets get utilized better; (2) convenience, for example because access becomes easier or faster; and (3) higher degrees of flexibility. Interestingly, users also feel that trust is really what makes the sharing work. If the trust is not there, the models collapse fairly quickly. Many of them have established their models so quickly that the local and national authorities are now playing catch-up games in terms of figuring out legal and tax issues, for example in the case of Uber in Germany, where questions such as proper insurance coverage, compliance with labor laws, and proper training requirements for the drivers are high on the agenda. While some of these concerns are definitely real and need to be addressed, it is also clear that some of the challenges are put forward in order to protect the old cartels.

The types of transactions that are being offered are surprisingly varied. Rentals, lending, pay-as-you-go (PAYG) or subscriptions, reselling, swaps, or donations are potential choices for the models in this space, which doesn't make life much easier.

How long will it take before these business models will be applied to mind+machine analytics? The race is already on at several levels, but some important elements are still missing. It is important to structure the thinking, as currently everything seems to be put into the same fuzzy blob of "sharing."

Let's start with Level 1 data: the hottest action is in the area of data sets and data streams of raw or curated data. Of course, data providers have always been around (e.g., Bloomberg, IMS Health, Thomson Reuters, and the like). Some of the information comes as data streams such as financial trading information, or as static data sets such as the monthly prescription data of medical drugs. Clearly, these players have built massive businesses, in some areas with almost oligopolistic or monopolistic power (e.g., in 2014 Bloomberg with about USD 9 billion, Thomson Reuters with about USD 12.6 billion, and IMS Health with about USD 3.3 billion).

However, there are new opportunities for data generators and creators whose main business might not be a data business. Here's something I recently heard: "Marc, we have been thinking about what to do with our data. Why not make a few bucks on the side, if someone is interested? We would also benefit from some data other people have. Maybe we can swap or barter."

It is clear from such discussions that most strategy planning departments of corporates don't see this as strategic opportunities yet, rather like some tactical opportunities to make some money. However, it seems that many marketing departments sell their data rather systematically. A 2014 Gartner survey with 300 marketers found that a surprising 43 percent of marketing organizations sell their data to other companies.[14] Of course, everybody says that they do it in accordance with the data privacy laws, but as we know from the chapter on privacy, several of these data sets might no longer be compliant with the General Data Protection Regulation (GDPR) or the EU–US Privacy Shield by 2018. There's some food for thought for the marketers.

Here is an interesting example of a marketplace selling data streams: Singapore-based DatastreamX lets customers buy bite-sized data sets or recurring data streams from data originators. If you are interested in topics such as "Prague:

Vltava River district weekly footfall traffic" for your real estate analysis of Prague, or "Mexican trade data of 222 million shipments" for your world trade analysis, you can buy these data feeds very easily online. The true innovation is not in the online buying of data sets; it is in the online buying of data *streams*; that is, you buy the right to data that will be produced in the future, and you will get it delivered as it happens.

Datacoup is a new model for commercializing your personal data, such as payment, demographic, and behavioral data. Datacoup will acquire your data and sell it to purchasers who want to understand consumers like you. In a way, it is supposed to become a big opt-in panel where you as the data originator get paid directly. Handshake is a very similar company offering the same peer-to-business model. This new breed of company is trying to cut out the existing intermediaries and data brokers such as Epsilon or Experian's credit reporting service. Such new models are clearly niche markets at this stage, but the interesting new angle is the realization that each customer's data has a value and that the incumbent set of data brokers are fundamentally nontransparent. Facebook is capitalizing on this data without compensating the data owner (i.e., you). Why should only the investors get all the value?

There is a great directory for such innovative models at KD Nuggets.[15] It lists a series of such data hubs and marketplaces, where data can be shared and bought. Are there any winning patterns at this stage? Not really, but it is likely that the economics of sharing will drive these companies' growth in years to come, if they deliver trusted and high-quality data, including the necessary audit trails. Whether the data will be subject to a lot of curation or value addition before being sold (as opposed to raw data only) will depend on the customer needs and the scale of the efforts.

Now, let's look at Level 2 information, Level 3 insights, and Level 4 knowledge. At these levels things become dire. Of course, a lot of it is driven by the confidentiality of insights and knowledge, since they are the source of competitive advantage. Would you share your most proprietary insights? Certainly not. There is, however, a very large opportunity for the sharing of analytics use cases. Platforms such as Microsoft Azure already provide a fantastic, modular IT infrastructure in the cloud for all sorts of data services, including the Internet of Things. If on top thousands or millions of analytics use cases could be shared and commercialized on such marketplaces, companies could save huge amounts of time and money in developing their next primary or secondary analytics use cases. Before this can happen, a common use case philosophy and language would be needed as the basis for a successful exchange of use cases. In this way, the business issue trees, data engines, analytic scripts and approaches, visualization templates, project plans, and resource requirements could be traded among companies, of course enabled by proper ownership rights and compensation models. In Part III, we will demonstrate how the Use Case Methodology could be at the root of such an evolution.

KNOWLEDGE MANAGEMENT 2.0—STILL AN ELUSIVE VISION?

In *The Hitchhiker's Guide to the Galaxy*, written by Douglas Adams in 1979, some highly intelligent multidimensional beings create a machine called Deep Thought to compute the answer to the ultimate question of life, the universe, and everything. The answer is 42. Here we are again—a true Level 3 insight delivered by AI! To my mind, the convoluted path of knowledge management to self-actualization could be described in similar terms.

Even though lots of software providers have promised Heaven on Earth achieved by way of wonderful knowledge management systems, Web 2.0, and social collaboration across silos and even company boundaries, the results of pure software-driven knowledge management are mediocre at best. A few years back a conversation with a partner of a law firm went like this: "We have tons of wikis. Off the record, I estimate that about 90 percent of the content is outdated by now. This is actually quite risky, as a large part of this 90 percent is not just outdated, but factually wrong. The system is clogged up, nobody cleanses it, and our practice lawyers are building their own local directories. We have truly built a white elephant. Of course, if you talked to our knowledge management people, they would tell you a totally different story."

Let's first understand the objectives of knowledge management. Wikipedia defines it in the following simple and clear way: "Knowledge management (KM) is the process of capturing, developing, sharing, and effectively using organizational knowledge. [K]nowledge management programs can yield impressive benefits to individuals and organizations if they are purposeful, concrete, and action-orientated." Indeed, the latter is the key: purposeful, concrete, and oriented for action.

Before we look at what works, we have to understand the pitfalls. Again, I need to state up front that the central knowledge management community is not likely to agree with my statements, but I am taking the perspective of the end user, the person at the end of the Last Mile. I am only summarizing tens of discussions with line managers who were wondering what knowledge management, oftentimes central knowledge management, had done for them. I should point out that there are some great examples of "almost best practice." Largely, these are companies whose business model is based on knowledge management (e.g., McKinsey or Boston Consulting Group [BCG]), or that have developed knowledge management solutions around very specific use cases (e.g., Procter & Gamble [P&G]).

Managing Research Flow: Workflow and Self-Service shows you a solution we built for a professional services company.

What has gone wrong in knowledge management during the past 20 years? Where are these pockets of quicksand? Why does everybody cringe when they hear the words *knowledge management*? Why has even academic activity on knowledge management dropped off? Let's look at the main reasons.

Tacit versus explicit knowledge: There are two fundamental forms of knowledge: tacit and explicit. *Tacit* stems from the Latin word *tacēre*, which means to be silent or to leave unsaid. So, by definition tacit knowledge will not be codified and will therefore not show up in any system, and, frankly, this will never change whatever the systems guys are telling you. This is the first big mistake many people make. They think that systems can solve this problem. As we have seen in the discussion of mind+machine analytics, Level 3 insight and Level 4 knowledge are still very much a Mind thing. So, the most interesting findings are and will remain buried inside the human brains, and also walk out of the door once the brain has decided to quit the job. Of course, there have been many efforts to capture the tacit knowledge, but codifying all sorts of knowledge is a very time-consuming, expensive, and largely futile effort if it has to be done as an add-on to the normal work.

A large industrial client had a period when it held four-hour generic exit interviews when employees left the firm. Someone would then transcribe the conversation and store it for future use. The ROI was dismal, and the practice was abandoned. McKinsey had already cracked this problem in the early 1990s through its pre-electronic knowledge directory (i.e., who knows what about what). So simple and so effective!

Insights and knowledge are things of the mind, and so are the incentives. Thinking that machines can run knowledge management is fundamentally flawed. If the minds do not have any incentives to do knowledge management, they simply won't. Either they get something very tangible and useful in return for their own specific situation, or they need an organizational incentive to do so.

In the former, the payback has to be direct and more or less instant. Sending some knowledge into a central wiki is a bit like stashing away the unused toys that your kids have outgrown in a cupboard in your basement. There is a very high likelihood that they will never be used again before you leave your house for good.

The latter is ultimately about money or promotions. Unless there are very clear incentives for people to create and share knowledge, not just in written form, they are no more likely to do it than make some philanthropic contributions. By contrast, at McKinsey a partner's evaluation depends 20 percent on whether the partner has come up with new knowledge, successfully applied it to client situations, and supported other partners with this knowledge—guess what—in client situations. Remember the three criteria: purposeful, concrete, and action-oriented?

Data and information versus insight and knowledge: In many companies knowledge management happens only at Level 1 data or Level 2 information, with lots of data lakes and expensive software and networks. Without context, even documents that had Level 3 insights when created turn into Level 2 information. How can the 100,000 share drives of that bank we discussed earlier all contain knowledge? Most likely, 99.9 percent is data or information only.

The good thing about insights and knowledge is that they are highly compressed data formats, especially in big data. Your marketing team just analyzed one terabyte of data and you ended up with a single sentence: "Cross-selling works mainly with customers where the bank already has a large share of wallet (i.e., most of the client's assets)." This sentence is about 200 bytes of (insightful) data volume—a true insight. It can help focus all future cross-selling campaigns and avoid a huge waste of resources.

You really don't need big data—or, even worse, data lakes—for proper knowledge management. Let's look at the Knowledge Directory in the case of McKinsey, which is probably the number 1 use case of knowledge management ever. Let's say each one of McKinsey's 11,000 consultants and researchers has a certain study history of about 20 studies for an average four-year tenure at McKinsey. Each study makes the consultant or researcher expert to some extent on some subject matter that gets updated at the end of each study. Assuming about 1,000 bytes per study (e.g., saying that the consultant/researcher understands the economics of superconducting magnetic energy storage plus some tagging information such as dates, study reference, etc.), this leads to only 220 megabytes of data volume for all of McKinsey. In today's world, this amount of data fits on one-tenth of a USB memory stick. Sounds more like a data droplet than a data lake, doesn't it? Nevertheless, it allows you to find the right person to talk to in a few seconds. That person will be able to give you the full tacit information plus any documents or further contacts that you might need.

Companies like Starmind of Switzerland can help in this endeavor, if there is no proper process to update the knowledge of each employee. Starmind can learn from the flow in your organization, if you are comfortable with it. It can find the right expert for you by monitoring the flow of emails, collecting recommendations, or overserving interactions between individuals. It even manages

Managing Research Flow:
Workflow and Self-Service

Context

Organization
Big 4 audit, accounting, and
advisory firm

Function(s)
Data analysis and delivery

Industry
Professional services

Geography
North America

Business Challenge

- Improve the research and analytics workflow resulting in productivity gains
- Improve the inadequate self-service architecture, reducing rework and redundancy

Solution

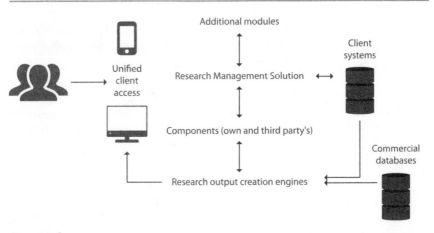

Approach

- Created Research Management
  Solution (RMS)
- Built RMS to be the content repository to
  enable repurposing of content and allow
  self-service
- Set up global team with local
  program management
- Governance framework underpinned
  by well-defined SLAs and MIS reporting
  enabled by RMS

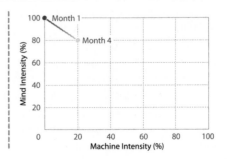

Analytics Challenges

- Providing global access to research and analytics for thousands of users while delivering a consistent experience
- Integrating client's IT systems and the RMS through single sign-on
- Innovative approach to workflow management, triaging, and reporting
- Coordinating the workflow with multiple preferences and rules
- Cross-training and knowledge management tools

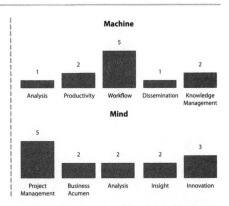

Benefits

Productivity	Time to Market	New Capabilities	Quality
• 10% up-front productivity gains over incumbent provider • Year-on-year productivity gains of ~5% • Total savings of ~$250,000 over a 3-year contract period	• Other network firms can plug & play system, significantly reducing time to market • No service disruption thanks to sound planning for transition	• Building and augmenting benchmarking capabilities in-house • New capability to reuse content and manage workflow of research	• Differentiated, consultative, and value-added service compared to the incumbent service provider • Specialized sector support leveraging vertical expertise

Implementation

- Included RMS, InsightBee, the productivity suite, and a subscription management automation tool
- Solution developed over 3 months by 4 FTEs, implemented within 1 month by 2 FTEs
- Team offers sector research and analysis; information retrieval; and vendor, contract, and subscription management services

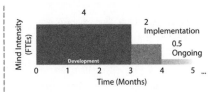

the workload for highly sought-after experts, and it has a built-in "forgetting" ability to get rid of outdated experts.

Knowledge management must center on use cases and be embedded in the workflow. Fuzzy pools of documents on SharePoint drives that can then be searched with linguistic search engines deploying AI is the hot topic of the day. Type in what is of interest, and the search engine will find you the right document in 500 terabytes of old documents with a latency of 100 milliseconds wherever in the company it may be, and whatever it may have been used for at the time when it was still relevant. This is a wonderful dream proposed by lots of search engine vendors! Unfortunately, it does not work well, as there are multiple hurdles. Many documents are confidential and should remain confidential (e.g., consulting studies in client situations). How will the machine determine whether the document is still to be considered confidential? A single mistake can cost millions or even billions if it includes market-moving information. Documents are rarely intelligible without understanding the right context, which is rarely described in Excel sheets or PowerPoint presentations. Even if a document is still relevant, it is highly likely that it will be in the wrong file format or template, and needs a lot of work to be made useful. So, generic search engines are hardly going to produce something that can be used as is or that brings the productivity advantages everybody is hoping for. There are too many false positives that need to be ranked for relevance, and 90 percent of documents are likely to be outdated.

This picture changes, however, if the knowledge management relates to a specific use case where the context is clear, say a pitch document for pension funds in asset management, or the knowledge directory in a consulting firm. Why? The knowledge management around specific use cases (e.g., the sales process to pension funds or finding the right consultant who knows something about superconducting magnetic energy storage) can be highly successful, especially if the knowledge management is built into the normal workflow. In this case, the machine might suggest an updated module for legal disclosures as the salesperson is producing the pitch, and everybody producing pitches will have access to the same up-to-date legal disclosures. This is productive knowledge management.

Knowledge management needs an "auto-death" functionality. Data, information, insights, and knowledge have different levels of half-life, as we have seen in the chapter on Trend 1: days and possibly weeks for data and information, maybe a year for true insights, and possibly one to five years for true knowledge. If we combine this with the fact that typical knowledge management systems largely store data and information and with the fact that insights and knowledge represent only a very small fraction of the data volumes, it becomes clear that the content of most knowledge management systems is well over 95 percent outdated data and information. There is a very high likelihood that nobody will ever use it again. However, such useless data tends to be very sticky, clogging up the system, making it harder and harder to find the real insights and knowledge. The 95 percent probably becomes 99 percent or 99.9 percent over time, and people become frustrated and start building their local wikis and SharePoint folders. This is the famous needle in the haystack analogy at work.

The vendors and the internal data scientist teams will then say that you should spend a few million dollars to buy modern AI, linguistic search engines, and some smart data warehouses. However, the generic AI engines cannot find the right nuggets of insight and knowledge, or, if they find them, they are hidden in tons of false positives. Of course, the false positives will need to be prioritized, the vendors will say. But there is a more fundamental issue: prioritization depends on the context and a lot of tacit knowledge, which isn't stored anywhere by definition. It would simply be unfair to blame the AI algorithms for this. How could the algorithms prioritize on the basis of things that don't even exist in the data? As we can see, this is an inherent problem with all such approaches. Over time, the systems keep clogging up, pretty much like a sewage system that does not get declogged, or in artificial reservoirs like those created by the Aswan Dam or the Three Gorges Dam where millions and millions of tons of sediment reduce their operational capacity.

What such systems need is an "auto-death" functionality for Levels 1–4, through which unused data gets either erased or at least automatically archived. Of course, this requires tagging of the analytic history of whatever is collected. As such functionalities hardly exist, today's systems keep clogging up.

Analytics use cases deserve proper knowledge management. In the demographics section of Part I we counted about one billion primary use cases in the world. It is surprising to see that companies knowledge-manage (or rather data-manage) almost everything such as emails, PowerPoint presentations, PDFs, and the like, but not analytics use cases, and certainly not the analytics use cases that did not work. Everybody seems to be so excited to get into analytics that there are no systematic end-to-end knowledge management processes for it.

Of course, the software providers of big data platforms allow you to create libraries of code written for their software platform, but there is no proper infrastructure for use case management. Given the explosion of analytics use cases currently under way, this will create a big opportunity for platform-independent providers. Part III will discuss this approach in detail.

There is currently a huge temptation to add big data and social media into knowledge management at Levels 1 and 2. Knowledge Management 2.0 (KM2.0) should focus on the insights, the "so whats," and the learnings at the meta level (i.e., "Who knows what about what?" or "Where can I find the purest source?") but not on storing basic data or information, which just leads to wasted efforts and huge sunk investments.

Let us once again look at those three words: purposeful, concrete, and action-oriented. They are the test bed for any knowledge management activity.

- **Purposeful and concrete:** No knowledge management activity is undertaken without a clear purpose. For example, the McKinsey Knowledge

Directory has a highly focused use case: bring the tacit knowledge to the client base. The two-page study reports capture the essence of the engagements in a sanitized fashion and make it available to all other consultants. The key point is that only the knowledge gets captured, but not all the data that was used to derive it. The functional and industry-vertical practices do their own knowledge management for improving proposals and methodologies. McKinsey has formalized its analytics use cases, and the knowledge management is done in and around these use cases in a highly focused manner.

- **Action-oriented:** The incentive systems are such that every partner and consultant at McKinsey has a very strong incentive to share knowledge. Sharing in this context means "successful delivery with clients."

Knowledge management in general has not evolved much during the past decade, and clumsy systems have damaged the notion of knowledge management. However, smart organizations have benefited a lot from knowledge management. KM2.0 puts the Mind at the center, sets the incentives correctly, and defines very specific, manageable use cases with tangible outputs. Interestingly, these models already worked in the 1990s, before elaborate IT support was available.

Knowledge objects as an architecture: Of course, in today's world technology can support the KM2.0 strategy in ideal ways if the right processes and architectures are chosen. InsightBee, for example, uses an information architecture based on knowledge objects. What is a knowledge object? It is a unit of knowledge (including data, information, and insights). For example, it could be a text box containing the executive summary of a presentation on the market for tunnel equipment in Switzerland. That knowledge object can then be tagged with a lot of meta information such as ownership, authorship of the original and alterations thereafter, context for validity, history of usage, and likely data for automatic archiving. Such a tagging-based architecture allows storing of contextual information, making searches much smarter.

I know that this was nerd talk, so let's use an example. You wrote a PowerPoint presentation three months ago. Its executive summary has been tagged as "executive summary"; that is, there is a little virtual tag hanging from it saying that you wrote the executive summary on June 3, 2016, for a market study on metal coatings in the United States in the context of a partial strategic review of your coatings business, that one of your colleagues changed the executive summary on October 10, 2016, that it was distributed to your department's distribution list for senior managers, that 57 people have looked up your knowledge object (not the whole presentation) since its creation, and that some of your colleagues annotated some value-adding comments about this particular market, giving some more context. It also says that your knowledge object is so well-liked that the planned data for auto-death is not until October 10, 2017. It also contains the link to the original presentation, not just the knowledge object. Of course, you did not actively have to write all the tags; the architecture settings either produced them automatically or prompted you to do so when missing.

Modern KM2.0 is people-centered, stores less data and information and focuses on Levels 3 and 4 instead, supports knowledge management use cases that drive tangible action, and uses more modern architectures such as the knowledge object architecture to enable useful things like audit trails, better prioritization of searches, and putting the knowledge into the right context. Part III will discuss the topic of knowledge management in more detail.

Trend #10

WORKFLOW PLATFORMS AND PROCESS AUTOMATION FOR ANALYTICS USE CASES

This chapter on workflows and automation is to analytics a bit like what the story of *The Force Awakens* is to the Star Wars universe. The movie came out in 2015, 30 years after *Return of the Jedi*. In it, the Rebels are fighting a new evil empire, the First Order, using lightsabers, which are individual weapons that take a lot of skill to use. Well, those of us who need analytics are fighting the complexity of an increasing number of analytics use cases using disconnected, simple tools with clumsy interfaces that make them next to impossible for the average end user to use.

Workflows and process automations at large scale have been around since computers came into their own in the 1970s. At a smaller scale, they existed earlier, such as when Alan Turing built one of the first computers to break the Germans' ciphers generated by their Enigma machine. That means one of the first automations in history was used for a use case in analytics—the breaking of German ciphers was pure data analytics and mathematics.

Since then a lot of progress has been made in creating workflows and automations for simple business processes such as opening bank accounts or ordering broadband connections from telecom operators. Such process workflows have been created for use cases with very large volumes. The amounts spent on such software and tools are staggering. The research firm Technavio stated that the global market for this area could reach USD 94 billion by 2020.[16]

For this reason there is a very large potential for analytics use cases supporting such relatively simple workflows and automations with so-called smart stuff, thereby achieving a leverage effect; that is, the analytics use case might not even take that much effort to set up but might achieve major savings or improvements for the overall workflow by, for example, smarter routing or smarter decision making. A key condition for such analytics to be successful is that they can be built into the end-to-end workflow. However, many small-scale end-to-end analytics use cases are not being automated efficiently at all. *Automation in Asset Management: Fund Fact Sheets* gives an example of what the still-hidden potential could be.

The benefits are amazing: a reduction of 75 percent of the human workload and a reduction of more than 30 percent in terms of time to proposal. These benefits do not even include the improved quality, the reduced legal risks in terms of using the right updated legal disclosures for the right countries, and the reduced opportunity costs for the smart employees who can now focus their time on value-adding activities rather than on boring manual work. The key in this example was clearly that the employees get an end-to-end solution for their use case (i.e., one where they don't need to switch back and forth between disconnected tools). As you might have guessed, it is really about the Last Mile again.

Part I showed that there are about one billion analytics use cases, give or take a few. The largest ones have been automated and are part of some workflow. It is hard to estimate the share of the small- and medium-sized ones that are yet to be automated, but even if another 20 percent could benefit from flexible automation and embedding into workflows, a lot of ROI could be generated. And this does not even account for all the new use cases being generated by the Internet of Things or new business issues.

Just to illustrate the end-to-end character once more, a use case from the world of banking will follow.

Not all use cases have enough scale for end-to-end workflows or automations. They might be too varied or too complex and the ROI of building such engines would simply not be high enough. However, even in such situations there are lots of micro-opportunities to improve productivity, time to market, and quality, or to build new capabilities that were simply not available beforehand. Such functionalities can be collected and integrated into optimization platforms in the form of embedded ribbons containing up to 20 or 30 micro-functionalities that can be called upon whenever needed. A good example is the investment banking ribbon (see *Investment Banking: Automating Routine Tasks*). It shows how 20 different functions got assembled into such a ribbon that gets embedded on every junior banker's desktop. The clean logos use case we discussed earlier is just one of these functionalities.

Of course, such optimization suites do not have the same improvement potential as large end-to-end platforms, but even then the cumulative benefits can amount to tens of full-time equivalents (FTEs) with surprisingly high ROI and side benefits like job enrichment, faster time to market, or audit trails.

Automation in Asset Management: Fund Fact Sheets

Context

Organization	Function(s)
Investment bank	Asset management marketing team

Industry	Geography
Asset management	Global, HQ in the United States

Business Challenge

- Automate and harmonize the production process for fund fact sheets and marketing presentations

Solution

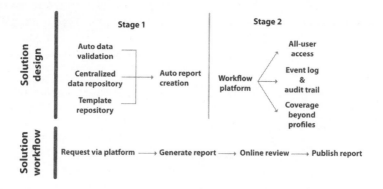

Approach

- Developed a prototype solution to automate report generation and template management
- Identified areas for streamlining the existing workflow
- Collaborated with the client team to set up rule sets for automated data validation
- Created structured storage and template repository
- Simplified data access and data mapping, and created a single data repository

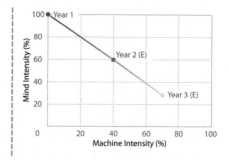

Analytics Challenges

- Information from multiple disparate sources feeding into final output
- Manual adjustments and validations at every step, resulting in high lead times
- Legal review and approval involved paper-based information exchanges with multiple iterations and no audit trail

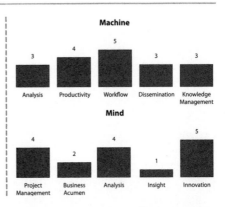

Machine

Analysis	Productivity	Workflow	Dissemination	Knowledge Management
3	4	5	3	3

Mind

Project Management	Business Acumen	Analysis	Insight	Innovation
4	2	4	1	5

Benefits

Productivity	Time to Market	New Capabilities	Quality
• Automation saves between 1 and 3 hours per report • Reports with same underlying data generated simultaneously • Streamlined proofreading process	• Time for first draft of fund fact sheet reduced from 2–3 days to instant • Total time reduced from 12–16 days to just the time required for legal review	• Workflow, disclosure, and template management • Audit trail and version control • User-based data control • Process compliance • Automated alerts	• No data errors thanks to rule-based mapping and automatic data validation

Implementation

- Streamlined process for data sourcing
- Automated data consolidation
- Created tool for automated report generation
- Defined data governance and control process
- Simplified quality control process

Per quarter	Reports	Before automation (hours)	Stage 1 (hours)
Profiles	22	219	139
Presentations	19	76	38
Strategy updates	6	15	8
Quarterly performance summary	1	10	1.5
Total effort		**320**	**186.5**

PROCUREMENT WORKFLOW: MANAGING AND DEVELOPING SUPPLIERS

Take the simple task of a business on-boarding a new supplier (i.e., loading a new supplier onto the IT systems so the business can transact with the supplier). There are a number of workflows that must be undertaken, such as basic data gathering upload (payment address, bank account numbers, contact details, etc.) through to the more complex ones, such as the checks of compliance (e.g., making sure that they have the right health and safety accreditation or insurance for their staff to work on-site).

The nature of these workflow automations is changing the way procurement works. In the past the majority of procurements' focus was on the request for proposal (RFP) or tender, which is when procurement approaches a number of suppliers to ask them to produce a proposal and quote against a set of needs. However, as workflow automation becomes more widely used in these areas of procurement, the focus is changing to initially working with stakeholders to understand the business needs, and then managing and developing suppliers.

One organization that has been focusing on automating the end of the procurement process and managing and developing suppliers is State of Flux. Its focus is on helping organizations come up with a standard supplier experience when dealing with their suppliers (think customer experience but flipped for suppliers). Given the complex and often global nature of modern organizations, the only way of achieving this is by standardizing and automating workflows.

To do this, State of Flux developed Statess, a system that uses workflow automation to support organizations in managing their suppliers across five key aspects: contracts, risks (including supplier vulnerability, accreditation and compliance, and supply chain risk), performance, innovation, and relationship. Through Statess, State of Flux has broken down the complex workflows associated with each of those five areas and automated them.

For example, take creating a key performance indicator (KPI); procurement should first look to understand where this KPI sits in the hierarchy in order to have a balanced scorecard. This requires each KPI to be weighted to understand its impact in the overall balanced scorecard hierarchy. In order to compare this KPI to others, it needs to be normalized, which State of Flux does by turning the KPI into a percentage by measuring score versus target. In addition to having a score and target percentage, bands are also required so you can see when the KPI is out of acceptable limits (red) or close to being out of acceptable limits (amber).

While complex, this is achievable when dealing with a single KPI, but some organization and supplier relationships may have hundreds of KPIs within their balanced scorecard and, in turn, hundreds or thousands of supplier relationships. The volume of data becomes enormous, so the only way to make this task manageable is to automate it through a system like Statess. Otherwise, you lose control and let suppliers self-manage and provide their own KPIs or balanced scorecards to you.

Alan Day, Founder of State of Flux

Evalueserve has created a systematic collection of more than 400 automation macros that can be bundled into modular ribbons, which leads to annual reduction of human workload of 5 to 7 percent at the overall level, and up to 99 percent in specific instances where the whole mini-process gets fully automated, which is not possible everywhere. Such functionalities are more about knowledge of the processes than the effort to create the software. Here is where specialized vendors have collected a lot of experience and where internal units (e.g., IT departments or captives) are frequently simply not up to date. What looks pretty straightforward for a specialized vendor still creates some big surprises when presented to clients.

The point of this chapter was not to give a full account of workflows and automation in analytics. This would simply not be possible, as the field is far too broad and complex. However, you should know that workflows and automations are massive levers for improvement and that you should now be in a position to ask your internal teams or vendors why they are not proposing such automation suites without being asked, and why everything should be built in-house.

Investment Banking:
Automating Routine Tasks

Context

Organization
Investment bank

Function(s)
M&A advisory and
capital markets

Industry
Financial services

Geography
Global

Business Challenge

- Improve the efficiency of the pitch book creation process
- Automate tasks that only add low value, including information gathering from internal and external sources and creation of tables and charts in PowerPoint slides

Solution

Mind Opportunities

- Standardize financial analysis frameworks
- Define knowledge object architecture for knowledge management
- Identify reuse opportunities
- Define rules for accessing knowledge repository

Machine Opportunities

- Create smart search engines and knowledge repositories
- Design web crawlers
- Set smart alerts
- Create standard document creation tools
- Build industry dashboards

Process Redesign

- Build workflow and queue management tool
- Introduce online collaboration tools
- Implement cloud-based comps builder
- Re-engineer process

Approach

- Designed workflow process and implemented workflow tool
- Standardized templates and analytical methodologies across sectors and offices
- Identified reuse opportunities
- Implemented knowledge management platform with access control
- Identified repetitive and low-value tasks requiring significant human input and automated them

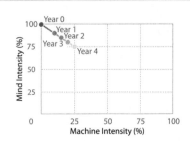

Analytics Challenges

- Lack of centralized knowledge repository made it harder to reuse internal knowledge
- No knowledge object-based architecture for effective reuse
- No standard financial and analytical framework across sectors and offices
- Effort-intensive manual collection of web-based data was subject to errors
- Extensive human effort in non-value-adding activities, including routine analytics and format conversions

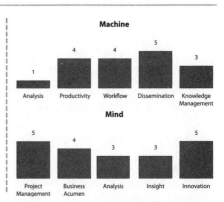

Benefits

Productivity	Time to Market	New Capabilities	Quality
• Overall productivity improved by 5% year-on-year • Up to 75% time savings through automation	• Overall cycle time down by 20% thanks to workflow and self-service knowledge management platform	• Business development support with new analytical and business intelligence tools • Online collaborations within deal team	• Improved accuracy of data collected from web • Standard guidelines resulting in consistent quality

Implementation

- Implemented:
  - Workflow in year 1
  - KM platform in year 2
  - Micro-automations (e.g., newsletter automations, web crawlers, and formatting tool kit) in year 3
  - More complex and customized tools (e.g., CRM alerts, comps builder, pitch book builder) and knowledge object-based architecture in years 4 and 5
- Early automations yielded the highest savings. Later animations gave high value but less savings due to their complexity.

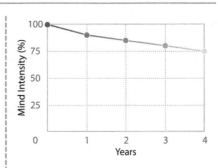

Trend #11

2015–2025: THE RISE OF THE MIND–MACHINE INTERFACE

In the *Iron Man* franchise, the characters use wonderful holographic technology for design, and control flight and weapons systems with their voices and eyes. Clearly, Tony Stark has cracked mind-to-machine interaction almost perfectly. The only thing missing is the suit also reading his thoughts.

In the real world, some drone control systems or fighter avionics are probably coming close to this level of interaction between the pilots and their machines, using augmented reality to project images into their helmets. Of course, the development of such systems has already consumed billions of dollars, largely driven by the defense industry. Some of this technology is now making it into civilian use cases; for example, the upscale car industry is already using such systems to make cars safer to drive or to provide information to the drivers. Some radical redesign has enabled retail versions for everybody's use (e.g., Oculus Rift, Google Glass, Microsoft's HoloLens, and soon-to-be bionic contact lenses). The software industry has also invested heavily in packages supporting such wearable devices for a variety of applications (e.g., archaeology, architecture, art, commerce, construction, education, gaming, design, surgery, navigation, sports, or tourism). It won't be long before regular citizens will be using such mind–machine interfaces in daily life. It's no wonder that the information giants such as Facebook, Google, and Amazon are competing heavily in this race for the mainstream consumer.

Clearly, machines are important, but the mind–machine interfaces are needed even more to make the machine work productively. Martin Ford and Jerry Kaplan describe a dire jobless future in their respective books *Rise of the Robots* (Basic Books, 2015) and *Humans Need Not Apply* (Yale University Press, 2015). They certainly have a point for certain job categories, where the humans are simply replaced 100 percent by robots, but as we discussed in Part I, the Mind will have a role to play for a long time to come in many current or future job categories. Efficient interfaces will be required.

This book is not about robots or factories, but about one billion analytics use cases. Of course, at the receiving end of many such analytics use cases there might be machines again, especially when looking at the Internet of Things, but in most cases human decision makers will be the hopeful requesters and the recipients of the Level 3 insights. So the analytics machines need interfaces with the minds of human decision makers. How have these interfaces evolved over the past 15 years? In preparing for this book I asked a number of colleagues and clients (80 percent antinerds, 20 percent nerds) what their preferred interfaces would look like, and where they are seeing the problems at this point. In order to understand their answers, we first need to understand who they are and what they need. We can get some help from user experience designers.

User experience designers use personas for their work; that is, they imagine real people representing certain user segments. For example, Persona 1 could

USER EXPERIENCE DESIGN: THE PREREQUISITE FOR SUCCESSFUL USER ACCEPTANCE

User experience is not a component for design; it is the sum of all the parts. All parties involved in the production have an impact on a product's overall experience. It begins with a user need, something a business, organization, or entrepreneur has identified as being worth focusing some time and effort on solving—they are often the driving force behind the change that needs to happen. A visual designer will contribute to the experience by ensuring that it reflects the personality of the brand, and users are delighted by how it looks and how easy it is to read and interact with. A front-end developer will deliver the fluidity and motion of the interface and ensure that it works on different devices. The back-end programmers will deliver the data with speed and efficiency so you're not waiting for ages for something to load and you are receiving what you have requested. The user experience designer's role is to help to define the flow of a product from end to end and to test it with users to assess suitability and usability. Some of these roles may be combined into one; however, all involved have an influence on the definition of these tasks and ultimately an impact of the success of the product's user acceptance.

Neil Gardiner, Every Interaction

be Mike, the 50-year-old, not very tech-savvy, office-based commercial banking sales manager of the US Northeastern territory managing a group of 10 branch managers, and Persona 2 could be Martina, the Gen Y, 30-year-old, tech-savvy, mobile operations manager servicing magnetic resonance imaging devices (MRIs) in Germany. Such personas even contain pictures to make them appear really human.

Persona 1, Mike, could say something like this:

"I don't have much time, and I really hate admin work. I am not one of these whiz kids, either, who have apps for everything on Earth. I want a very simple way to capture and communicate what I want to know, and I want the 'system' (whoever that might be) to give me exactly what I need, when I need it, and in a format that is easy to use for my daily work. I don't want a lot of tables and documents, just the 'so whats' (e.g., if my territory is dropping against the other territories). I certainly don't want to fire up three or four different programs on my computer, where I need to copy and paste between them. Once I've made my decision (e.g., given an approval for something), it must be easy to document and communicate it. In the future, I also want to be able to find it again very easily. Plus, if something substantial has changed, I want to be alerted. There must also be a very easy way to interact with whoever is going to give me the analysis, as playing voice mail ping-pong drives me and my people absolutely nuts. And finally, I want the central team to under-stand what I am doing."

Persona 2, Martina, could sound like this:

"I am on the road all the time. I need to be able to access everything remotely and I need it in a mobile-friendly format on my handheld. My activities should be logged automatically, so I don't have to spend much time on admin, and I should get alerted to important changes rather than me having to log on using dual log-on procedures that take me a lot of time to then find out what has changed. Of course, my three key applications need to fully interoperate so that I don't have to reenter my requests. Approvals need to be communicated electronically. I don't have time to call my boss all the time. This is highly inefficient: I want a live chat feature on my mobile app. Of course, the audit trail needs to be done automatically, and my activity log should be sent to my bosses and my clients automatically."

Mike and Martina agree on the current situation. In summary, one could say that the user experience in analytics use cases has hardly evolved during the past 15 years, especially when compared to what was discussed earlier. Most of the use cases are still delivered in the form of post facto voluminous Excels, PowerPoint presentations, and PDFs, with a lack of "so whats" and event-driven alerts, requiring too much unnecessary administrative work, suffering from lack of interoperability between applications, with decisions not integrated into the normal workflow, and with phone calls required for everything, creating inefficient loops in scheduling. Mike and Martina also wish that the central teams understood better what their daily jobs and requirements look like. They agree that good user experience design for analytics use cases is essential to the end user's acceptance. To put it bluntly: *user experience design can make the difference between success and failure of analytics.* And the current situation is rather bleak.

These are the typical statements by line managers suffering from the Last Mile syndrome. If you ask the central teams, you get different answers. They say that the line managers are not clear about their needs, that they want impossible things, that it will take large IT budgets to complete such projects in-house, that they don't have the resources to satisfy all these needs, that compliance is a critical factor, and that interoperability between systems, geography, and businesses is a nice dream. However, you very rarely hear the topic of user experience or mind–machine interfaces. Granted, lots of these constraints are real, but at least for the use cases that are operational, the user experience makes a huge difference.

Interestingly, the consulting world seems to have woken up to the topic of user experience, and there seems to be a race for acquiring design firms. McKinsey bought design firm Lunar in 2015 after collaborating with it since 2013. Especially when McKinsey's Digital Labs collaborate with Lunar, things become interesting as they create mind–machine interfaces or digital user experience designs. McKinsey states on its website that industrial design and user experience design are closely related. Of course they are: that is about how humans interact with products. Whether such products are digital or physical does not really matter anymore. Accenture bought design firm Fjord in 2013 for its "transformation of digital businesses." Google and Facebook also went shopping with the acquisitions of Mike & Maaike and Hot Studio, and Adobe bought design firm Behance. The cultures of design firms are very different from the cultures of consulting firms or corporates, which is probably why the acquired companies are usually not fully integrated, but remain somewhat autonomous. Evalueserve hasn't bought any design firm, but closely collaborates with US-based Infusion and UK-based Every Interaction for all its user experience design work.

It is very clear why there is a rush to buy design firms. User experience design can mean the difference between success and failure of an analytics use case. "The rise of the mind–machine interface" is certainly for real, also in analytics.

Mind–Machine Interface: Game Controller shows how a couple of creative students used mind+machine to make their lives easier. It is an elegant interface

USER EXPERIENCE: USER-CENTRICITY AND AGILE DEVELOPMENT

If you invest millions in a product that is developed in isolation, based on assumptions and led by a technically minded team without involving the end user, it's doomed to fail. Any part of the experience can turn people off and drive them to your competitors.

Online, the smallest user irritations can affect users' feelings toward a service: load time, unnecessary questions, wrong links, untrustworthiness, inappropriate tone, or an overwhelming number of features—they all make it hard to perform the essential tasks. User time is precious, and they can leave you as quickly as they arrived.

In a business environment, if users are forced to work with a badly designed piece of software on a daily basis, they might not be in a position to leave, but you can imagine the impact this can have on productivity. Rather than enabling staff, the tools designed to help become a hindrance.

Every user's experience with your brand or product has multiple touch points. Online and offline interactions all influence the user's view of your service. If you deliver a great online ordering experience but the delivery is shockingly late or the end product doesn't live up to expectations, then obviously you will lose customers unless you gather feedback, learn, and make changes.

If you take a user-centric approach, you get early adoption and the impact can be significant in uptake, cost saving, and profit. In recent years, development best practice has moved on from that isolated approach. Agile development is about building quickly and deploying early, so assumptions can be tested. But at the same time, user experience designers, along with business owners and business analysts, can begin to solve the key business challenges by growing their understanding of the end users, building flows around what end users need to be able to do, and moving quickly to test interactive prototypes.

There is an obvious advantage to testing your product as early as possible on end users. Telling people how great something is going to be and actually getting them to use it are two very different things. This is something you want to learn quickly, not a year into the development process when the team has built your product. User experience is not the icing on the cake: it's something that needs to run throughout your business from the start and continually through the life span of the product.

Neil Gardiner, Every Interaction

with a cleverly written underlying code that allowed them to conquer the online gaming world in their sleep–literally! It plays the game while they are away from their computers. The players just set the strategy a few times every day and several collaborating game controllers execute commands automatically on their behalf. The students reached the game's global top rank after a few weeks.

Mind–Machine Interface:
Game Controller

Context

Organization	Function(s)
Eric & Flo's minds	Bots and interfaces

Industry	Geography
Online gaming	Europe

Business Challenge

- Accelerate mind–machine interaction with the help of a bot
- Automate mundane tasks and enable players to focus on strategic tasks
- Play the game on behalf of players while they are offline
- Solve captchas automatically on behalf of players

Solution

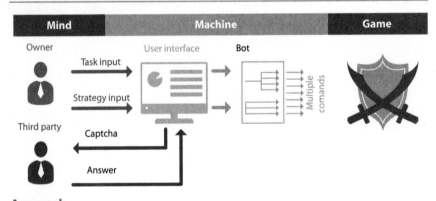

Approach

- Interface designed for maximum possible inputs (clicks, mouse movement, keyboard, etc.)
- Designed bot to record and plan numerous actions
- Implemented copier functions to reduce playtime for the player
- Introduced HTML reading and execution algorithms

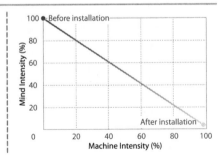

Analytics Challenges

- Analyzing and finding regularities within thousands of lines of HTML
- Developing shortcuts for the user
- Develop controller interface to handle manual input at multiple tactical and strategic levels
- Solve captchas automatically on behalf of players

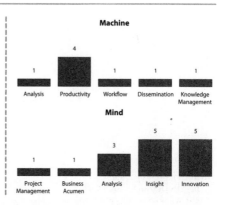

Benefits

Productivity	Time to Market	New Capabilities	Quality
• 70% time reduction • Bot continues the work while player is offline • Automated bot's responses more timely than human input	• Development time of 20 hours	• Ability to increase score while player is offline and thanks to increased efficiency	• Very positive results—reached top lists in global game rankings

Implementation

- Very limited implementation due to legal and ethical implications
- As proof-of-concept to show efficiency gain from a well-designed interface, it was successful
- Bot took 20 hrs of programming time to develop

Trend #12

AGILE, AGILE, AGILE

A gile methodologies, originally developed by the IT industry for software de-velopment, are almost ideally suited for cracking analytics use cases. The ag-ile approach was used for InsightBee and it brought speed and flexibility. There are several key advantages, but after having run several such product develop-ment cycles, we have found the five most striking advantages to be:

1. **Shortening time to market by factors:** There is the concept of the min-imum viable product (MVP). Especially in today's fast-lived world with truly global competition in many industries, speed is of the essence. The MVP 1 defines the simplest possible product that will have a market: no bells and whistles, just the essence of what the early adopters will re-quire to buy the product. Future evolutions of the product will then add sets of features one by one. In the case of InsightBee, we probably saved 75 percent of the development time that a classical approach would have required.

2. **Rapid evolution of functionalities:** Agile uses "sprints" to add new func-tionalities or adapt existing ones. For InsightBee we used a series of se-quential three-week-long sprints over a period of two years. All sprints were based on market feedback. This allowed us to morph the product according to market needs. Especially when introducing new use cases, it is highly likely that the initial specifications will change, as the Last Mile users ask for new or changed features when they see the product for the first time in reality. Based on experience, one should simply not expect the end users to even be able to describe perfectly and in detail what they will need. How do you describe something that does not exist yet? This is the nonlinearity or serendipity of product development. Minds work in iterative and intui-tive ways, not in 100 percent deterministic and linear ways, in spite of some

internal IT departments or central data analytics units handing out such guidelines. Many analytics use cases addressed in slow and old-fashioned ways have failed to deliver results due to this basic human characteristic.

3. **Ability to get end user feedback quickly:** This is similar to rapid prototyping. Wire frames can be developed based on MVP 1 within a few weeks or months, depending on the size of the use case. These are simple graphic but not yet functional representations of what the user experience is going to look like. The Last Mile users can already give very important input early on, which avoids major rework down the road. Once a working product is ready, the Last Mile users can test the functionality and the workflow. This is critical for the acceptance of the product.

4. **Flexibility by design for the future life cycle:** Agile assumes future change. It does not actively invite it, but it prepares the architecture for flexibility. Analytics use cases fit this profile perfectly. The business questions, the data feeds, the users and their requirements, and the organizational structures all change. This saves a lot of time, money, and mind resources down the road. Life cycle management of use cases is critical. In analytics, the initial development costs are only a relatively small fraction of the lifetime costs. Depending on the dynamics of an analytics use case, lifetime costs can be factors bigger than the initial development costs in approaches where rigid structures are being used.

5. **Agile platforms enable scalability for groups of use cases:** InsightBee is a great example of an agile platform where consecutive products can be launched in shorter and shorter cycles. While the initial platform took about six months to develop, the consecutive launches of new use cases are now down to six to eight weeks. Moreover, basic core functionality built for the platform becomes available to all use cases on the platform right away. The example of Live Chat shows this nicely. Once Live Chat was introduced, all solutions and their users could immediately benefit from this new capability. The platform approach also simplifies the life cycle and portfolio management tasks considerably.

Agile also extends to the organizational concept of getting things done. Which internal IT department can credibly claim to have all the necessary skills in-house? Agile allows various players to be embedded in flexible ways. For InsightBee we realized very quickly that we did not have all the required skills, not even in India where Evalueserve has a very capable knowledge technology organization able to deliver dashboards, portals, macros, productivity suites, and other tools. Therefore, we work with Swiss-based Acrea for the architectural design and overall program management, Swiss-based MP Technology for code development and integration, UK-based Every Interaction or US-based Infusion for user experience design, Kaizen Search for search engine optimization (SEO), Swiss-based Squirro for artificial intelligence (AI), UK-based Earnest for content and campaign design, and several other partners for other types of functionalities, such as Chinese natural language processing (NLP). Evalueserve's internal IT function focuses on the technology integration and the interfaces to internal systems (e.g., finance or customer relationship management [CRM]), and Evalueserve's marketing department focuses on the rapid and agile integration of the content and the campaigns.

This approach is very similar to the automotive industry, which uses tier 1 suppliers for the first-level subsystems (e.g., the power train), tier 2 suppliers for second-level subsystems (e.g., the gearbox), and tier 3 suppliers for third-level subsystems (e.g., components of the gearbox). The big car manufacturers themselves focus on product design, assembly, and marketing rather than trying to have the full value chain in-house. Tiered partnerships of specialized players using similar development methodologies will be critical for mind+machine in the future given the large numbers of use cases and types of skills required. We are experiencing this need in a CRM use case where the client wants to improve the value addition of its CRM data by adding multiple services focused on business development to its platform. For this use case, we are collaborating with a CRM integrator, a user experience design agency, and an NLP provider.

As we work very closely with Acrea for the architecture of our solutions, we invited them to contribute their view of the use case, describing the key aspects from the perspective of IT architecture and program management.

AN IT ARCHITECTURE THAT SUPPORTS AGILE

Nowadays *agility* is the buzzword in any digital business project. Agile teams implement new business functionality rapidly in short sprints and test its user acceptance throughout the development. Learnings from customer reactions are then quickly incorporated into the product.

One of the key challenges of such an approach is designing an IT architecture that can keep up. In a traditional IT world, legacy systems are often built as monoliths (think of a massive mainframe or other all-encompassing server-side applications) that implement more than 80 percent of all business capabilities. In many cases, such monolithic applications are built as single logical executables and don't follow a modular approach.

A monolithic design hinders agile development. Change requests for monolithic applications have to be serialized, and the task list of the singular development team is often stacked to the moon, unfortunately. A modern IT architecture built on the greenfield, like the one of Evalue-serve's InsightBee, better supports agility and flexibility by design.

When we developed InsightBee we tried to decouple and modularize as much as possible. Each component had to be self-contained, including owning and managing its own data. In order to achieve this goal, each component had to be scoped along business domains and business capabilities. (See Figure II.5.)

For example, one component contains all functions related to customer interactions (log-in, ordering, alerting, etc.). Another component deals with market intelligence (handling research requests and facilitating effective processing by mind+machine interaction). There is even a component focusing on the effective management of knowledge objects and knowledge documents. All components encapsulate a clearly defined set of closely related business capabilities.

And to further simplify things, all core components use the same proven technology stack (operating system, supporting application, etc.).

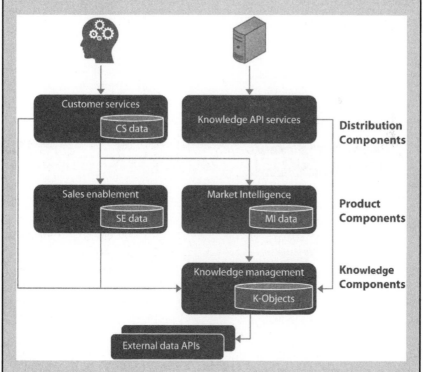

Figure II.5   Acrea Agile: Loosely Coupled Components of InsightBee

(*Continued*)

HOW DOES SUCH AN APPROACH SUPPORT AGILITY?

Since all components of the system are self-contained (including the respective data) and communicate only via well-defined service contracts, they can easily be decoupled from each other. Components don't induce side effects to other components when changed. Each component can be advanced and tested separately, and thus efforts can be made parallel to increase delivery speed and agility.

In addition, low technology diversity further increases the effectiveness of agile teams, because development resources can be shared among components. Such an approach is similar to how cloud-based Internet services from well-known companies (like Google or Expedia) are designed and operated.

It is good to see that proven Internet paradigms have finally arrived in the corporate world.

Michael Müller, Acrea AG

(MIND+MACHINE)^2 = GLOBAL PARTNERING EQUALS MORE THAN 1+1

In 2003, Evalueserve was featured in an *Economist* report on outsourcing in the investment banking space. We got a call from an equities analyst in London telling us that his COO of research (of one of the bulge bracket investment banks) wanted to meet me for 15 minutes in London. I was based in the Austrian Alps at the time. Flying to London for a 15-minute meeting? Okay, I said, I will give it a shot.

Two weeks later I entered the meeting room in London together with our UK head of sales. After a few very brief introductions, the COO came right to the point: "What do you guys know about equities research?" Truthfully, I answered that we did not know much, but that we would do anything to learn it. Then the COO said: "Because you are so honest, you are going to get a pilot project. If this goes well, you might get up to 200 FTEs [full-time equivalents] from our bank."

A few years later we were the largest outsourcing vendor in sell-side research for that investment bank. It is simply amazing what has happened in these 13 years since then. The sophistication of outsourcing solutions has exploded. These days the solutions are specialized by industry desk or by functional topics such as index calculations, all mind+machine. And all such collaborations use multiple operations hubs around the globe in fully integrated management structures. Risk and compliance have also taught us a lot. Just one example: these days we are talking about "intertectonic BCP." Ouch. What an acronym! It is actually the very simple idea of business continuity planning across Earth's tectonic plates When there is a big earthquake on one tectonic plate, say in Chile, some of the most critical processes can be transferred to other hubs, in India or in Raleigh,

177

North Carolina, for example, within a few hours. This actually happened in the big 2010 earthquake (8.8 on the Richter scale), and within two hours India started picking up the work from Chile.

The point is that outsourcing in analytics, be it internally to a captive or a central function or externally to global partners, has gone from an era of almost complete ignorance in the late 1990s to high degrees of sophistication and thought leadership in only 15 years. But the race is on, and only innovators will survive.

The purpose of this chapter is to give you an understanding of these eras, what you as a line manager can realistically expect from your internal and external partners, and what questions you should ask your internal procurement teams, but also your central IT and analytics functions when deciding on where to get the Minds and the Machines for your use cases. I am not trying to give a market overview with a comprehensive list of the key players and their pros and cons, as there are enough market research reports or analyst firms specializing in this field. However, I am going to focus on the topics that are usually not mentioned in these market research reports.

Having founded Evalueserve, my views would obviously be biased. Therefore, in writing this chapter I consciously put on my independent consulting hat, taking a critical look at what works and what doesn't. We are not going to look at all areas of outsourcing (e.g., not real estate or finance). This chapter focuses on the one billion analytics use cases, explaining the eras of outsourcing, the main drivers of innovation, the available solutions, and generally what drives success but also failure in achieving positive ROI.

Rather than just giving abstract descriptions of what happened, I use my personal experience in the Evalueserve context. Nevertheless, our experience is quite representative of what other firms in knowledge process outsourcing (KPO) or business process outsourcing (BPO) such as EXL Services or Genpact would have gone through, at larger scales due to their predominant BPO character.

ERA 1: PURE GEOGRAPHIC COST ARBITRAGE (2000–2005)

We hired our first 10 employees in Gurgaon, India, in early 2001 directly from Indian business schools. When we started in 2001, the salaries in India were about 20 to 25 percent of comparable Western salaries (or less). After significant training in terms of methodologies, cultural differences, and data sources, they quickly became billable analysts and got us the cash flows we needed: we became profitable in February 2002, after just 14 months. We trained them in research and analytics and found our first clients in the Western world, largely in the United States and Northern European markets such as the United Kingdom, the Nordics, the Benelux, Switzerland, and Germany. The reports we produced at the time were good, but would certainly not make the cut anymore today. Clients gave us very specific tasks (e.g., profile their competitors or research some markets) for a few hundred or thousand dollars per report. The model was novel, and many corporates tried it out. Of course, we got a few bloody noses on our rapid and steep learning curve. Fortunately, I had already collected quite some experience by sitting on the board of McKinsey Knowledge Center in Gurgaon, India, which allowed us to avoid the basic mistakes at least.

Growth was fast. We more than doubled pretty much every year. There was a bit of political backlash in the United States and Europe regarding outsourcing, but it was limited. Of course, this meant growth pains everywhere. We could not hire and train people quickly enough. In parallel to hiring for operations, we also expanded our sales force. Their pitch was relatively simple: give us your work and save money. It worked, though. There were quite a few start-ups that had set up their operations between 1999 and 2003. There were also spin-offs from large corporates (e.g., Genpact, which is the listed former captive of GE Capital).

At the time, it was land-grab mode. Everybody would perform almost any kind of work in order to get going, although the start-up players had their areas of specialization based on their founders' respective backgrounds. In our case, it was intellectual property (cofounder Alok Aggarwal had been the head of IBM R&D Strategy and the head of IBM's Indian R&D center) and business research (due to the McKinsey backgrounds of our COO Ashish Gupta and me). Other start-ups, such as Amba Research, were driven by equity analyst backgrounds, and still others by former bankers.

Of course, the Forbes 2000 companies around the world had heard of the "India model." Moreover, given that they usually had some managers of Indian origin, it was not long before they all raced to India to set up captives. Every week there were announcements of new centers promising wonderful skills at practically no cost. I used to call this the 24- to 36-month honeymoon phase for captives. Their business development was far simpler compared to free-market vendors. The work was *mandated* to come to them. The companies' CFOs or CEOs would ask for the work to go to India. Jack Welch's famous statement was: "Prove to me why you are *not* sending work to India." In these years, hundreds of captives were set up in India. They could be compared to broadband antibiotics: one-size-fits-all processes.

As the captives were largely cost centers and did not really have to earn the right to grow in the open market, they could afford to set artificial internal transfer prices that were quite high. This meant that they could pay higher salaries to new employees, sometimes up to 30 percent higher than ours, which were already at the higher end of the spectrum due to our KPO positioning. This was the heyday of the poaching war. Whenever a new captive opened in our vicinity, we knew that it was only going to be a matter of time before the poaching would start. The less loyal employees would leave for a few thousand rupees more.

Just as an aside: when you look at the CVs of people who have been in this industry, you can immediately tell if they were generally loyal to their companies, simply by looking at how often they changed jobs. Some people left before they had even joined, some after six months, some after one or two years. These days we simply do not hire such people anymore, and their problem is that the past is the past and the CV is the CV. Such moves will always be on their CVs. Interestingly, the same effect can be found again in data analytics, just with an offset of about 10 years.

Fortunately, there were great numbers of very loyal employees as well, and we kept growing quickly to over 1,000 employees in India. Given that we were entirely focused on research and analytics, these were pretty big numbers. Of course, the BPO players would grow to 20,000 or 40,000 employees during this phase.

ERA 2: GLOBALIZING OUTSOURCING (2005–2015)

Our clients were largely Forbes 2000 companies. This meant that their needs were also global. In 2005, an existing client (a leading investment bank) asked us if we were interested in setting up a China center for Asian work. We said yes and agreed to do a pilot in Shanghai, as it was simply impossible to analyze the gaming market in Macao from India, and Chinese employees could not be attracted to come and live in India. We performed well during the pilot, but ultimately the contract was given to Accenture, which had a preexisting setup in China. (To our big satisfaction we won this work back in 2014 based on the specialization we had achieved by then.) In spite of this setback we went ahead and set up our China center, which quickly reached about 100 analysts. We went through a very steep learning curve during these years. How do you integrate highly intelligent but culturally diverse employees, establish global management processes, and cope with differences in terms of time zones, labor law, and client requirements? We know now!

Then in 2007, the same investment bank asked us if we were interested in setting up shop in Latin America. We said yes again and chose Chile for our endeavor, since the then (and current) president of Chile, Michelle Bachelet, was really interested in getting her country into the knowledge economy, and the Chilean universities produce excellent talent at scale. This time we actually did get the contract from the banking client, and the Chile center grew quickly to over 100 analysts. This time the cultural challenges were smaller, but we had to create the "follow the sun" processes, with India and Chile working in tandem to cover essentially the full working day. Chile's value proposition was centered on covering the US time zones and Latin America, as well as providing 24/5.5 coverage in conjunction with India.

Then in 2008, the same investment bank was looking to outsource some Russian work. We set up our Romania center, since we wanted a near-shore operation inside the European Union for reasons of EU data protection for our data analytics work. We set up in Cluj-Napoca, since the Babes University had a large quant faculty, which produces great data analytics talent.

And finally, in 2014 we set up our near-shore center in Raleigh, North Carolina. After 2012 there was an increasing demand for onshore and near-shore outsourcing in the United States. The Research Triangle area of Raleigh–Durham produces excellent skills. This center is currently growing very quickly, as many clients want to have a part of their global, outsourced workflow done in the United States. Similarly, we also set up an in-office operation with a big law firm in London.

Financial Benchmark Analytics: Environmental Index shows a project where our global team pulled together to provide a consistent service.

This phase of globalization was driven by our clients' needs, and we chose the locations almost entirely on the basis of the availability of skill and talent. As an aside: we always smiled when we saw companies hire expensive consulting firms to determine the locations for their captive centers. Such consulting firms would then build huge models with all sorts of factors, while we could have told them very easily where to go, as the only thing that really counts is the availability of skill. But then again, management needed the official stamp of approval by some well-known consulting brands.

In this phase, many vendors and clients went through similar approaches. For Asia, they set up centers in the Philippines or China, for Europe largely in Poland or Romania, in Latin America mostly in Chile, Argentina, Costa Rica, or Mexico, and in the United Kingdom mostly in Birmingham, Manchester, or Northern Ireland. In the United States, banks would set up units in cities such as Jacksonville, Florida, or in Salt Lake City, Utah, or in Raleigh, North Carolina. What differentiates the successful ones from the less successful ones is how well they integrated the centers into the global workflows.

Several clients also chose two or more vendors or captives to de-risk their operations. Dual sourcing became the name of the game, and it still is a very good approach to keep everyone on their toes, including the captives. Very successful companies, including some of the well-known top management consulting firms and some of the global investment banks, have developed very sophisticated governance models for making captives and vendors work together in very successful ways. Best practices in managing outsourcing relationships and captives would probably fill another book, but I will apply wisdom passed on to us by His Holiness the Dalai Lama in 2000. We were listening intently to his speech on overcoming negative feelings, together with several hundred other listeners in Delhi, sitting cross-legged on the floor of the hall (which made all Westerners cringe with pain). After two hours, His Holiness opened the forum for questions. Then, after about 30 minutes of answering questions, he granted a single, last question. While the session had been extremely enriching, we were all looking forward to stretching our legs again. Then came the question: "Please tell us something about the difference between life and death." I will never forget his response, when everyone thought that this would require much time to explain. He simply said, "Yes, there is one. Thank you for listening to me. Good-bye." So, best practices in managing such outsourcing relationships will not be part of this book.

Financial Benchmark Analytics:
Environmental Index

Context

Organization
Major financial
benchmarks provider

Function(s)
ESG products

Industry
Financial services: Indexes

Geography
Global team, HQ in Europe

Business Challenge

- Build a Environmental Index (EI) product for a major financial benchmarks provider
- Analyze and monitor 1,650 companies globally on an annual basis

Solution

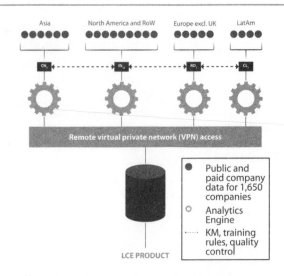

- Public and paid company data for 1,650 companies
- Analytics Engine
- KM, training rules, quality control

LCE PRODUCT

Approach

- Set up team of 20 FTEs across 4 global centers, with leadership at HQ
- Contributed to the development of data entry interface for remote global access
- Created SLA framework for quality control, time to delivery, and error rates

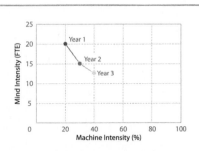

Analytics Challenges

- Global-level project management with team spread across multiple locations
- Consistent analyses across geographies and verticals for the analyzed companies
- Application of analytics framework globally across several teams in a short time frame
- Building a new index product in a virtual environment, requiring innovation
- Coordination of workflow with 100s of rules

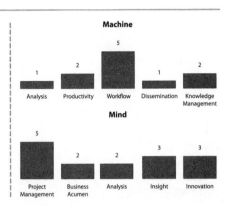

Benefits

Productivity	Time to Market	New Capabilities	Quality
• 1,650 companies analyzed in 6 months • 15% productivity gain via automation and web interface enhancements	• Product built in 6 months • 20% reduction in time to delivery in year 2	• New revenue-earning product • Full audit trail • Full KM of rules • Non-English language research	• High-quality product with significantly low error rate compared to the SLA of 5%

Implementation

- From 0 to 1,650 companies in 6 months
- 20 FTEs for first 6 months (setup)
- 10 FTEs to support thereafter
- Recurring 20 FTEs each Q2 (index data)
- Budget of USD 0.25 million in year 1
- Capex of USD 0.1 million for software and data

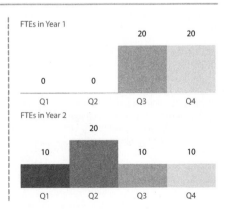

ERA 3: PROCESS REENGINEERING (2007–2015) AND SPECIALIZATION

Vendors started improving their knowledge of the clients' processes, sometimes to the point where the vendors knew the processes better than the clients did. They started building capabilities by hiring or acquiring the right skill sets. Often these were people who had had long careers in Western markets and industries and had deep insights into what the clients were looking for. Increasingly, vendors started suggesting process changes to their clients based on what they had learned from other clients, but also based on idea generation in their own back-office operations. Evalueserve embarked on a program called KPO Transformation with the goal of providing better value to clients by helping redesign the outsourcing processes. The analyst teams would conduct idea generation sessions to find opportunities to improve the delivery process of the outsourced work. The success was amazing. Productivity improvements of 20 percent were the lower limit. Over time we actively approached clients with client-specific innovation agendas, which soon became the standard for all governance meetings. We had Knowledge Olympics, which gave financial and nonfinancial awards to the best ideas.

Of course, the killer idea was not just to focus on the scope of the outsourced work, but to think of the *end-to-end process* also including the client's work. Saving a working hour onshore had the quadruple effect of saving an hour offshore. Of course, this implied that the vendors needed the skill sets onshore to assess the client's workflow and processes. We called these consultants solution architects. During this phase, the vendors started setting up consulting teams that would help clients improve their processes, leveraging outsourcing at the same time. Clearly, this required specialization in the certain processes, which is why the vendor base started focusing on certain use cases they were really good at. At Evalueserve we kept focusing on knowledge process in research and analytics.

This was the first era where captives experienced significant issues in being able to perform at the same level as the vendors. Captives by definition had only a single client, their owner. Therefore, they did not have the same broad exposure as the vendors for many processes. Increasingly, the value proposition of vendors became stronger, and captives needed to play arguments such as compliance (i.e., "Things need to be kept in-house") or cost (i.e., "Our hourly rates are lower, because you don't have to pay for the vendors' sales force and profits"), which may be valid in some cases, but certainly not in all cases.

ERA 4: HYBRID ON-SITE, NEAR-SHORE, AND FAR-SHORE OUTSOURCING (2010–)

Increasingly, the clients required on-site and near-shore skills. We would provide hybrid solutions in multiple centers and also in the client's premises; for example, an overall team of about 100 analysts could be spread as follows: 15 analysts in China, 35 in India, 10 in Romania, 20 in Chile, 5 in Raleigh, and 5 each at client sites in New York, London, and Hong Kong. Of course, this demands good process control and strict governance. Such hybrid setups are increasingly common, and clients like their flexibility and also the ability to mix and match various skill sets.

Since 2015 US clients are increasingly asking for joint near-shore operations in the United States, where we would even go to campus together. Applicants would hear that they will work for Evalueserve but on behalf of the client for about two or three years, after which period they will then be eligible for front-office roles, for example, in New York as the client's employees. The benefits for the clients are obvious. Evalueserve takes care of the hiring and training, and the client then gets to pick the cream of the crop. Again, such integrated models are not things that captives can offer easily.

ERA 5: MIND+MACHINE IN OUTSOURCING (2010–)

Three factors are driving mind+machine in outsourcing: clients becoming more demanding in terms of the benefits they can expect from their vendors, the advent of machines enabling vendors to provide specialized solutions, and a geographic cost arbitrage that is still there but reducing in relative terms. Clients want improved productivity, faster time to market, better quality, and new capabilities that will make them more successful in their markets. This is a tall order for vendors, but it is the reality. Vendors are adding Machine into the mix of their solutions, because Mind-only is not able to deliver such benefits consistently. Clearly, this means that the vendors have to cannibalize their own revenues. Evalueserve is automating away about 5 to 10 percent of its overall manual workload on an annual basis. This means that in order to grow in the double digits as a company, it needs to grow the work produced by at least 15 to 20 percent per year. But the message is clear and simple: if Evalueserve doesn't do it, somebody else will, so it is better to be the leader and win market share.

This time, captives have even bigger problems following suit. They usually don't have the degrees of freedom or the resources to develop significant Machine solutions, unless they are embedded in global programs with such a focus. But more important than this, they don't have multiple clients and the ensuing specialization and knowledge required for specific analytics use cases. Moreover, vendors can amortize their investments into specific use cases over a large client base: captives cannot do this. Therefore, by definition, the ROI will suffer.

Mind+machine solutions are increasingly enabling global workflows so that outsourcing becomes possible and seamless. Analyzing the outsourcing potential of mind+machine solutions can definitely create opportunities for better ROI. The cloud increasingly enables such collaboration models without requiring major IT projects. In the early 2000s the decreasing costs of telecommunications enabled the Mind-only outsourcing models to India. Now it is the cloud

Industry Sector Update:
Marketing Presentations

Context

Organization
Investment bank

Function(s)
Sector research

Industry
Financial services

Geography
United States

Business Challenge

- Generate analytical pack of sector KPIs every quarter (involves data extraction from websites to populate over 100 charts)
- Automate time-consuming task of manual data extraction and chart population to free up time for value-adding insights and reduce the possibility of errors

Solution

Approach

- Analyzed source codes of websites and formats of marketing presentations
- Examined terms and conditions of data extraction policies to ensure compliance
- Automated data extraction process and pasting of charts and tables
- Executed parallel runs (manual and automated) to identify discrepancies and close gaps

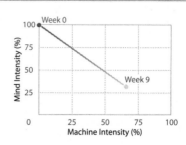

Analytics Challenges

- Source code varies across websites
- Compliance with the data extraction policy of individual websites
- Presenting data cohesively
- Creation of a dynamic and robust platform to incorporate any future changes in website and presentation design

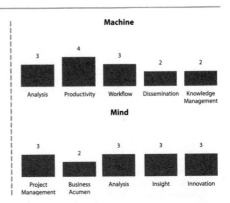

Machine

Analysis	Productivity	Workflow	Dissemination	Knowledge Management
3	4	3	2	2

Mind

Project Management	Business Acumen	Analysis	Insight	Innovation
3	2	3	3	3

Benefits

Productivity	Time to Market	New Capabilities	Quality
• 87% productivity gains through automation	• 75% faster delivery	• Increased scope of analysis with 4 new sector metrics	• Consistent chart and table dimensions in all presentations • Complete automation leading to a zero error rate

Implementation

- Developed customized automation tool in 5 weeks
- Tested the tool for 4 weeks in parallel runs alongside the manual method
- Trained client engagement team to do maintenance and support; no dedicated FTE is required
- Teams continuously increase scope of work by adding new metrics and enabling better analysis

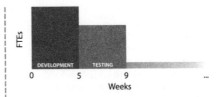

FTEs

DEVELOPMENT   TESTING

0   5   9   ...

Weeks

Investment Banking:
A Global Offshore Research Function

Context

Organization
Investment bank

Function(s)
Investment banking and advisory

Industry
Financial services

Geography
Global offices with HQ in Europe

Business Challenge

- Build a research function that efficiently and effectively supports the client's business needs
- Set up analytical team supporting 1,000+ bankers globally
- Deliver high-quality work consistently across the product line in a cost-effective manner

Solution

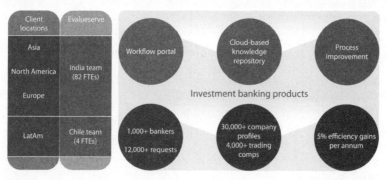

Client locations | Evalueserve

Asia

North America | India team (82 FTEs)

Europe

LatAm | Chile team (4 FTEs)

Workflow portal

Cloud-based knowledge repository

Process improvement

Investment banking products

1,000+ bankers
12,000+ requests

30,000+ company profiles
4,000+ trading comps

5% efficiency gains per annum

Approach

- Deployed workflow portal for transparent, real-time engagement
- Developed cloud-based knowledge repository for effective re-use of knowledge assets
- Introduced a robust governance mechanism that includes customized MIS reporting, meetings with gatekeepers, roadshows, and feedback workshops
- Developed process automations over time

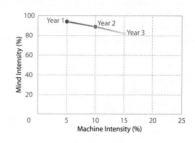

Analytics Challenges

- Lack of centralized workflow tracking and lack of systematic knowledge management
- Lack of collaboration across client offices
- Very limited standardization of work products, limiting automation
- Requirements for language support
- Significant time spent on repetitive, low-value tasks
- Low motivation from some client stakeholders to change the status quo

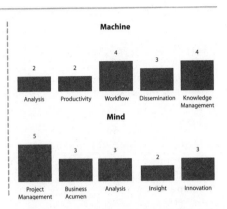

Benefits

Productivity	Time to Market	New Capabilities	Quality
• 5% annualized efficiency gains via standardization, re-use, and automation • Request volume growth of ~45% with a head count growth of only 16%	• Reduced turnaround times for standard recurring tasks • Enhanced efficiencies by building sector expertise	• Non-English language research • Robust internal knowledge assets • Support in launching and managing new products	• Adherence to strict service levels for quality and project management • Reduced errors in data-intensive tasks through automations

Implementation

- Started an 8-member pilot team to understand expectations and set delivery standards
- Team increased to 86 FTEs by year 3
- Developed and launched a cloud-based workflow portal
- Created a comprehensive knowledge repository for efficient re-use of information
- Implemented process automations, resulting in significant efficiency gains

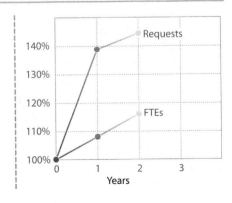

technology that enables more efficient mind+machine solutions for many analytics use cases.

State-of-the-art outsourcing combines hybrid engagement models and mind+machine. Especially for the analytics use cases described in this book, finding the right talent globally is not only an option, but often the only way to find it and integrate it into the global workflows.

PRICING AND PERFORMANCE BENCHMARKS

The more advanced procurement departments are able to integrate mind+machine into their make-versus-buy decisions and vendor selection models. However, they are a minority. Even today, the so-called rate tables by location and service are still the predominant way of comparing the commercials of vendors. Instead, models should compare the benefits of mind+machine. Why?

Let's compare the two models for a simple use case, say a piece of data analytics involving 10 analysts for one year of work for a Chicago-based client.

1. **Model A—"rate table"**: The procurement department compares Vendors A and B, and Captive C by way of rate tables for the 10 FTEs. Say the India-based Vendor A charges USD 35 per hour for the 10 data scientists in a largely manual staff augmentation model. Vendor B (United States/Latin America) proposes a hybrid mind+machine solution involving 30 percent near-shore United States and 70 percent far-shore Latin America with an average hourly rate of USD 45. India-based Captive C charges a variable cost of USD 30 per hour. If the comparison is based on hourly rates, Captive C will be chosen, Vendor A comes second, and Vendor B comes third.

2. **Model B—"value-based"**: The procurement department now includes productivity benefits across the *end-to-end* use case (i.e., both savings in the outsourced part and savings due to internal process improvements) in the calculations and properly allocates overheads to the captive rather than just looking at variable salary costs. If done properly, now Vendor B might come out to be the winner by a good margin (assuming a 30 percent productivity benefit), but Vendor A would probably match Captive C in terms of overall value.

Obviously, Model B is more accurate than Model A. Granted, productivity advantages need to be measured, but this is very much feasible given today's vendor's maturity. In this example, the productivity benefits stem from two sources: the automation tools, and the superior engagement model for the US client with better fit in terms of proximity, ability to travel to Chicago at short notice (which is not possible from India without a proper visa), and better time zone coverage for the United States.

A more advanced assessment would also include the other benefits such as shorter time to market for the deliverables due to process reengineering and automation, enhanced quality, and new capabilities for the client (e.g., being able to display the results on mobile devices or getting push notifications for major changes).

Mind+machine can produce productivity benefits of up to 75 percent for certain processes, improvements in terms of time to market of more than 90 percent for highly automated products and around 30 percent for workflow platforms, as well as significant improvements in terms of quality and client capabilities. Just an example: if the InsightBee Sales Intelligence platform produces a hot lead once per month, which the classic approach might not have produced, the added revenues and margin on the additional deals would already produce a very significant ROI for the client.

Whatever use case you have in mind, please ask your procurement department or internal service units to provide you with the apples-to-apples comparisons. It might take a little more time to come to a conclusion, but it is definitely worth it.

Let's now just look at the Mind part and its cost and availability around the globe. For analytics use cases, the skill groups you might be looking for are MBAs, chartered financial analysts (CFAs), financial risk managers (FRMs), statisticians, mathematicians, data scientists, user experience designers, and IT folks with modern skill sets in agile, cloud, and mobile technologies and methodologies. Where do you find them and at what cost? It is very hard to generalize. Factors such as training and experience influence the productivity of these skill groups significantly. In a mind+machine model, human skills such as creativity, excellent nerd/antinerd communication skills, independent thinking, the ability to use constructive push-back, onshore experience, and business understanding are significantly more important than whether or not someone has an MSc or a PhD in statistics. In fact, we had better results in big data analytics and advanced forecasting with outside-of-the-box thinkers (e.g., one had a background in agricultural engineering) than with amazing data scientists who could not communicate or work in teams. These soft factors can make huge differences, and Evalueserve changed its hiring practices accordingly.

In terms of pure salaries for the Mind, India is still the lowest-cost, highest-skill location in the world for such sought-after skills. With improvements in the Indian school system, the employability of people has improved over the course of the past 15 years. For the purpose of this comparison, we will index India salaries to 100 percent for fresh graduates. Another great skill pool for quantitative skills is China. Salaries will be at about 130 to 140 percent for comparable skills. In Latin America (e.g., Chile or Argentina), great skills are available at about 150 percent. Near-shore (i.e., in Eastern Europe or in second-tier US cities), the index is probably about 170 percent. Places like New York or London or Zurich would be in the medium 200 percents.

Financial Benchmark Analytics: Index Reporting

Context

Organization
Major financial benchmarks

Function(s)
Index development, production, and reporting

Industry
Financial services: indexes

Geography
Global team with HQ in Europe

Business Challenge

- Help to facilitate the handling of increased volume of index requests
- Resolve difficulties in report creation, dissemination, and knowledge management
- Reduce risk of errors due to system complexity and manual report generation

Solution

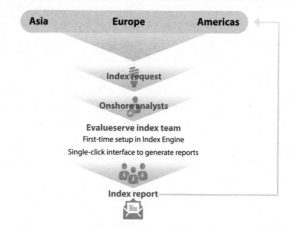

Asia   Europe   Americas

Index request

Onshore analysts

Evalueserve index team
First-time setup in Index Engine
Single-click interface to generate reports

Index report

Approach

- Created dashboard connected to the index history database with index–client mapping
- Predefined report formats
- Programmed automatic client report generation with an option to automatically transmit the report to the client

For each index, two reports are possible on a given price date: the end-of-day index level report; and the index ingredient and makeup report

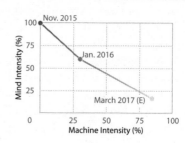

Analytics Challenges

- Different asset classes run this process for different clients with a possible overlap in the list of indexes
- Different report format required for different asset classes
- The process is not scalable to the increasing number of indexes that require reporting
- The process is error-prone due to manual creation of the reports

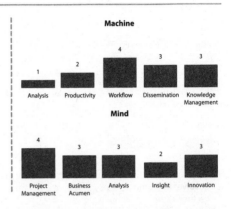

Benefits

Productivity	Time to Market	New Capabilities	Quality
• Standardized reporting • Easy report setup • Fast and efficient run-time process	• New asset classes added quickly • Easy to rerun reports in case of errors • Reports generated and sent instantly	• Scalable • Customized reporting • Multiple file types (.xml, .xls, etc.)	• Reduced errors in data collation • Consistent report formats • Intuitive user interface

Implementation

- Reporting for multiple clients can be done in one go
- Client-specific folders are automatically created and reports are saved in a well-managed, auditable way
- All reports go out in one new format
- Total development effort of 200 person hours

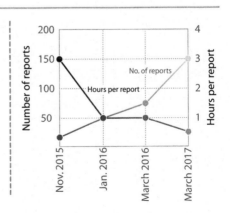

Now we take on the famous topic of salary increases in India, which is badly understood by most. Of course, it is true that salaries increase by about 8 to 10 percent for every year of tenure, which is certainly a lot compared to an average wage inflation of 2 to 3 percent in the West. But let's not make the mistake many people in the West make when they predict the demise of outsourcing to far-shore destinations. They compare apples and oranges, or pay-for-tenure with average wage inflation. Paying salary increases for increases in tenure is *not* the same as general average wage inflation. Even in the West, we pay high increases for every year of tenure in the group of knowledge professionals. My annual increases in my years at McKinsey were easily 20 to 25 percent per year. Did anyone speak of a general wage inflation in Switzerland because of this? No. Let's compare apples and apples. We should compare the salaries of person A with exactly three years of experience in 2010 and of person B with again exactly three years of experience in 2015. If we do this calculation, the picture is far less dramatic.

One of the biggest differences, though, in terms of onshore markets and near-shore/offshore markets is the availability of good midlevel management and people with experience. Again, this is a factor that procurement departments rarely consider. However, the ROI of analytics use cases depends critically on the quality of the midlevel program management. In this category, clearly onshore markets rank highest. Finding good middle management in China is possible, but very difficult. India has a more experienced workforce in outsourcing, which is why it is possible to find good middle management, albeit at almost Western prices. In places like Chile, Poland, or Romania a good group of middle management has started emerging, but they are rare and highly sought after.

In spite of such differences, the total cost of ownership from an outsourcing perspective is pretty much the same across all centers these days. True, onshore or near-shore centers might be more expensive than centers in India, but they have clear advantages in terms of onshore travel, time zones, and languages. This gets reflected in the increasing demand for near-shore centers in the United States, for example. Nevertheless, India remains the largest skill pool available and will have some position in the future, regardless of what people who have a political agenda against outsourcing might say.

THE FUTURE OF OUTSOURCING IN KNOWLEDGE-INTENSIVE PROCESSES

Here are eight tentative predictions about the next 10 years of outsourcing as it pertains to analytics.

1. Mind+machine will dominate in outsourcing. Costs in offshore locations will continue to go up for the aforementioned skill sets. This implies increasing degrees of automation until a balance is achieved.

2. Cloud and mobile will go mainstream in outsourcing. Cloud platforms with mobile delivery will be critical for mind+machine for analytics use cases.

3. Outsourcing will continue to grow. As vendors will continue to specialize, the competitive advantage of vendors over internal units will grow.

4. There will be more near-shore, less offshore. The percentage mix between onshore, near-shore, and far-shore will change driven by strong forces that favor near-shore outsourcing.

5. Global, hybrid models will dominate. Client needs are global in nature and require global solutions. In all likelihood, global will be a multiregional model spanning the Asia-Pacific (APAC) region, Europe, and the Americas.

6. Vendors will be far more efficient than captives. Mind+machine will require specialization, multiple-client exposure, onshore presence, the ability to amortize IT investments in platforms, and generally a new breed of skill sets. Captives by definition cannot have multiple-client exposure. Therefore, it will be hard for them to build mind+machine solutions that have global impact. Changing the situation will take time. The occasional sale or partial closing of a captive will be common, but captives as a whole are sticky. Compliance and regulatory reasons will probably remain the only real argument for keeping captives open.

7. There will be consolidation in the vendor space. The big outsourcing companies have already bought up many of the independent specialists, having realized that mind+machine needs specialized skills and process know-how as well as size.

8. Vendors will be adding consulting skills. Some of the big firms have acquired consulting firms to reengineer their clients' processes, and this trend is likely to continue.

PART II: CONCLUSION

These are the 13 trends that are going to shape the evolution of Mind+Machine. As with every new development, there are big opportunities, but also significant potential risks to be avoided or at least managed. Overall, I believe that the trends are very much good news for you, the business owners and end users. The balance of power has very much shifted in your favor. The ingredients for successfully managing thousands of existing and new use cases are in place—we just need to assemble them into a consistent methodology that addresses the opportunities and challenges of the one billion use cases. In Part III, I will propose the Use Case Methodology (UCM), which could provide a common language to develop and manage individual use cases and portfolios of use cases on an ongoing basis.

PART III

HOW TO IMPLEMENT THE MIND+MACHINE APPROACH

As the Hubble space telescope demonstrates every day, zooming away from a focus on individual stars and planets allows us to see first the solar systems and then the beauty of the billions of galaxies. We can recognize the existence of elliptical, spiral, and irregular galaxies—three patterns or arrangements that we cannot perceive without a distant vantage point. Think of it as the ultimate big picture view.

Replace the solar systems and galaxies with analytics use cases and replace the Hubble telescope with this book, at a far smaller scale, of course, and you'll understand what I'm trying to do in Part III. I want to pull back far enough from the one billion primary use cases to let you see the big picture: broad patterns, relationships, and connections. When you zoom in on any given use case, you'll be better able to understand its position and relationship within the bigger whole. I hope it will create an understanding that mind+machine is not as complex as some people are trying to make it.

To achieve this, I am going beyond just looking at the big picture to offer these perspectives packaged as a methodology. It should help you keep a set of fair expectations from your internal and external analytics providers and give you some ready-to-use surgical questions that will keep everything transparent and everybody on track. The focus is entirely on *your* benefits and the ROI that mind+machine analytics provides to *you*, the end user.

Come with me on this journey to see how to successfully implement the mind+machine approach.

THE ANALYTICS USE CASE METHODOLOGY: A CHANGE IN MIND-SET

The energy of the mind is the essence of life.
—Aristotle, The Philosophy of Aristotle

As life changes, so must our minds. In Part II, we looked at the current and future trends driving mind+machine. The current nonarchitecture is bound to fail or, at the very least, be highly inefficient for companies, managers, and, most important, end users who are in need of timely and actionable insights. A change in mind-set is essential.

We know that there are about one billion primary analytics use cases and about 50 billion secondary use case variations annually, with thousands of new use cases added every year. Managing such vast numbers of use cases, most of which span multiple types of minds and machines, requires a new, common language that uses individual use cases at the core and can be understood by everyone. Over the past few years we have seen that the systematic application of this use case concept simplifies matters dramatically, increases transparency, weeds out methods that do not and will not succeed, improves the ROI of many use cases, and, most importantly, helps decision makers like you get what you need, when you need it, and in a format that makes sense.

In this part of the book, we propose our Use Case Methodology (UCM), which addresses the topic of mind+machine analytics as a structured portfolio of individual use cases. It deals with the end-to-end management of individual use cases, but also with the governance of whole portfolios of use cases. Figure III.1 gives a top-down overview of the framework.

Companies need to be able to handle the complexity of their various portfolios of mind+machine use cases across their functional, regional, or business unit entities. The number and type will vary: the US sales force of a construction equipment manufacturer might have a portfolio of 200 analytics use cases along its sales cycle, while the European maintenance function of the medical imaging division of an industrial conglomerate might have 500 use cases in the Internet of Things. However, the right approach is still fundamentally the same.

The UCM addresses the following questions:

- Use case level: How should **individual use cases** be managed end-to-end? In other words, how should we:
  - Define the business issue, the clients, and the client benefits?
  - Determine the resources, skills, infrastructure, time lines, and management?
  - Ensure success in terms of ROI and client benefits?
  - Manage the life cycle and the risks?
  - Ensure proper knowledge management?

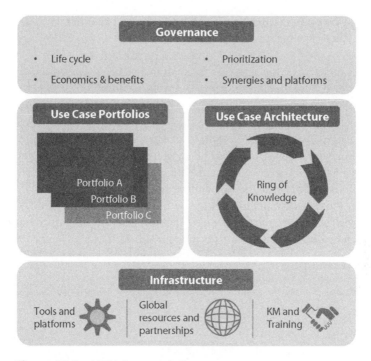

Figure III.1 UCM Framework Overview

- Portfolio level: How should **portfolios** of use cases be managed?
  - Which use cases should be created, life cycle managed, or terminated?
  - What are the right priorities and resource allocations?
  - Are there any platform benefits across the portfolio?
  - How can we ensure positive ROI across the portfolio?
  - How should governance and program management be performed?

In the next few chapters we will discuss the management of individual use cases, and then we'll move on to discuss portfolios.

We've already looked at several analytics use cases but not discussed them in terms of the Use Case Methodology. To help focus on the details, we will first look at a few more use cases, each of which of course has many more details but the same core descriptive concept—in fact, it's the same straightforward concept we can apply to every single one of the billion primary use cases.

Every single use case can be described with the UCM acting as a *single common language*. Using a common language in mind+machine analytics is as important as using a common language from guest to server or server to kitchen in a restaurant.

The UCM is trying to serve the community as a common language that is understood by all parties: the business users, analysts, techies, vendors, controllers,

Energy Retailer:
Competitive Pricing Analytics

Context

Organization
Retail energy provider

Function(s)
Pricing and analytics

Industry
Energy services

Geography
United States

Business Challenge

- Improve understanding of competitor pricing strategies and reduce time to market
- Increase granularity and quality of data
- Reduce core team's workload on low-value tasks associated with reporting

Solution

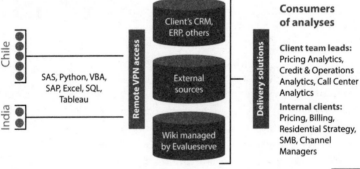

Consumers of analyses

Client team leads: Pricing Analytics, Credit & Operations Analytics, Call Center Analytics

Internal clients: Pricing, Billing, Residential Strategy, SMB, Channel Managers

● KM, Training, Governance
— Team members

Approach

Stage 1: Automated large portions of each reporting process
- Defined detailed roadmap of workload transition associated with reporting
- Defined KPIs to track efficiency gains
- Established dedicated team
- Restructured existing delivery schedule to capitalize on time zone differences

Stage 2: Improved granularity and quality of existing metrics in line with the client's long-term strategic goals

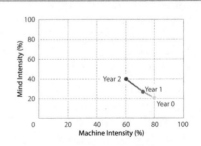

Analytics Challenges

- Aligning dozens of metric definitions and sources for 20+ business stakeholders across 8 different channels
- Midcampaign experimentation and refocusing: adjusting product and channel performance tracking when reacting to release of a disruptive competitor product
- Channel manager expectations: applying midcampaign changes in business rules led to discrepancies in perceived performance metrics, affecting channel goal benchmarking

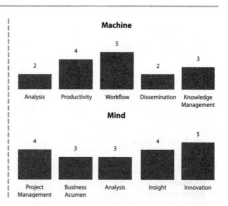

Benefits

Productivity	Time to Market	New Capabilities	Quality
• Team's reporting capacity rose 4-fold • Doubled ad hoc analysis capacity without an equivalent team size increase	• Tracking online competitors four times per day meant quicker reaction to disruptive launches • Quicker adjustment to new product structures	• Tracking three times more competitors • Automation of several software	• Automated highly detailed quality controls 2 to 4 levels below main KPIs

Implementation

- Dedicated wiki and KM best practices improved new team member onboarding
- Time for complex ad hoc analyses reduced from 1 year to 4 months
- Developed and deployed a process to allow tracking of 20 competitors four times per day (previously 8 competitors once per week)
- Increased automation so the amount and level of difficulty of the work produced outpaced the growth of the team

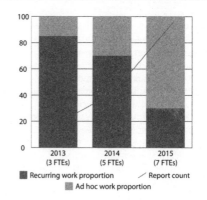

Intellectual Property:
Identifying and Managing IP Risk

Context

Organization
Electronics company

Industry
Consumer electronics and
telecommunications

Function(s)
IP strategy and analysis team

Geography
Global

Business Challenge

- Build a high-quality, cost-effective solution to help assess patent risk from competitors
- Categorize and benchmark large patent portfolios for competitive intelligence and ensure knowledge reuse for better analyses, higher quality, and quicker decision making

Solution

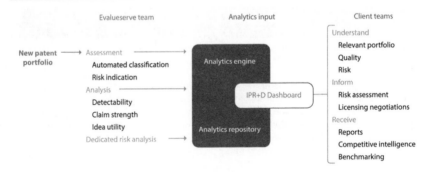

Approach

Development phase:
- Built the taxonomy with product feature-based categories
- Developed the relevant training set for text analytics-based classifiers

Implementation phase:
- Tested the classifiers by comparing the results with data curated manually
- Further modified and enriched classifiers to ensure high result quality
- Built platform on IPR+D Dashboard for patent portfolio data analyses

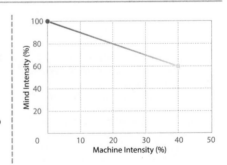

Analytics Challenges

- Generating exhaustive training set for each product feature category
- Fine-tuning classifiers and feature set, which needed repeated iterations to ensure high quality (more than 90% accuracy)
- Creating workflow for combining Mind+Machine process for gaining impactful efficiency without compromising on quality
- One-click report generation required new templates to ensure transmission of meaningful insights

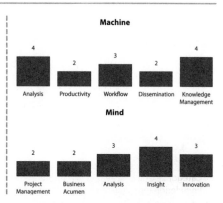

Benefits

Productivity	Time to Market	New Capabilities	Quality
• 40% efficiency gains through efficient workflow platform • Delivery time cut from 6–8 weeks to 2–3 weeks	• Solution built over 3 months • Deployment for new clients can be done within a few weeks	• Patent portfolio categorized for product features • Quick CI and portfolio benchmarking reports • Monthly patent monitoring reports	• Manual analysis of all patents ensures 100% quality control • Categorization helps allocate right engineer from right team for final risk assessment

Implementation

- Using Evalueserve's existing IPR+D Dashboard as a delivery platform with custom workflow functionality.
- Using KMX text analytical tools and classifiers to categorize patents onto product features
- Working with 2 other corporate clients to build similar risk mitigation solutions
- Potential for USD 0.5 million from licensing clients in year 1

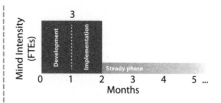

Market and Customer Intelligence:
Market Inventories

Context

Organization
Global staffing and recruitment firm

Function(s)
Market & customer intelligence

Industry
Human resources

Geography
Global, HQ in Europe

Business Challenge

- Set up a market intelligence (MI) function at holding level
- Ensure consistent approach to various research and analytics initiatives
- Build market inventory reports to promote data-driven decisions in sales and marketing
- Competitor benchmarking to understand business strategy and gain first-mover advantage

Solution

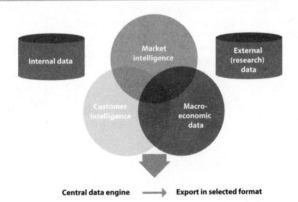

Central data engine ⟶ Export in selected format

Approach

- Set up a dedicated team of business analysts with local market insight and data analysts for data-heavy initiatives
- Designed central data engine for storage and reuse of internal and external market information
- Developed over 15 market inventory reports covering key verticals and largest geographical markets
- Aggregated key market information in dashboards and set up a document repository platform

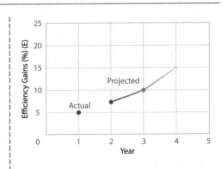

Analytics Challenges

- Lack of a consistent approach to data usage and dissemination
- Low organizational maturity to data-driven planning and decision making
- Internal data scattered across multiple platforms and formats
- Complex research framework, including hundreds of different internal and external sources

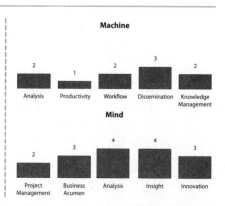

Benefits

Productivity	Time to Market	New Capabilities	Quality
• Reuse of market data in multiple MI reports • Productivity gains of over 80% via automated generation of company profiles	• Quicker decision making and prioritization of initiatives through more harmonized and standardized reporting	• Market intelligence on new verticals and geographies • Improved knowledge management thanks to report repository	• Higher level of insights in market inventory reports • Consistent approach to market sizing and market share analysis • Easy-to-read reports and visualizations

Implementation

- Set up a 3-analyst team to support newly built market intelligence function—delivery started from day 1
- Covered inventories from 5 different verticals in year 1
- Developed 100+ competitor profiles
- Disseminated market intelligence reports to 20+ business stakeholders

and compliance specialists. From a more behavioral perspective, it also tries to serve as the common language between the different Myers–Briggs personalities we discussed in Part I—even between our nerds and antinerds! It is fundamentally designed to be open source. It allows management tools and platforms to be created that all use the same frameworks. Moreover, it would ultimately enable use cases to be shared between companies, allowing more people to benefit from Level 4 knowledge created elsewhere.

As the analytics use case is the pivotal element of the UCM, here is its definition again as a reminder:

An analytics use case is the **end-to-end analytics support solution** applied once or repeatedly to a **single business issue** faced by an **end user** or homogeneous group of end users who need to make decisions, take actions, or deliver a product or service **on time** based on the **insights** delivered.

Let's now dive into the world of analytics use cases, starting with the definition of the business issue and the benefits the use case is expected to deliver.

FOCUS ON THE BUSINESS ISSUE AND THE CLIENT BENEFITS

Simplicity is ultimately a matter of focus.
—Ann Voskamp, *One Thousand Gifts:*
A Dare to Live Fully Right Where You Are

The most common issue resulting in low or negative ROI is that analytics is often started without any clear definition of the specific business issue, the clients or end user(s), and the expected client benefits. Instead, a collection of resources is put in place with statements such as "We first need to create an analytics capability. Then that central team is going to find out what can be analyzed." Interestingly, defining these three essential things isn't even that difficult. It just needs to happen with the necessary rigor and discipline, and always *before* any analytics efforts.

State the precise business issue: What problem are we trying to solve? There are three simple rules:

- Rule 1: **One business issue deserves one use case.** We frequently see that analytics use cases get overloaded. Somebody has a good idea. Various functions chime in, adding new requirements and complexities, and we end up in that familiar trap of complexity, interdependencies, defocusing, delays, escalating costs, and lack of ROI.
- Rule 2: **Keep the business issue narrow, and focus on the first minimum viable product (MVP 1).** The business issue should be as focused as possible; for example, it should initially be one function and one region. Time to market is critical. Anything that takes more than a few months is too long. The initial goal should be MVP 1, which is defined as the simplest possible product

for a given business issue that creates the first wave of ROI. Once it is in place, agile sprints can focus on creating MVP 2, 3, and so on with the hope of increasing levels of ROI. Overloading the specs to try to serve multiple regions and multiple functions or do too much just complicates the first situation.

- **Rule 3: Simplicity wins.** The simpler your use case, the better. Don't start with big data or AI if you don't have to. Most use cases deliver ROI through simple improvements (e.g., with a better workflow or a first set of small data). The bells and whistles can be added later, once there is proof that it works. Of course, there are certain use cases that simply need big data to start with, but then try to run some initial tests limited to the data feeds you really need.

Define the end users explicitly: Who are the end users for this particular business issue? Again, we have three simple rules:

- **Rule 1: Keep it to a single user group.** You might be surprised how quickly your end user group can expand, with lots of free riders joining the bandwagon even though the use case is intended for another group. Since expectations vary by type of end user, this will quickly create conflicting objectives.
- **Rule 2: Analytics is for end users, not for central teams or vendors.** Such projects can become loaded with hidden agendas, letting analytics become its own purpose and absorbing large budgets. It is critical to know whose objectives need to be served.
- **Rule 3: The end users rule.** Nobody but the end users should judge whether the solution has been successful. Controlling's role is to support them, not to judge success.

Define the client benefits. What are the expectations regarding the client benefits to be achieved for the specific use case? There are five simple rules:

- **Rule 1: Use the client benefit framework for each use case.** Define quantified targets for each dimension of benefit: productivity, time to market, quality, and new capabilities. Make sure you consider the *end-to-end process*, and not just the analytics part of the process. Many people will try to shy away from clear target setting. Don't allow this to happen. Not every use case has targets for all four categories in this framework, but there must be at least one nonempty category. Typically, two or three categories are involved.
- **Rule 2: Agree on a common, simple, and transparent ROI framework.** Remember your market first—the client benefits drive ROI. The question must be output based: "Will this use case make us more competitive? Will it help us sell more?" Agree with your finance function on a simple and transparent calculation framework that is commonly accepted across your company. Anything that is longer than a page won't work—it might be intellectually stimulating, but nobody will have the time to do the complex calculations. This might save your job, as your use case *will* be reviewed at some point in the future. Be prepared for it, and get everybody aligned around it.

Clearly, productivity is easiest to quantify in terms of impact on ROI. However, the other dimensions might be even more important for ROI; for example, if your sales pitches reach the clients faster than your competitors' do, this might have a large impact on your revenues. It is therefore important to understand the precise market impact of the Level 3 insights the use case delivers to the decision makers. This factor probably drives ROI more than anything else. It also helps in prioritizing use cases relative to each other in a market-based impact assessment as opposed to a prioritization based on internal factors.

- Rule 3: **Define the expectations up front for each use case.** The expected benefits need to be defined before the work starts—and that means defined in writing! Once the work has started, internal or external parties will have their contracts in place already and won't move anymore—or if they do, it will be at additional cost.

- Rule 4: **Define the budget by use case.** Companies often make the mistake of not having budgets "defined" by use case, meaning that the line units will ultimately get some nontransparent overhead allocations from some central units, leading to a lot of not-so-happy payers and ultimately useless distractions for the stakeholders.

- Rule 5: **Stringently track progress against the client benefits.** Everything else is nice to have, but this is the most important element. It will keep everybody on their toes and oriented toward a common goal. Keep this tracking going for the whole lifetime of the use case, and revise it when the use case goes through some life cycle management (e.g., for the next MVP). Client progress reviews for permanent analytics relationships at Evalueserve always include tracking the progress against the client benefits: it's essential for both sides to manage expectations and results.

Life cycle management: Use cases evolve over time. They have to go through their consecutive MVPs until they stabilize. The actual user needs might change in various ways: scope, frequency, format, delivery channel, and mode. There is a tendency for other users to try to piggyback on existing use cases by latching onto them. The ROI of the use case might no longer justify its existence, in which case its execution should be either stopped or streamlined so that the ROI comes back into positive territory. Changes require resources, and the business owners need to prioritize any actions.

Based on our experience, the more user types there are, the stickier use cases become; that is, they become extremely hard to kill and continue to absorb resources. This is another reason for Rule 4. It is highly unlikely that all user groups will decide at the same time that they do not need a use case anymore. Keeping use cases focused and modular and avoiding complex spaghetti architectures with lots of interfaces and interdependencies can save millions.

Customer Churn Analytics:
B2B Dealer Network

Context

Organization
Manufacturer of heavy machinery

Industry
Automotive

Function(s)
Machine parts sales

Geography
North America and China

Business Challenge

- Improve understanding of controllable and uncontrollable drivers of churn
- Identify customers at risk of defection
- Develop a strategy to retain the most loyal and profitable customers

Solution

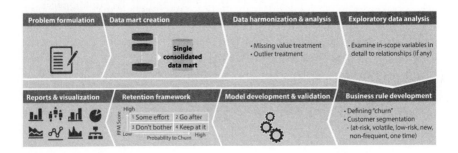

Problem formulation	Data mart creation	Data harmonization & analysis	Exploratory data analysis
	Single consolidated data mart	• Missing value treatment • Outlier treatment	• Examine in-scope variables in detail to relationships (if any)

Reports & visualization	Retention framework	Model development & validation	Business rule development
	High 1 Some effort 2 Go after 3 Don't bother 4 Keep at it Low Probability to Churn High		• Defining "churn" • Customer segmentation - (at-risk, volatile, low-risk, new, non-frequent, one time)

Approach

- Developed business rules to define churn and segment customers
- Excluded new, non-frequent, and one-time customers from the analysis
- Scored customers on their recency, frequency, and monetary value (RFM) behavior
- Regressed customer behavior against hypothesized variables to identify key triggers of attrition
- Developed a retention framework using model results and RFM scores
- Developed a dashboard for refresh and end consumption

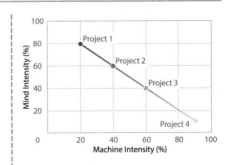

Analytics Challenges

- Integrating data from multiple sources with varying formats and quality, including missing values and variables
- Heterogeneous dealer network made it very difficult to develop a scalable retention framework
- Identifying the right analytical technique with a good mix of ease of interpretation, execution speed, and accuracy

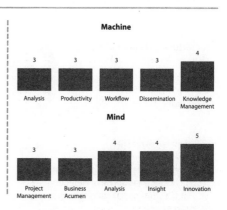

Benefits

Productivity	Time to Market	New Capabilities	Quality
• 93% productivity gain via automation • ROI of ~$25 million per dealer	• First model built in 12 weeks • 50% reduced time for second dealer (time to delivery)	• More effective and efficient retention campaigns • Data monetization opportunity for the client	• Average model accuracy of over 80%

Implementation

- 4 dealers analyzed in 6 months
- 4 FTEs for 12 weeks to develop the first model and 3 FTEs for 8 weeks to develop the second model
- 1 FTE to refresh the model every quarter
- 3 versions of dashboard developed: Executive, Operational, and Tactical

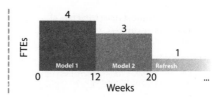

Preventive Maintenance:
Analyzing and Predicting Network Failures

Context

Organization
Major telecom operator

Function(s)
Service assurance and operations

Industry
Telecommunications

Geography
HQ in Europe

Business Challenge

- Combine multiple data sources in order to identify root causes for network downtime incidents
- Predict future network failures

Solution

Link and harmonize data from sources	**Identify events leading to failure**	**Perform predictive analytics**

Alerts	Devices
Ticketing	Inventory
Incidents	Performance

Approach

- Load raw data and identify links and keys between data sources
- Aggregate, cleanse, and harmonize data to standardize formats
- Join all data sources into a consolidated master dataset
- Identify cascades of events leading to network failure (path analysis)
- Identify a prediction model based on past pattern analysis

Analytics Challenges

- Processing large volumes (around 500 GB) of data
- Understanding and aggregating multiple data sources from different systems
- Using path analytics to identify root causes of network incidents

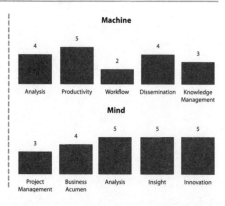

Benefits

Productivity	Time to Market	New Capabilities	Quality
• Streamlined root cause analysis • Created framework for incident prevention	• One month thanks to the data discovery methodology used • Future runs largely automated	• First successful data integration project for client • Ability to trigger preventive action based on complex patterns in network	• Reduction of number of errors thanks to the automated scripts used for implementation

Implementation

- Project team: 2 data scientists, 1 data engineer and 1 subject matter expert (SME)
- Workshop: SME, data scientists, and business stakeholders prioritized work based on feasibility and alignment to business drivers
- Data extraction: Team spent 2 weeks extracting and aggregating samples from all relevant sources
- Data preparation: Team spent 1 week cleansing raw data to create a master dataset
- Modeling: Multiple iterations of path analytics implemented over the course of one week

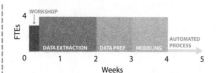

Perspective #2

MAP OUT THE RING OF KNOWLEDGE

Before you read this chapter, I suggest you watch the short movie *Powers of 10*. It's available online in both a version from 1977 and a newer one called *The Ultimate Zoom*. Both show how zooming in and out can help put things in perspective and reveal the proper overview of something. It is very easy to get lost in the details when we look at anything—and it's the biggest risk in mind+machine analytics.

Usually, it starts innocuously: some scope creep, running into complex interfaces, a lack of specialist skills, a few emerging data quality problems, a sudden reorganization or shifting of priorities, the key data scientist leaving for better pastures. Suddenly the use case fails because the details and distractions have overwhelmed the ability to keep the overview. In the Use Case Methodology (UCM), the Ring of Knowledge can help maintain that high-level overview.

- Rule 1: **Map the use case onto the Ring of Knowledge.** The Ring of Knowledge (see Figure I.4 in Part I) provides a framework that captures the main aspects of the use case, making sure none of them are forgotten—but remember that the Ring of Knowledge shows the use case in its final operating mode. It is not a project plan for its implementation.
- Rule 2: **Prioritize the stages relative to each other, and budget accordingly.** The Ring can help prioritize and spot deviations in resource spend. Usually, people work sequentially starting with the data. Of course, they encounter lots of data problems along the way and get mired down, absorbing a large part of the resources, losing sight of the later stages and their resource needs. If planning does not take each coming stage into account, there will be less time and money for the user experience design, audit trails, and knowledge management.

- Rule 3: **Keep track of any changes.** The Ring provides a simple one-page tool to capture changes and assess their overall impact on the life cycle of the use case.

The Ring of Knowledge also helps in bringing our nerds and the antinerds together with a common language focused on the benefits of each stage, and not the technical details. It enables the business owner of the use case to ask the right questions and facilitate the creation of a minimum viable product. For example: "Should we spend the time on improving the end user experience? Or should we take the data scientists' suggestion to integrate an unstructured data feed from social media, which would require AI for screening?" The user experience might prove far more important than an additional social media data feed. Asking the right question helps the business owner decide to allocate the resources to the right stages in the ring.

The following use case is a good example of successfully applying the Ring of Knowledge to create a working solution and then improve it over the following months.

Supply Chain Framework:
Bottleneck Identification

Context

Organization
Leading postal company

Function(s)
Supply chain

Industry
E-commerce

Geography
Nordic region

Business Challenge

- Identify bottlenecks in the e-commerce delivery system at each stage
- Optimize the supply chain to achieve next-day delivery to B2B customers
- Recommend improvements based on warehouse and transportation systems data

Solution

Business Issue   How to improve logistics performance for next-day delivery

Level 1 Levers

Process   Benchmark warehouse process   Benchmark transportation process

Level 2 Levers

✔ Failures in batching   ✔ Failures in receiving
✔ Failures in picking   ✔ Failures in sorting
✔ Failures in packing   ✔ Failures in delivery

Output   Reports & configurable visualization

Approach

- Mapped business process into small, measurable steps from order to delivery
- Analyzed last 2 years' relevant data to create models of expected performance
- Measured regular data feeds from each step for several cycles and benchmarked with the expected performance
- Automated daily refresh
- Identified on-the-ground bottlenecks causing the delays in the entire process

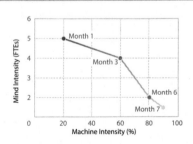

Analytics Challenges

- Data harmonization
- Multiple factors impacting lead time for delivery: warehouse location, order time (morning, afternoon), month (peak vs. non-peak season), type of product (fast vs. slow-moving goods)
- Limited historical data

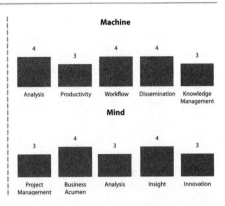

Benefits

Productivity	Time to Market	New Capabilities	Quality
• 50% reduction in delivery time from warehouse to customers • Enabled focus on removing on-the-ground bottlenecks	• Product built in 6 months	• In-depth supply chain analysis, trend monitoring, process benchmarking, and social media insights • Supply chain analytics dashboard	• Successful identification of transportation and warehousing bottlenecks • Automated tools helped remove manual delays and inaccuracies

Implementation

- 0 to 95% automation in 6 months
- 4 FTEs for 6 months for solution development
- 0.25 FTEs for solution implementation from month 7 onwards
- Daily dashboard for monitoring supply chain assisted in continuous improvement

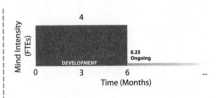

Perspective #3

CHOOSE DATA WISELY BASED ON THE ISSUE TREE

The biggest temptation in analytics is to fall for the "more data is better" principle. Let's collect all the data we can think of, find all the internal data in all the data silos that might potentially be relevant, throw in all the social media data and all the other free sources, and overlay this with all the paid data sources we can afford. This is exactly what happens when people buy data lakes.

There is a simple fact that shows how wrong this is: in most analytics projects data structuring and cleansing absorb 80 to 90 percent of the total project cost. That means only 10 to 20 percent is left for the actual thinking and analytics part, where Level 3 insights are getting created. As it happens, most use cases can be reduced to a few significant data dimensions, say 20 percent of the fields that might potentially be available in whatever data warehouse. This implies that up to 80 percent of the marginally relevant fields could easily be dropped from the analysis. If you spend the time to integrate these marginally relevant data fields, performing the required structuring and cleansing, you have wasted 64 to 72 percent (80 percent of 80 to 90 percent) of the total project time. In addition, you are subject to a much bigger risk of some data feeds changing their characteristics, meaning a lot of downstream maintenance cost.

Here are 11 simple rules to avoid this unnecessary wastage:

- Rule 1: **Create an issue tree.** This is probably the oldest consulting tool on this planet. Whole generations of consultants have been trained in it. At McKinsey, this concept became part of the consulting DNA. It involves breaking down the overall business question into manageable, logically independent subquestions, possibly in two or three hierarchical levels. Ultimately, each leaf sitting on the final branches represents some data or information that needs to be collected to conduct a successful analysis, and the nodes contain the models of how the data needs to be analyzed. Analytics use cases can be broken down in similar ways. The big advantage of this method is that the users are forced to come up with hypotheses that can be tested, thereby automatically introducing rigor into the selection of data fields. This is how we can avoid "boiling the ocean"—or, more to the point, boiling the data lake!

- Rule 2: **Define the minimum viable data set.** The first minimum viable product (MVP 1) requires an initial data set based on the issue tree. The point is to keep it to the absolute minimum while still ensuring inclusion of the data that is most likely to lead to new insights, i.e., the first minimum viable data set (MVD 1). This is the time to consider including alternative data and data from other silos, as new combinations of data often provide surprising insights. The concept of MVD 1 means increased speed and reduced complexity. If you want to show quick results, don't overburden the project at the outset. Additional data sets can be integrated once you are successful.

- Rule 3: **If you can avoid big data, avoid it.** As discussed in Part I, big data has great benefits, but only in about 5 percent of all use cases. The working hypothesis is therefore is to use small data until the need for big data is proven—just like "innocent until proven guilty" in a court of law. The issue tree can help in limiting the data fields where big data is actually required. As discussed in Part I, the proponents of big data will say that handling big data does not cost much these days. This might be true for the storage and tool-based manipulation of the data, but it is not true for structuring, cleansing, establishing the cross-functional interfaces, managing the data flow and quality, integration with other sources, authorizations, compliance, and risk. All of these *do* require expensive data scientist and decision maker time.

- Rule 4: **When you need big data, do it professionally and measure its ROI.** Five percent of use cases do require some level of big data. However, our experience shows that many data fields do not really add the expected value to the analysis. Maybe the information doesn't exist in the data set, the quality is not sufficient and cannot be fixed, or there is too much noise in the data. Whatever the reason, be on top of the ROI. Kill the big data fields that don't provide value, and keep only the ones that do. Unused data fields will cost a lot of time and money downstream—they are *not* cost-neutral.

- Rule 5: **Prototype using subsets of data before expanding the MVD.** The MVD is should be a documented set. Be aware of sneaking expansions, a data field here or there, or your use case might quickly nose-dive into negative ROI. Any additions should be justified and prototyped before full implementation into the ongoing operation of the analytics use case.

- Rule 6: **Establish hard criteria for data quality entering your use case.** Bad data quality continues to be one of the biggest problems in any analytics use case. Simple problems such as incomplete data sets with empty fields, inconsistent duplications, differing time stamps, similar but different spellings of field names, and many other problems can lead to fundamentally flawed calculations. But then there are also "smarter" problems. A good example is the weekend problem in financial data series. Trading halts over the weekend but time stamps keep running, so in order to calculate the right growth rates and statistical distributions, the weekend needs to be mathematically removed. In Evalueserve's index operations, we need to correct the data in hundreds of similar areas. The picture gets really bad when uncontrolled external data or unstructured data enters the picture, and AI won't be able to fix the problem. Your risk and compliance department will be very happy if you can show them audits of data quality, especially if you use the data for critical decisions or, even worse, sell products containing the data.
- Rule 7: **Stay with the source and don't create copies.** Ultimately, the owner of the source will agree to the results of your use case only if the owner can be assured that the data enters your analysis in a controlled fashion. Creating interim copies destroys this "bond of accountability" and creates the opportunity for denying anything your use case might produce.
- Rule 8: **Ensure intellectual property rights and compliance with regulatory requirements.** Are you sure you are allowed to use the various data sets you are planning on using? Do you really have all the right contracts and licenses in place? Did you check which compliance rules might affect your data sets? This is particularly important if you use the data to create commercial products. Violating intellectual property rights or regulations might cost you dearly.
- Rule 9: **Plan for future changes in data sources.** It is an illusion to believe that data sets and their characteristics will remain static. You are lucky if all the data origination is under your control. In reality, data comes from various places where the use case owners don't have jurisdiction. What happens if the characteristics of your data source change overnight and you are not informed? Suddenly, all your downstream work might turn useless. When you take on a data set, make sure there is a process to check with the owner for changes and that there is no assumption of perfection.
- Rule 10: **Keep an audit trail and document the learnings.** Given the risks involved, it is essential to be able to demonstrate that your team applied a sufficient level of diligence in dealing with the data sets. Essentially, you will need an end-to-end audit trail of the data set, the accountability for its ownership and quality, the process of inclusion, the decisions on whether and how to use it, or any enhancements or alterations performed on it. Also, important findings or prototypes in dealing with the data sets should

be documented, *even if or especially if they were negative and led to the exclusion of the data set.* Whoever takes the job from you at some point should not be forced to make the same decisions all over again.

- Rule 11: **Monitor the end-to-end costs of the data and the data work.** As 80 to 90 percent of any analytics use case can end up being Level 1 data work, monitoring the investments and running costs of collecting, structuring, and cleansing the data is important. Constantly finding ways to reduce these costs can free up valuable resources such as data scientists or analysts for work that adds more value.

Spend Analytics:
Category Planning Tool

Context

Organization
Major water, energy, and hygiene services provider

Function(s)
Procurement & supply chain management

Industry
Energy services

Geography
Global with HQ in the United States

Business Challenge

Standardizing global spend data of the client and its acquired subsidiary:
* Segmentation of spend data for integration into ERP
* Harmonizing data from disparate systems

Solution

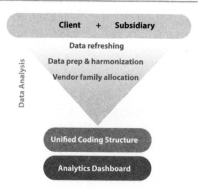

Approach

* Analyzed business needs and study of client tech and data landscape
* Set up a combined team of data analysts, business analysts, and technology experts
* Designed a unified category coding structure to classify client's spend data
* Classified 5,000+ codes of different entities into a unified structure and integrated 1 million+ spend data lines
* Represented structured spend data in a dashboard to allow scenario modeling
* Established an efficient process for automatically classifying all future transactions

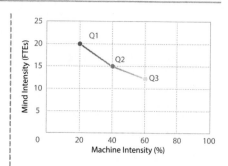

Analytics Challenges

- Integrating several hundred contracts and goods & services codes with varying formats in a standard analytic framework
- Defining the workflow with hundreds of business rules
- Building a unique solution to address users with different profiles and needs while ensuring performance and quick adoption

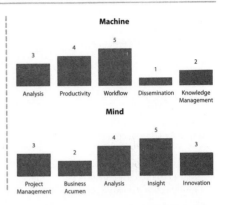

Benefits

Productivity	Time to Market	New Capabilities	Quality
• Cost savings of ~5% for the client post implementation • 70% productivity gains thanks to automated spend classification	• Complete solution in less than 5 months (compared to 1 year for an IT-fronted approach)	• Entirely new process • Interactive dashboard for scenario planning • New levers for supplier negotiation	• More than 98% first-time-right and on-time delivery

Implementation

- Required just 3 FTEs for 4 months for development
- Reduced worker input to only 100 hours per quarter (0.2 FTEs) thereafter
- Classified 1 million+ spend data lines and 10,000+ vendors in 6 months
- Built 30+ analytic frameworks revealing business insights

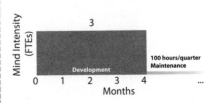

Predictive Analytics:
Cross-Selling Support

Context

Organization
Major telecom operator

Function(s)
Marketing

Industry
Telecommunications

Geography
United Kingdom

Business Challenge

- Increase the average revenue per user by cross-selling a key product to existing customers
- Maximize the ROI for direct marketing through efficient targeting

Solution

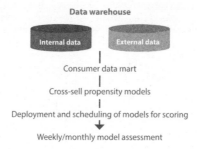

Data warehouse

Internal data   External data

Consumer data mart

Cross-sell propensity models

Deployment and scheduling of models for scoring

Weekly/monthly model assessment

Approach

- Split the modeling audience by services to enable:
  – Campaign predictors to be optimized for different customer bases
  – Different propositions and treatments to be made according to the current product portfolio
- Aggregated consumer attributes to create modeling-ready data sets
- Performed data cleansing to reduce ~900 variables to the 30 most significant predictors
- Applied statistical and machine-learning techniques to develop the best-performing model
- Scored customer base with propensity models every week to ensure relevance to campaign objectives

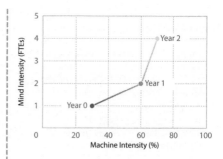

Analytics Challenges

- Size and complexity of the database combined with the inconsistencies across different tables required significant data understanding and skill to build robust models
- Proper data quality mechanisms and checkpoints needed to be put in place
- Lack of sufficient examples in the historical data to build models from: need for continuous innovation and performance enhancement of the models

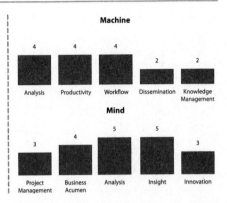

Benefits

Productivity	Time to Market	New Capabilities	Quality
• 70% effort reduction around models • More than 70 predictive models can be scored and assessed every week	• Scores refreshed weekly, reducing time to customer from 6 weeks to 2 weeks • Daily scoring of key models for real-time decision making	• Application of new (to client) modeling algorithms • Ability to deal with complex and huge data sources	• On average 60% of the new adopters identified in top 20% of the base • 100% right-first-time and 100% on-time delivery

Implementation

- 4-analyst team to develop and maintain the propensity models
- Robust assessment framework to continuously monitor the performance of the model with indicators: green at 60%, amber at 45%, and red below 45% (adopters in top 2 deciles)
- Rebuild occurs whenever there is a decline or a new data item becomes available to improve prediction
- Several direct marketing campaigns with 2- to 3-fold improved performance
- Models used in call centers to make best offers, resulting in 30% increase of product take-up

Perspective #4

THE EFFICIENT FRONTIER WHERE MACHINES SUPPORT MINDS

Mind only is too expensive and too slow. Machine only doesn't deliver the real insights or knowledge. Success lies in knowing how to mix mind+ machine—and not just in terms of proportion, but also type.

This chapter is about the Machine part of the equation. Of course, the selection of the right Mind with cross-functional skills and the right background is also very important. We'll deal with that in the next chapter.

Each use case has an efficient mix of mind+machine that optimizes its ROI and helps achieve the client benefits in terms of productivity, time to market, quality, and new capabilities. Overautomating can be too costly and inefficient, whereas underautomating might not deliver the client benefits or might simply render the use case uneconomical. Investment professionals would call this the *efficient frontier*: the optimal mix of various assets (e.g., shares, bonds, real estate, etc.) that optimizes the returns given a certain overall risk of the portfolio. The thought is actually very simple. Each asset class has a certain risk attached and a certain expectation for returns. Financial wizards can calculate the overall performance and risk of the portfolio as a function of the mix of the underlying asset classes, using the rules developed by Harry Markowitz, who won the Nobel Prize for his theory in 1990. The idea is to apply this concept to analytics use cases. Finding this efficient frontier is the goal of this chapter.

To illustrate this point, please have another look at some of the use cases in this book. Each use case shows an increasing degree of automation over time. The first minimum viable product (MVP 1) focuses more on implementing the solution in the first place. Future releases improve the degree of automation until a steady state is reached, sometimes after a few years of running the process. This is when the efficient frontier has been found for that use case. As you will be able to see, some use cases have up to 99 percent automation, while some others manage maybe around 10 percent at the overall level. The more varied and complex the work, the lower the degree of automation. But whatever the use case, some degree of automation is always possible: probably not in the insight-focused analytics work, but certainly in the other parts of the process. While this is certainly not a hard rule and there are big deviations from use case to use case, **average improvements of about 30 percent in productivity and about 30 percent in response times** seem to be possible, depending on the starting point.

The following rules for finding the efficient frontier are based on experience, both positive and negative:

- Rule 1: **Analyze the end-to-end use case for automation potential.** The most common mistake is to focus on the data and analytics but forget the other parts of the process, namely the workflow, the dissemination to and interaction with the end users, and knowledge management. In one case, the client was super-happy and proud of its SAS scripts for analyzing telecom product usage data. However, the client had not thought of distributing and knowledge managing the results. Ultimately, this led to bigger losses in the end users' productivity than what had been gained by further improving the data scripts.

- Rule 2: **Apply all five types of automation, but keep it simple.** Remember the five areas of automation that can be applied to each use case: data and analytics tools, including AI; productivity tools; workflow platforms; publishing and dissemination engines; and knowledge management tools. At the beginning (i.e., for MVP 1), focus on the low-hanging fruit and do not try to be fancy. Easy wins are usually *not* in the areas of big data, AI, or unstructured data. They can be found in better workflows along the manufacturing line, improved visualization and formatting, better and more efficient interaction with the end users (the Last Mile) while making their lives easier, and in better knowledge management. In the interests of development time, follow the 80/20 rule. Trying to build in too much automation from the start might be unproductive and very expensive downstream. Many analytics use cases evolve strongly during the first few cycles. Keep improvements such as AI, big data, or unstructured data for later in the process, if they're appropriate at all—unless your use case is one of the 5 percent of use cases that need big data, in which case it is obviously part of MVP 1.

- Rule 3: **Keep things as off-the-shelf and modular as possible.** Don't try to reinvent the world. In all likelihood someone (internal or external) has already developed a tool or a mind+machine solution that can address part of your use case. Keep use cases and their functionalities as modular as possible, and avoid spaghetti architectures with tons of interfaces to other

Operating Excellence Analytics: Efficiency Index

Context

Organization
All operating units
(business and support)

Function(s)
All functions

Industry
Service industry

Geography
Global

Business Challenge

- Establish a standard model to measure the impact of efficiency improvement initiatives (across different teams and operating units)

Solution

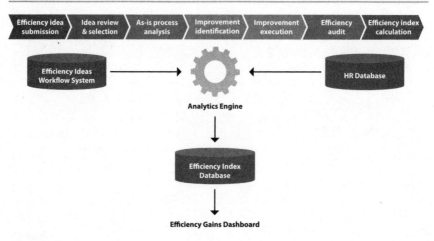

Efficiency idea submission › Idea review & selection › As-is process analysis › Improvement identification › Improvement execution › Efficiency audit › Efficiency index calculation

Efficiency Ideas Workflow System → Analytics Engine ← HR Database

Analytics Engine

↓

Efficiency Index Database

↓

Efficiency Gains Dashboard

Approach

- Created a centralized project management office (PMO) to train teams to identify and analyze efficiency improvement opportunities
- Created a standard definition for the efficiency gains index, agnostic of the nature of the work being done by the various teams
- Established rules for efficiency gain sharing, hierarchical roll-up, and location indexes
- Created a live dashboard to summarize data along with multilayered analysis

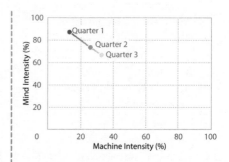

Analytics Challenges

- Maintaining correct roll-up data despite changes in team and reporting manager during the year
- Distributing efficiency gains when there are multiple beneficiaries of an initiative
- Aligning common matrix despite different working hours for each location
- Verifying the correct calculation of expected and actual efficiency gains
- Regular and accurate update of the Efficiency Gains Dashboard

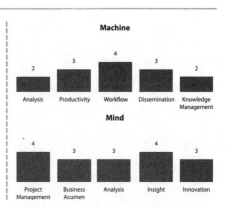

Benefits

Productivity	Time to Market	New Capabilities	Quality
• Efficiency gains of 8% (525,000 hours in 2015) • Efficiency gains index calculation effort reduced by 60%	• Improvement in turnaround times from 5% to 40% across different teams • Efficiency index calculation time reduced from 4 days to 0.5 days	• Optimization (Automation) Suites for different domains • Process Improvement consulting for client processes • Strong pool of automation experts	• Overall quality improvement in process deliverables across different teams by reducing manual effort • Efficiency gains calculation error reduced to zero

Implementation

- Introduced efficiency gain as a parameter of evaluation
- Identified team representatives and created their mapping with employees
- Up-skilled employees on Lean and Visual Basic for Applications (VBA)
- Weekly meetings with COO and business and location heads to drive the process
- Automated a significant part of the efficiency gains calculation and notification process

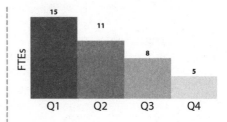

use cases. To illustrate this point: a machine manufacturer could develop a single standardized dissemination module for distributing any insights of all its preventive maintenance use cases to its dealerships. This reduces the complexity of use cases, speeds up their development by way of reuse, and generally keeps the solutions simple, less risky, and less costly over their life spans.

- Rule 4: **Apply continuous improvement.** As you can see from most of the use cases in this book, improvements over time can be very substantial. The most successful approach is to have a team or teams whose role it is to find, prototype, and implement improvement ideas for the use case portfolios. For a global law firm with more than 2,000 lawyers, we had a team of three full-time program managers who continuously worked on finding new use cases and improving existing ones. Once they had trialled the improvements, they handed the use cases to the line for steady-state operation. At any given point in time, they had a live pipeline of about 50 to 80 new use cases or improvement ideas, prioritized together with the client.

  Such program managers work at the intersection of technology and business and have very strong backgrounds in program management. It is a very special skill that normal line organizations usually do not have. Moreover, these are the people who know what is going on across the company (i.e., across various use case portfolios). They are the ones who can spot improvement opportunities (e.g., because someone else has come up with a smart platform for Portfolio A that could serve Portfolio B as well).

  The ROI on these program managers was highly positive, as the cumulative savings and improvements for their use cases more than compensated for their costs.

- Rule 5: **Find opportunities for platforms and modules.** Certain use cases in a portfolio (e.g., preventive maintenance in packaging machines) have a lot of similarities. For example, the sensor packages and configurations create similar types of data streams (type of data, velocity, and variability), use similar analytics algorithms and tools, and require similar communication channels to the dealerships in various countries. Of course, each use case is different nevertheless, but the synergies are obvious. Similarly, the Last Mile platform of InsightBee allows the bundling of interactions with similar types of end users in a single platform. It is clear that this requires investment and planning, but a smart modular architecture can speed up the development of future use cases manyfold, as we have seen in the case of InsightBee. More importantly, any improvement in a module or functionality of such a platform becomes available to the whole portfolio of use cases running on it right away. A good example of this is the generic alerting capability of InsightBee, which pushes short alerts with insights to the decision makers.

- Rule 6: **Document performance, learnings, audit trails, and best practices.** We're back to knowledge management. Of course, this needs to be supported by machines as well, as we will show later. There is no way that 450 new use cases can be handled without a tool and a governance process. The machine parts of any new use case are critical ingredients and need to be documented. Interestingly, it is almost more important to document what didn't work than what did work. Why? When new use cases are being created and prototyped, it is hugely useful to know what people have already tried and why it did not work. This can save a lot of time and money, time probably being the more important angle.

The efficient frontier for any portfolio of use cases will become apparent over time. Imagine a world in which one billion analytics use cases are approaching the efficient frontier! While this is obviously an elusive vision, just achieving a part of this for your own portfolios would create a lot of ROI and many happy clients.

THE RIGHT MIX OF MINDS MEANS A WORLD OF GOOD OPTIONS

The right mix of minds is critical for the success of any mind+machine use case. Even in situations where machines dominate the execution of the daily workload, minds are critical for the creation of the use case and the creation of the Level 3 Insights.

What are the seven biggest Mind-related mistakes companies typically make?

1. Control is delegated to the central technical teams rather than the business owners or end users.
2. There is not enough business knowledge in the analytics team.
3. The business analysts and technical experts are not colocated during the design stage.
4. There is no end-to-end transparency on the total resources for the use case by phase.
5. There is too much reliance on in-house, central analytics resources—best practice solutions or knowledge is not bought from the market for the appropriate parts of the use case. It is highly unlikely that all the right skills will ever be in-house.
6. The team rushes into prototyping the solution with little thought about the downstream maintenance and life cycle resource and control requirements, which tend to be very significant, especially when not actively managed.
7. There is little knowledge management around who knows what about certain classes of use cases. This relates to siloed lock-in of use case specialists and insufficient transfer of knowledge to other units.

Common sense can avoid most of these issues, but it seems that common sense gets lost somewhere along the way when it comes to analytics. I am not going to give a class on the basics of program management in this chapter, but instead will focus on the challenges specific to mind+machine.

- Rule 1: **Plan for the full life cycle, not just the adrenaline rush.** The optimal Mind mix changes over the life cycle of the use case. Don't just consider who you need for phase I (design and prototyping); consider what phases II (going live and steady-state delivery) and III (maintenance and life cycle management) will look like.
- Rule 2: **Control remains with the business owner.** Avoid the inferiority complex that many business owners develop when it comes to analytics, which leads them to delegate ownership. While the business owners might not have all the prerequisite skills, they are the ultimate clients and the best to judge whether the benefits are there. The business owner must remain in charge of the full use case throughout its life cycle.
- Rule 3: **Inject sufficient business and regional knowledge into the team.** It is not good enough to have some generic business know-how in the team or, say, a data scientist with an MBA. Only the real end users can judge whether the use case meets the client's needs. For global use cases, multiregional staffing might be required. Western companies particularly underestimate the need for local Asian staff on their teams. Japan, South Korea, China, Hong Kong, and the countries of Southeast Asia are all very different geographies with very different market dynamics.

  Without the regional context that our local environmental, social, and governance (ESG) analysts in China, India, Romania, and Chile provide, Evalueserve would not be able to deliver the same results in our considerable body of sustainability work, which involves scanning more than 2,000 companies worldwide.
- Rule 4: **Allocate the roles.** Deciding which people should take on which tasks on the team is obviously important and needs careful consideration. Don't forget that you may need external people to fill some of the roles if you don't have the competencies in-house (see Rule 7 and Figure III.2)
- Rule 5: **Colocate during design and rollout.** I refer to this as removing the glue from the office chairs. I've never been able to understand the inertia to be overcome in getting people to colocate. How about getting the data scientists to spend a few weeks on the road with the end users in order to gather that real-world experience? Chat, emails, phone, and other channels are vastly inferior during the design stage when compared to sitting less than 10 feet away from each other. There is a very creative

range of excuses not to colocate: "I am working on multiple projects" or "I need my workstation" (this in the days of virtual desktops!) or even "Our coffee machine is better"—I kid you not! Colocation does not happen naturally. It needs to be enforced and checked, but the benefits are considerable.

- Rule 6: **Keep close tabs on all resources on the team, and monitor the forecasts frequently.** As 80 to 90 percent of the costs come from data work, it is essential to keep resources under control. Small topics can lead to big resource needs; for example, going from small data to big data can cause personnel costs to explode because of the work on data quality, compliance, and so on that is required.

- Rule 7: **Why make it, if you can buy it?** Create your mind availability matrix early (see Figure III.2). Mind+machine use cases require broad sets of skills, many of which might not be available internally.

  Here is an example: despite specializing in mind+machine and having an internal knowledge technology team of almost 100 people, for the creation of InsightBee, Evalueserve did not have the right skill sets in-house for user experience design, search engine optimization, or software development for the front-end and the back-end engine. What did we do? We outsourced a lot of the specialized work to a network of partner firms in the United Kingdom and Switzerland. We had the right business analyst skills and people who understood the various databases extremely well, but we identified this lack of onshore program management skills early on.

  In our experience, getting the right specialized skills for the project is the only way to get a project delivered on time. Depending on the use case, 10 to 15 different skill sets may be needed. There are essentially two models of buying: resource augmentation and solution provisioning (where the solution can be simply a part of the whole use case). In order to keep costs under control, a mixed onshore/offshore model might help. Pure offshore models are not likely to work well in mind+machine analytics due to the high number of iterations required to stabilize the use cases. This almost always requires onshore resources.

- Rule 8: **Before building anything, check if someone has already done it, inside your company or outside.** Don't reinvent the wheel. In all likelihood, someone has already built similar use cases, inside your company or outside. By now there are lots of specialist companies that have libraries of existing use cases that can be adapted to fit your specific needs, which might be much faster than developing the use cases in-house. The Use Case Methodology (UCM) helps to establish a common language for such exchange, and we have built a tool to capture the knowledge and make it available for exchange. But even now it would easily be possible to learn from other people's experience.

Mind matrix	Use case:		
	Phase I	Phase II	Phase III
Minds	Design & prototyping	Going live & steady state	Maintenance & life cycle
Business owner	Active leadership	Cruise control	Innovation peaks
End users (by region / function)	Design, feedback, & testing	Improvement ideas	Design, feedback, & testing
Program management	Full control of use case	Launch & monitoring	Monitoring & change control
Process reengineering	Process design	Process audit	Process design
Business analysts	Precise business knowledge	Ongoing delivery	Adjustments
Financial quants	Precise functional knowledge	Ongoing delivery	Adjustments
Data scientists	Analytic methodology	Ongoing delivery	Adjustments
User experience design	Focus on client benefits	Improvement ideas	Adjustments
Editorial & publishing	Visual design	Ongoing delivery	Adjustments
Knowledge management	KM concept	Document learnings	Updates
Technology architect	Use case tech architecture	Improvement ideas	Innovation ideas
Software design	Use case dependent	Bug fixes	Adjustments
AI for levels 1 / 2	Focus on a few areas	Learn & improve	Adjustments
IT infrastructure	Integrate & support	Helpline	Adjustments
Finance & controlling	Sign off on benefits	Ongoing benefits controlling	Improve ROI
Compliance	Determine setup	Monitor risks	Assess changes

Figure III.2 Mind Availability Matrix

Once the right skill sets have been determined, the business owner needs to choose the right engagement model. There is no one-size-fits-all way to achieve this, but there are a series of options the business owner can choose from. The efficient frontier also applies to the Mind part of the equation. The choice depends on several factors that vary between the three phases of the use case: skill availability, skill cost, implementation speed, and implementation efficacy.

At Evalueserve we've seen plenty of approaches that worked and that didn't, taking the occasional beating along the way. Here are some of the learnings:

- Learning 1: **Standardize the models and give them names.** With the growing number of mind+machine use cases, it is important to have a set of standard or default engagement models that work for a known need, user group, or situation (Figure III.3). By ensuring that each engagement model is named and has a clear definition of the offering to a given user group, you can be confident that people are applying the right solution at the right cost and effort, and not overspending or using an approach that can't deliver.

  Think of commercial products that exist in a range, from high-end models loaded with features and customization possibilities to simple, focused models with more of a plug-and-play nature. Examples include cars and motorbikes, computers, home security systems, sewing machines, and carpenter's workbenches. I'm sure you could think of many more examples. You get the model that has the offering you need: you don't buy a high-end desktop computer with a subscription to a suite of design software if all you need is to check emails and browse the Internet; and you wouldn't get a portable sewing machine that only does two stitch types if you're planning to make bespoke suits.

- Learning 2: **Slot your use cases into a fitting engagement model early on.** The target operating model should be known quickly, as it will determine the governance model and clarify responsibilities and accountability.

- Learning 3: **Have enough onsite/onshore capacity—especially in Phase I.** Some people think that they can save money by getting things done offshore only (e.g., in their captives in India). This is a mistake. Especially in Phase I, hundreds or thousands of design decisions need to be made. Even if the right skills were available offshore, the client benefit and the user experience design processes require face-to-face presence, not just at headquarters, but also in the regional offices that are supposed to benefit from the use case.

- Learning 4: **Adjust the resource mix over time.** During Phases II and III, an increasing degree of automation will (it is hoped) reduce the need for resources, both onshore and offshore. Therefore, the target resource mix should be actively managed. Maintenance activities should be automated as much as possible or delegated to a low-cost offshore environment if automation is not the right solution. However, significant life cycle improvements requiring a lot of creativity and onshore presence should be dealt with like the initial design and prototyping phase (i.e., largely onshore).

- Learning 5: **Avoid the temptation of hourly rates.** Evaluate vendors and internal analytics service departments or captive centers entirely on the basis of medium-term return on investment (ROI) and their ability to deliver the client benefits *on time*, and *not* based on hourly rates. Especially in mind+machine, the cost savings and leverage come from specialized skills creating and inventing the right machines, not from getting a few dollars off the hourly rates of some individuals. Also, resist the temptation of comparing internal salaries with the full price of external vendors. The delta between fully loaded internal rates and variable salaries can easily be 50 percent. While it might look attractive in the short run, the full sledge-hammer of overheads will come back to you via allocations one day.

- Learning 6: **Great quant and data scientist skills can be found around the world, in places you wouldn't expect.** Data scientists obviously play important roles in such projects, but companies sometimes forget that there are hot spots of great skills worldwide. If compliance dictates permit, look outside the United States and Western Europe to find great quant and data scientist skills in Latin America (with the added advantage of favor-able trade agreements with the United States), Eastern Europe (with the added advantage of being EU member states), and Asia. While salaries are increasing in these countries, the cost differential will remain significant for many years to come. The cultural and geographic proximity of Latin America and Eastern Europe to the United States and Western Europe, respectively, creates a level playing field with the far-shore locations such as India in terms of total cost of ownership. Second-tier cities in the United States are a very interesting new trend, as discussed earlier. Analysts from such centers can reach the US destinations without a visa in just a few hours.

Now, I know that this question is already burning in your brain: how much? I am going to do something some people will not like. I am going to give some costs for highly sought-after data scientists and financial quants with risk back-grounds at 2016 price levels or fully loaded cost levels that can be found in the market for permanent engagements.

Beware: These cost figures are fully loaded, including all overheads such as management, real estate, human resources (HR), training, office equipment, and so on, not just the employees' salaries. Your captives will tell you that they can get people at much lower salaries, but if you add in infrastructure, HR, management, expat packages, travel, and all the other hidden costs, I would seriously doubt there are any cost advantages for captives.

- Second-tier US cities: USD 150,000 per annum for analysts and USD 200,000 p.a. for managers.
- Chile: USD 110,000 p.a. for analysts and USD 160,000 p.a. for managers.
- Romania: USD 95,000 p.a. for analysts and USD 140,000 p.a. for managers.
- China: USD 90,000 p.a. for analysts and USD 135,000 p.a. for managers.
- India: USD 75,000 p.a. for analysts and USD 110,000 p.a. for managers.

Engagement models

| Typical clients | Enterprise, FTE models | | | |
	Banks	Financial and professional services, corporates	Professional services, corporates	Small and medium business, corporates
Location				
On-site	Possible worldwide and recommended	Possible worldwide and recommended	Possible worldwide and recommended	Temporary on-site team possible
Near-shore	Possible (1 to 2 locations)	Possible (1 to 2 locations)	Possible (single location)	Possible (single location)
Far-shore	1 to 4 locations	1 to 2 locations	Single location	Single location
Commercial model				
FTEs	100–250	50–150	5–50	2–3
Project costing	Possible	Possible	Possible	Possible
Per-unit payment	Possible	Possible	Possible	Possible
Pay-as-you-go	Not possible	Not possible	Not possible	Not possible
Unified global governance	Recommended	Recommended	Recommended	Recommended
Compliance, IT, and security				
Banking level	Recommended	Not required	Not required	Not required
Dedicated enclosure	Recommended	Recommended	Recommended	Not required
Standard, open space	Not recommended	Possible, depending on project	Possible, depending on project	Recommended

Figure III.3   Engagement Models

Engagement models

Typical clients	Cloud, pay-as-you-go models		On-demand models
	Professional services, corporates	Small and medium businesses	Professional services, corporates
Location			
On-site	Not possible	Not possible	Temporary on-site team possible
Near-shore	Possible	Possible	Possible (single location)
Far-shore	Possible	Possible	Single location
Commercial model			
FTEs	N/A	N/A	N/A
Project costing	Possible	Possible	Possible
Per-unit payment	Possible	Possible	Standard
Pay-as-you-go	Standard	Standard	Possible
Unified global governance	Recommended	Recommended	Recommended
Compliance, IT, and security			
Banking level	Not required	Not required	Not required
Dedicated enclosure	Not required	Not required	Not required
Standard, open space	Recommended	Recommended	Recommended

Quants and data scientists command a 20 to 25 percent premium over the regular financial or business analysts and knowledge technologists running some of the machines. I leave it to you to determine the cost differential to your own organization. Our observation has been that fully loaded costs in expensive places such as New York or London can easily be 50 to 100 percent higher than what I showed here, especially for such skills with limited availability.

The efficient frontier of Minds can be found relatively easily. At Evalueserve we have found that working with a relatively constant set of partners for special skills in standardized engagement models delivers a lot of benefits in terms of speed, mutual understanding, and synergies across all use cases. While too much coordination stifles innovation, the approach of letting a thousand flowers bloom might create a hothouse of different approaches and technology stacks, leading to high complexity and the inability to share the knowledge across portfolios of use cases.

THE RIGHT WORKFLOW: FLEXIBLE PLATFORMS EMBEDDED IN THE PROCESS

The right workflows enabled by flexible platforms represent the biggest source of productivity increase and faster time to market, but are often underestimated or not thought of in the initial rush to analytics. In mind+machine analytics, most people focus on the analytics question and the data, but not on the end-to-end workflow involving all the participants (e.g., the in-house lawyers for sign-off of pitches or search strings, or the actual end user). All the great data work gets done, but approvals are stuck in some email in-box or the end user gets some hard-to-understand Excel sheets that first need a lot of work to match the data structure of the system.

Again, I'd like to give you a few simple rules:

- Rule 1: **Map out the use case's workflow early on and identify the participants.** Almost all use cases involve several participants. The typical roles are contributions in terms of data, analytics, visualization, feedback, decisions, use, and knowledge management. All these functions interact somehow along the Ring of Knowledge. Especially in distributed environments, tasks can get stuck for a long time without anyone doing any work. We saw use cases where approvals held up the whole process by several days just because the approvals sat in very patient email in-boxes. Moreover, occasionally some filters would move urgent approval emails into the wrong folders, which would then lead to some detective work on where things had

Financial Services:
Investment Banking Studio

Context

Organization
Investment bank

Function(s)
Advisory and M&A

Industry
Financial services

Geography
Global

Business Challenge

- Reduce the time spent on repetitive and mundane tasks (non-deal analytics and pitch books)
- Reduce demotivation and attrition among junior bankers

Solution

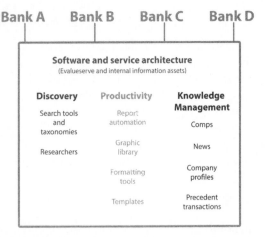

Bank A **Bank B** **Bank C** **Bank D**

Software and service architecture
(Evalueserve and internal information assets)

Discovery	**Productivity**	**Knowledge Management**
Search tools and taxonomies	Report automation	Comps
	Graphic library	News
Researchers	
	Formatting tools	Company profiles
	Templates	Precedent transactions

Approach

- Established an internal incubation team to conceptualize and develop solution
- Improved productivity through better information discovery, automation of routine tasks, standardization of reporting and visualization, and improved knowledge management
- Partnered with leading design, digital, and software firms to develop specialist assets

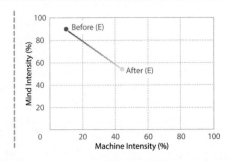

Analytics Challenges

- Developing a new solution to precisely address customer needs
- Assembling disparate analytics modules into one platform with a robust workflow management system
- Developing content and information assets that can be applicable across clients

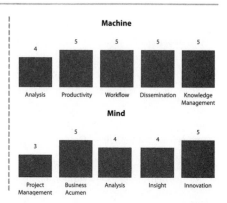

Benefits

Productivity	Time to Market	New Capabilities	Quality
• 40–50% (E) productivity gains on routine tasks • Scalable automation features for enhanced knowledge management	• Faster production of non-deal client material combined • Faster collaboration and analyses	• Faster team collaboration • Mobile solutions for client-facing meetings	• More time spent on insightful analytics as opposed to data management

Implementation

- Product is in development
- 12 FTEs have worked for 12 months on the concept, design, and development of the minimal viable product

been held up. Just this unnecessary overhead work absorbed more than approximately 15 percent of the overall workload.

- Rule 2: **Use the big picture overview to identify the top three improvement areas.** The 80/20 rule applies: the top three bottlenecks have about 80 percent of the improvement potential in the majority of use cases. The first minimum viable product (MVP 1) should focus on these. Interestingly, they are relatively easy to spot with a bit of common sense and process understanding. The bigger issue is the psychological state of the people involved. Not everybody is happy with their processes being simplified, as their resources and budgets could potentially get cut.

- Rule 3: **Define the mind+machine target workflow to deliver the client benefits.** For MVP 1, briefly check how close the target workflow will get you to achieving the client benefits.

- Rule 4: **Get into the platform as MVP 1—keep it simple and iterative initially.** Especially for new use cases, don't go for the grand design of a full enterprise platform right away: do the pilot using simple macros. Granted, they might not give you a fully scalable and robust platform, but learnings can be built into them very quickly. Once the macros stabilize, the workflow has probably stabilized. MVP 2 or higher can then look into more robust platforms.

- Rule 5: **Base the life cycle of the platform on ROI.** How long will the use case exist? Is it really worth creating a large platform? Thinking of the use case's life cycle while calculating the ROI will make this decision much easier.

- Rule 6: **Leverage existing platforms, if possible.** A workflow is a workflow. The generic functionalities are almost always similar. Why not use a configurable off-the-shelf cloud platform? Why develop the workflow in-house? Some analytics vendors also offer some workflow capabilities as well.

The end user is often both at the beginning of the workflow as requester and at the end as beneficiary. The interaction with the end user has two major components: the distribution to the Last Mile and the user experience. The next two chapters will deal with these topics.

SERVING THE END USERS WELL: FIGURING OUT THE LAST MILE

Who are your end users? Let's go back to the definition of a use case. These are people who need to make decisions, take actions, or deliver a product or service on time based on the insights delivered. They could be a set of 20 key account managers (KAMs) in heavy industrial goods in Asia, or 15 relationship managers in the high-net-worth segment of a wealth management firm in Germany, or 10 global product managers in a consumer goods company, or 100 service technicians at 20 truck dealerships across Europe, or several hundred consultants at a large consulting firm spread globally, or a few thousand retailers around the world.

What is common to all the use cases? You have a large number of end users with very different needs and usage profiles. Consultants actively request research every now and then for their projects. Service technicians need push alerts telling them that something is wrong with some specific trucks in their region. Retailers are interested in benchmarking weekend sales. However, there is a set of five characteristic patterns driving the Last Mile.

1. **One-to-many mapping:** The KAMs mentioned before are a good example. They require prequalified sales leads for their region and get it from a single source (e.g., a central research function or an external cloud solution). Similarly, the wealth managers get some profiling insights for their wealthy clients or prospects from a central research department or an external provider—for example, a trigger when one of the clients has gone public with a start-up and therefore has a lot of liquidity, potentially leading to some net new assets for the wealth manager. Time is of the essence.

2. **Many-to-many mapping:** This is a bit more complex. Let's look at the use case in the staffing industry. There are thousands of data providers—the staffed personnel, hundreds of staffing consultants, and hundreds of client organizations. This is one of the more complex mappings, a triple mapping m:n:l topology with m data providers (i.e., the staffed personnel), n consultants in need of insights, and l client organizations. This is probably as hard as it gets for any use case.

3. **Push versus pull, or interaction-based:** Research and analytics used to be largely pull-based; a requester had a need, sent an email to someone who had the data, and expected some answer within a few days or weeks. However, there is a strong trend toward a push model, where alerts get pushed to the end user, triggering some action. The Internet of Things is going to drive a lot of push-based use cases (e.g., a truck needing the preventive replacement of a mechanical part). The future standard will be both push and pull (i.e., interaction-based).

4. **Offline versus live decision making:** The service technician gets the alerts and acts on them. The truck needs to be called for maintenance. The alert becomes a maintenance event in the workflow system. This is an example of live decision making where the end user is part of a workflow. Offline use cases are not necessarily synchronized with any immediate decisions and might not become part of a workflow.

5. **Interactions between end users and central staff:** Many use cases require iterations between the analysts and the end users. The ease of interaction and the level of responsiveness drive adoption. Live chat features help avoid lengthy voicemail back and forth, and mobile enablement improves the user experience for mobile end users.

The logistics involved in serving the Last Mile increases dramatically with the number and the interconnectedness of end users. While simple one-to-few use cases might still be handled via email distribution, one-to-many or many-to-many use cases create large amounts of traffic and interdependencies, and therefore need to be handled in different ways.

Here are some steps to identify such complexities early on:

- Rule 1: **Give the Last Mile the right level of attention right from the start.** The Last Mile tends to get lower priority, while analytics get all the attention, but it is the Last Mile that will decide on the success or failure of the use case.
- Rule 2: **Identify the use case topology.** You have identified the end users already, as in Perspective 1. We need to find out who else is involved in the use case. It could be the in-house lawyers having to sign off the pitches to the pension funds or the central research department or the data providers.
- Rule 3: **Find out how the end user should be served best.** End users are not always clear about how they want the analytics to be delivered, because

many don't know what is possible these days. When do they need to make their decisions? How does the use case fit in? Are the end users office-based or are they mobile? Do they need time-critical alerts? What formats? Whoever leads the development of the use case should spend some quality time with the end users. Involve the user experience designers early on.

- Rule 4: **Identify potential bottlenecks early.** There is a reason why city planning departments simulate new bridges or intersections before they build them. They want to understand how the traffic flows will change in the future. A new bridge might remove one bottleneck but create a new one elsewhere. Analytics use cases, especially mind+machine, are not much different. The bottlenecks are typically the humans somewhere along the value chain of the use case; for example, a central research department whose budget got cut might not be in a position to deliver anymore.

- Rule 5: **Bundle analytics use cases in the Last Mile, if possible.** I call this "the fight for app space on my mobile phone." How many separate platforms and channels can humans manage on a daily basis? How many logins? And don't forget that this count will include their personal channels. Anything beyond 20 becomes hard. Therefore, the delivery of analytics to specific users (e.g., key account managers) should ideally be bundled and mobile. Of course, this implies that there is some kind of modular architecture in place that allows simple additions and removals of analytics use cases for specific user groups.

- Rule 6: **Determine the highest ROI technology solution.** The ROI calculation should include the time end users spend on accessing and interacting with the analytics. We have seen cases where the end users were mobile and had to spend a lot of unnecessary time accessing the analytics. Apart from the fact that they were very annoyed, they could have done much smarter things during that time. Portals are great ways to address the one-to-many topology, especially when generic insights (e.g., competitive intelligence) need to be pushed out to many users. However, they are hard to connect to the workflows, or they become complex when user-specific content needs to be pushed out, in which case the end users need to be attached to workflow systems. If people are mobile, apps linked to the workflow are probably the answer. And if multiple companies are involved (e.g., various dealerships or independent financial advisers interacting with an automobile manufacturer or bank), cloud-based solutions can take out a lot of complexity. The general rule should be to keep things as simple as possible, but not at the price of wasting the end users' time.

With the increasing number of analytics use cases, the Last Mile is really gaining in importance. Being able to manage the logistics of flow of requests and insights will be critical.

Sales Enablement:
Account-Based Marketing Support

Context

Organization
Global enterprise connectivity

Function(s)
Marketing, strategy, & sales

Industry
Telecommunications

Geography
HQ in India

Business Challenge

- Build account-based marketing support to increase up-selling
- Push qualified sales opportunities and leads to salespeople
- Generate deeper competitive insights

Solution

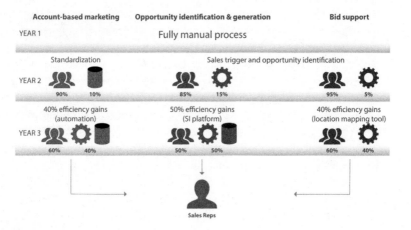

Account-based marketing	Opportunity identification & generation	Bid support
YEAR 1	Fully manual process	
Standardization	Sales trigger and opportunity identification	
YEAR 2 — 90% / 10%	85% / 15%	95% / 5%
40% efficiency gains (automation)	50% efficiency gains (SI platform)	40% efficiency gains (location mapping tool)
YEAR 3 — 60% / 40%	50% / 50%	60% / 40%

Sales Reps

Approach

- Set up a team of 13 FTEs to provide customer and competitor insights; mapped team members to sales reps in different regions
- Created standardized templates for deliverables; automated information extraction from databases
- Developed a sales intelligence (SI) platform to identify relevant and quality sales opportunities and leads
- Created a tool that provides information on competitive positioning by location

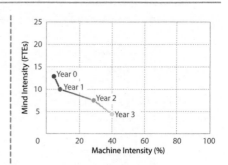

Mind Intensity (FTEs) vs Machine Intensity (%)

- Year 0
- Year 1
- Year 2
- Year 3

Analytics Challenges

- Reduce delivery time and improve deliverable quality despite high volume and velocity of client requests
- Increase efficiency in existing engagement
- Improve quality of business opportunities identified for sales representatives
- Analyze and report sales opportunities with validation based on historical sales data

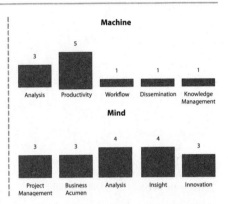

Benefits

Productivity	Time to Market	New Capabilities	Quality
• Saved ~3,000 hours in 2015; expected 6,000+ hours in in 2016 • Pushed 150+ opportunities to CRM with 19% increase YoY • Actioned 60+ bids in the current year	• 27 hours faster for structured deliverables (average) • 40% faster for bid support (average) • 50% faster push of opportunities and leads to salespeople	• SI platform-based process (70% machine and 30% mind) • Database of network capacity that presents information on world map	• 30% increase in acceptance of opportunities pushed to salespeople • Analysts access CRM and take part in on-site workshops with salespeople and senior executives

Implementation

- 0 to 8 months: Manually performed account-based marketing; identified and agreed on common needs of sales reps
- 9 to 16 months: Created templates, identified databases, and automated sections of deliverables
- 17 to 24 months: Started developing the opportunity search and identification process, which was supported by creating a library of sales triggers; ran a pilot
- 25 to 32 months: Automated the location mapping tool to handle increasing volumes of bid support; started building the SI platform
- Ongoing from month 33: Identified opportunity leads for ~150 accounts

THE RIGHT USER INTERACTION: THE ART OF USER EXPERIENCE

L et's now look into what is required for good user experience design. In the May 2010 UX *Magazine*, psychologist and cognitive scientist Dr. Susan Weinschenk explained a human-centric view of what good mind–machine interfaces should focus on. There are 10 guidelines:

1. **Minimize the work for the mind.** Give only what is absolutely needed at each stage. Use default settings that learn from each human's behavior. Let people decide to drill down, if they need it.
2. **Accept the mind's limitations, and accept that different minds work differently.** Providing a minimum amount of text, intuitive visualization, and no demand for multitasking is the way to go. Tell the mind exactly what it needs to do. Avoid confusion. Assume that the end user is a generalist, not a specialist. Allow some degree of customization to user preferences.
3. **Expect that minds make mistakes.** Anticipate mistakes and try to prevent them. Ask for confirmations. Allow undoing. Perform robust user testing before rollout.
4. **Assume that minds keep forgetting.** People remember three or four things maximum.
5. **Remember that minds are social, but machines aren't.** People are social and seek social validation (e.g., through ratings and reviews). Collaboration strengthens the bonds between minds. Find ways to communicate easily with others essential to the use case. For example, use live chat rather than asking people to call each other. Setting up phone calls is clumsy and takes a lot of time. Live chats are social, but at the same time very efficient.

6. **Grab the mind's attention.** Get the user to focus on the task at hand by way of visually changing elements. Highlight changes. Send concise alerts.
7. **Remember that minds crave information.** People need feedback on what is going on. Where are we in the process? How many steps are still to be done?
8. **Recognize that minds perform unconsciously.** Pictures, interactive elements, and stories work well. Build the psychology into the messages; don't just give what a machine would need.

   A good example: Our innovation platform analyzes patent landscapes and displays the information in a star diagram with circles at the end of each ray. The circles are clickable for further drill-down into specific subareas. Our programmers programmed them to wobble a little bit when clicked. The patent professionals find this very appealing in an otherwise rather dry and technical patent domain.
9. **Figure out the mind's mental model of a use case.** Different people have different models in their minds. A nerd will have a different approach compared to an antinerd. The user experience needs to mirror the actual end user's mental model, not the programmer's.
10. **Remember that minds prefer visuals.** Guide the users visually: things that are closely related should be grouped on the screen. Visuals are more effective than text. If text has to be used, it should be large fonts.

I found this psychologist's view very interesting, as the normal descriptions of user experience design focus more on the technical side of things. That's not surprising—they were most likely written by technologists!

But there is more to it than just the Last Mile interface with the end user. User experience design needs to be thought of at the very beginning of the work on any analytics use case. Bad user experience design is certainly one of the top 10 reasons for negative ROI of analytics use cases. But then how can successful user experience design be ensured?

- **Rule 1: Find out if you need external help for user experience design.** Not everyone can buy user experience design firms, nor should they, especially when the company cultures are very different. We made the decision to go external for user experience design, and we were very happy about this decision.
- **Rule 2: Understand the end user's needs and ways of working.** Here is again where psychology and ergonomics come in. How can the payload be delivered? How do we get the end user to adopt the deliverables? It's essential to colocate and watch people in their daily work.
- **Rule 3: Use rapid prototyping.** Did you know that kindergarten kids perform better at the "spaghetti tower with a marshmallow on top" game than MBAs, as Tom Wujec explains in his TED Talk?[1] This is a game where

groups of up to five individuals have 30 minutes to build a self-standing structure from a bunch of about 30 dry spaghetti strands. The structure needs to be able to hold the weight of a marshmallow. We played this game at a management offsite in India. Why is this relevant? Kindergarten kids use rapid prototyping without knowing. They try things out quickly, learn from failure, try again, learn again, and fix things until they work. MBAs are more likely to fight the endless ego game over the right design and ultimately fail.

- Rule 4: **Test with different personas.** It is not good enough to test the user experience with only the easiest-to-convince early adopters, who are probably so-called cryptonerds; that is, they do programming in their personal lives at home. Test with a range of people, especially those hardest to convince.
- Rule 5: **Develop some standard patterns for the company.** Learn from successful use cases and make these user experience designs the standard for the company. Don't reinvent the world all the time. Why do Amazon, Apple, and many other giants have only a single channel for user interaction? The mind is lazy and does not want to work too much, and does not want to remember too many different mind–machine interfaces. Simplicity wins.

The sidebar contains some practical advice from Neil Gardiner of Every Interaction.

PARTNERING FOR USER EXPERIENCE DESIGN

How do I commission user experience, and what sort of team do I need?

The dream scenario is to have a user experience design team in-house. The hard part is finding the right people (knowing what you're looking for) and convincing them to work solely on your product. This approach can work well if you plan to have everything under one roof and if you have the space and the funds to do so. If that's not a possibility—and at the outset it often isn't—then engaging with an agency is the best way forward. It's rare to get one agency that can deliver on all your needs. In our experience the team is often best constructed out of a collective of specialists: user experience designers, user interface designers, developers, analytics and search engine optimization (SEO) experts, and so on. A good user experience team will be able to connect you with their partner network and help you find the best people for the job.

How do you short-list agencies? Ask around: reputation helps. Google "user experience designers" and you will quickly find the cream of the crop. Some companies have a bias toward research, others toward visual design; some are spread more evenly across the two. You have to work out what your product needs. Once you have a short list of agencies you want to approach—three is a good number—meet them face to face and see how you get along. You want to find a company that can be honest with you and tell you how it is. It's important to have your ideas challenged and tested with users. Find out exactly whom you will be working with and how they plan to run the project.

Fit is the most important thing; find a company that gets what you're trying to achieve and is able to help you with the things you can't do yourself. If they've worked in your sector, that's a benefit but it's not critical. A good user experience firm can solve problems no matter what the sector is. The skills are transferable.

Proximity is a benefit. It's always useful to be able to sit around a table to develop ideas and make decisions. However, it's not essential: many teams work remotely using Skype or Google Hangout for meetings. Screen-sharing tools like Join.me make it easy for everyone to see what's being discussed.

It's not essential to have a large team on a project, but of course that depends on what you need to do and how quickly you need to do it. The larger the team, the more coordination is required. So it doesn't necessarily translate into being more productive.

On the client side, you need one or more experts to drive the requirements, act as a sounding board, and answer the many questions that will follow. This is often just one person, but it's sometimes better to have multiple experts, as this allows them to be more critical and less concerned about just getting the job done. You also need a product owner, a CTO for example, who will drive the production of the project forward. This role should be held by one person. Making the right technical decisions early on is critical to long-term success.

On the user experience design side, you need a lead user experience architect, someone who will drive the underlying organization and flow of the product. This person will help capture user needs and business requirements, produce flow diagrams, and develop wireframe prototypes. They will test and iterate the concept, and work with the developers and user interface designers to move to a refined product you can release and test.

(Continued)

InsightBee:
A UX Design Study by Every Interaction

Context

Organization
Research and analytics provider

Function(s)
Digital user experience design

Industry
Business market intelligence

Geography
UK and Europe launch, global scale

Business Challenge

- Convert Evalueserve's best-in-class reporting into a self-service, on-demand, digital solution
- Enhance user experience and satisfaction through interaction improvements

Solution

UX Design Process

Learn - Iterate and repeat the process

Understand - Gain insight on the industry and the client's vision

Deploy - Launch this version

Analyze - Understand the client's proposal and competitor landscape

Build - Create a working minimum viable product

Plan - Define how we will tackle the the problem

Design - Define the look and feel

Sketch - Create a quick prototype to test main user flow

Iterate - Improve the experience

Test - Test the prototype with users and client

Approach

- Formed a team of technology, vision, and design partners to take the original team's vision and turn it into a web-based solution
- Began by researching the proof of concept and defining the user experience
- Defined and built a bespoke transactional order process minimum viable product to test the market
- Went through an iterative learning and development process
- Expanded the product range once the customer base was established

Solutions to Challenges

- The small team meant quick decisions and changes.
- The global team allowed the people with the best skill set to be found, regardless of their location in the world.
- Business teams were able to adapt the business model from pay-as-you-go to corporate plans quickly.
- The focus on user experience meant decisions were based on usability.
- Testing helped identify what people were struggling to understand.
- Creating a solid design language means that new products all have a familiarity and consistency.

Benefits

Productivity	Time to Market	New Capabilities	Quality
• Faster turnaround for certain report types	• 50% faster than any comparable approach	• Easy management for large accounts • On-demand ordering	• High-quality, affordable reports with no up-front investment need

Implementation

- 6 months from concept to minimum viable product (MVP) launch
- Consistent monthly growth of 30% in the first year

Provided by Neil Gardiner, Director at Every Interaction

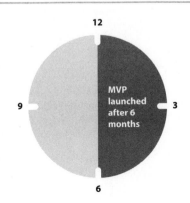

12

9   MVP launched after 6 months   3

6

You need to be prepared to iterate your product's design. It's rare that something will be perfect from the get-go. Iterations and changes may become more granular over time, but it depends on the findings of each test. Testing with a small group of people may be enough to confirm any concerns you might have. Testing with a broader group is required if issues surface that you didn't suspect. You need to be careful not to change or redevelop features based on one user's opinion. A common pitfall is to invest in a feature that a client insists is required only to find that he's the only person who wants it.

Aspire to continually improve your product. You cannot afford to stand still. Improving doesn't necessarily mean just adding features: it may mean taking things away. It just means continuing to listen to your users and trying to stay ahead of your competition.

Minimum viable product (MVP) is a term that is used a lot. It's supposed to be the leanest version of your product that you can release. It's a term people like to use but very often find it hard to stick to. This is where the power of your team comes in. Having more than one person on the client side helps rationalize the decision process about what should be in and what should be out of your first release—ideally one of those stakeholders will be focused on staying lean. It's very easy to spend a lot of time on features that aren't essential to releasing something people can use. It's a hard task, but you have to keep asking yourself, "If I were to launch this tomorrow, what would I leave out?"

Neil Gardiner, Every Interaction

INTEGRATED KNOWLEDGE MANAGEMENT MEANS SPEED AND SAVINGS

Knowledge management needs to be **purposeful, concrete,** and **action-oriented** in order to get the payload delivered. Great knowledge management can significantly improve the ROI of analytics use cases, but it has to be integrated into the planning of any use case early on. The opportunities for knowledge management exist at five levels:

1. **The content delivered.** Level 3 insights and Level 4 knowledge should be stored for reuse (not to be confused with storing the Level 1 data or Level 2 information). Especially in large organizations, the likelihood that several people ask for the same or a very similar analysis is very high (e.g., in consulting or in banking). In research and analytics we have seen reuse of about 15 to 20 percent. Reuse lowers the cost, but more importantly it speeds up delivery for the repeat use, either by way of self-serve or by reduced time spent on modifying the original deliverable. Of course, the workflow needs to be constructed such that the insights get stored and tagged properly without much human interaction or none at all, and are searchable and accessible easily for reuse.

2. **The use case framework.** Analytics contain lots of models and built-in logic along each step of the Ring of Knowledge. It is not just the one killer statistical analysis in R or SAS. There is logic in how the data is collected, cleansed, and structured to ready it for the analysis. There is a lot of logic in the visualization and dissemination of the analysis, and in what goes into knowledge management. Most importantly, there is also a lot of logic in what was *discarded* along the way, such as data that was not robust enough,

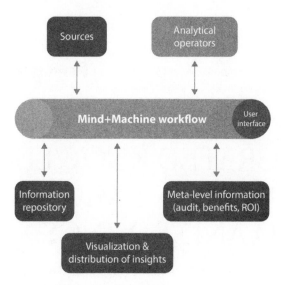

Figure III.4 The Use Case Framework (UCF)

AI algorithms that were tested but rejected, statistical models that did not work, or visualizations that weren't accepted by the Last Mile users. Storing lessons learned will avoid reinventing the world in the future. Figure III.4 shows a simplified, top-down view on an analytics use case, starting with the data and ending with the dissemination. This Use Case Framework provides a modular approach for storing and reusing the various elements of any use case.

3. **The meta-level information.** Each use case produces a lot of meta-level information (i.e., information that describes the process of creating and running the use case): the project plan, team involved, accountable individuals, usage, costs, changes made, audit trails, and of course ROI. The benefits are shorter development cycles for improvements of existing use cases or new use cases, and better management of the commercial elements, risks, and liabilities.

4. **The use case portfolio.** Companies have to manage growing numbers of use cases. The use case portfolios can easily become unwieldy and nontransparent. Imagine a company having a portfolio of 500 use cases in the Internet of Things. Governance becomes much easier if the portfolios can be managed at the portfolio level. Of course, easy-to-use tools are needed, but this is where the Use Case Methodology (UCM) philosophy can provide the necessary common language.

5. **The knowledge directory.** This is the "who knows what?" in the company. Even though the usefulness of this model was proven many years ago, very few companies actually have it. It is really a no-brainer with very high ROI.

We now know what to do, but the key is really in the implementation. Here are 10 low-hanging fruit rules for successful knowledge management.

- Rule 1: **Plan for knowledge management ahead of time for every use case.** The Ring of Knowledge helps us think through the knowledge management aspects of each use case early on. If it can play a significant role, early identification will set the priorities right. Smart knowledge management might have a much bigger and easier-to-achieve client benefit than trying to force complex AI and machine learning into the use case, for example.
- Rule 2: **Set organizational incentives for knowledge management.** As discussed in Part II, true knowledge management does not happen in an altruistic fashion. "What's in it for me?" is the ultimate question. Such incentives must have teeth in both directions. Unless knowledge management is a part of performance management and is actually monitored and evaluated, the impact is going to be limited. It is as simple as that. The criteria should be strict, simple, and output-based, and not just input-based; for example, it's not important how much time was spent on it or how many pages of text were written.
- Rule 3: **Focus on Level 3 insights and Level 4 knowledge, avoid data lakes of Level 1 data, and be very careful about Level 2 information.** Resist the temptation to store everything just because you have it or used it once, unless you are forced to store it due to regulatory requirements or compliance-related rules (but even then make sure to challenge statements such as "We need to do this—I have heard that Compliance said so"). Data lakes or general-purpose wikis storing used input data are *not* good knowledge management, especially given how quickly Level 1 data is outdated. Level 2 information should be retained only if there is a high probability of reuse. The real value lies in Level 3 insights and Level 4 knowledge that have longer life cycles and drive action.
- Rule 4: **Focus on high-ROI use cases.** Knowledge management should focus on clearly defined use cases that drive real action and generate ROI. There is a series of low-hanging fruit use cases along the Ring of Knowledge: data sources with their structures and limitations; data mappings for data structuring ; data cleansing logic and algorithms; analytics models, including the programming scripts (both used and discarded earlier); analytic insights delivered; visualization templates and algorithms; or reusable and updated assets such as the knowledge directory, credentials, tombstones, legal disclosures, and pitch templates. The logo database mentioned earlier is a good example of a high-ROI use case in knowledge management.
- Rule 5: **Exploit the meta-level information, ensuring consistency across the use case portfolio.** There are multiple use cases to exploit meta-level information, as discussed earlier. The use case's client benefits and its ROI are certainly the most important ingredients for the overall portfolio

management, while the compliance-related information might save your job one day, and learnings from earlier use cases might help you save a lot of time and money. The trick is to capture the information systematically as a part of the normal workflow, which requires the right tools and processes. One-off exercises may help fill some gaps, but they do not deliver the benefits at the portfolio level (i.e., where resources need to be allocated to different use cases).

- Rule 6: **Embed it in the workflow, and use simple tools.** Knowledge management does not occur naturally, which is why Level 3 insights or Level 4 knowledge should be tagged and stored when they arise. This means that the normal workflow needs to support the Minds in a semiautomated fashion. Experience shows that special offline efforts to create knowledge absorb too much productive working time and are abandoned relatively quickly after initial bursts of enthusiasm.

- Rule 7: **Have accountable knowledge stewards maintain pure knowledge assets.** Specialized knowledge assets (e.g., the logo database, banking tombstones, credentials, CRM data, or templates) should be maintained centrally by knowledge stewards who are fully accountable for their quality. This is far more efficient and effective than having decentralized, nonspecialized approaches without any clear accountabilities. Our experience is that knowledge stewardship can fix significant quality issues very quickly, and save a lot of the direct and indirect downstream cost of working with bad data. Ongoing maintenance also benefits highly from specialization, lowering the life cycle cost of any asset by more than 50 percent.

- Rule 8: **Auto-expiry as the guiding principle to declog your knowledge management.** Life spans of usefulness vary, as discussed in Part II. Determine the expected life span for Levels 1–4 of your use case, and program it for obsolescence unless it is refreshed in the meantime. The principle should be: autoarchive unless there is proof that the use case or its content should continue to exist, not the other way around, which is still the predominant mode in most companies.

- Rule 9: **Use modern concepts such as knowledge object architecture and the UCM.** Of course, the UCM philosophy requires an information architecture to manage individual use cases and portfolios. Tools based on this open-source architecture can help perform the tasks described earlier efficiently and effectively, even in distributed environments. InsightBee's K-Hive is a good example of an implementation of the knowledge object architecture. It is fully integrated into InsightBee's workflow, and allows for efficient reuse of the deliverables or parts thereof.

- Rule 10: **Manage the portfolio.** Use the meta-level information of each use case to manage your portfolios. The UCM makes use cases comparable and manageable across their lifetimes. Life cycle decisions can be made based on facts and figures rather than on personal preferences.

DATA ARCHITECTURE IS THE HEART OF KNOWLEDGE MANAGEMENT

What is a company strategy? What is the benefit of a data analytics use case?

Understanding these questions seems straightforward to a human being, but a machine requires some structure before it can process and store content, turning it into knowledge. A data architecture defines such a knowledge structure.

Designing proper data architectures takes time and often requires multiple iterations. We always strive for results that are well thought through but as simple as possible.

With InsightBee and the Use Case Framework (UCF), we faced similar data modeling challenges.

For InsightBee, one of the key challenges was to define a data architecture that supports machine processing but at the same time allows for efficient mind intervention. For example, all raw input data collected from external application programming interfaces (APIs), such as Dun & Bradstreet, had to be transformed into a common InsightBee data model for further machine processing. Furthermore, the same data model also needed to provide specific elements for human researchers to verify data inputs and write executive summaries as a conclusion of the research process.

After several iterations of the data model we were satisfied, and we called it the "K-model." It consists of structured elements called "knowledge objects" and is InsightBee's standard way of describing companies, executives, and industries in a mind+machine-compatible fashion. (See Figure III.5.)

For the UCF the situation was even more complex. The biggest challenge was to find a data model that can represent billions of potential analytics use cases and is not too complex for a human mind to understand and work on. The data model has to allow business users to ask all kinds of questions regarding key aspects of an analytics use case—for example, "What business benefits can I get from analyzing my customer data?" or "How valuable are my customers over their full lifetimes?"

We ended up with a data model that contains well-defined structures for key attributes but also includes more generic text elements to capture unstructured data. For example, "cost/benefit type" is a structured element that defines the expected benefit of the solution, and one possible

(Continued)

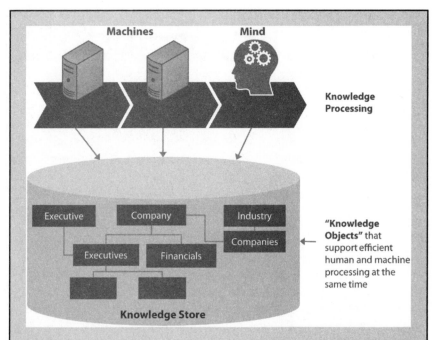

Figure III.5   Mind+Machines Working on the Same Optimized Data Model

value is "sales growth." "Business question" is a less structured element for the solution architect to record a manager's question (which needs to be answered by the analytics use case).

In order to handle model complexity, we introduced three abstraction levels for analytics use case content. (See Figure III.6.) At each level more details are added to an analytical use case. The content of the top level (solution) can be shared among companies without revealing sensitive company information, whereas the lower two levels contain company and project information (e.g., links to company-specific data sources).

You can breathe a sigh of relief now, as you don't have to understand the details of our model. Our goal was to illustrate some examples. It took a lot of hard work until we were satisfied with our current UCF data model. However, I am sure that we will have to develop it further in the future. Nowadays, even data models need to be somewhat agile.

During the creation of InsightBee and the UCF we discovered that structuring knowledge in the right way is crucial to enable minds and machines to work together seamlessly and manage the knowledge efficiently. As with all models, you have to be careful not to overcomplicate things. A very sophisticated, very structured, complicated knowledge model might

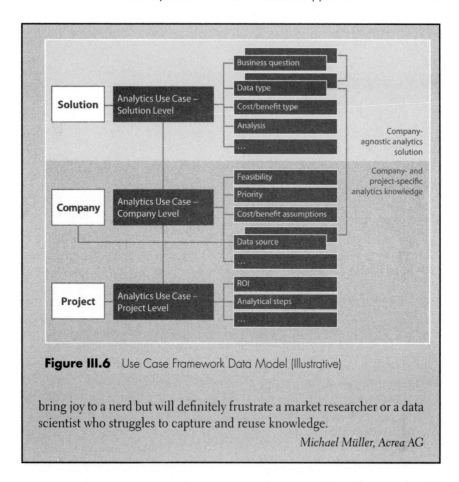

Figure III.6   Use Case Framework Data Model (Illustrative)

bring joy to a nerd but will definitely frustrate a market researcher or a data scientist who struggles to capture and reuse knowledge.

Michael Müller, Acrea AG

This chapter demonstrated the benefits of effective knowledge management. Think of your own organization and try to identify opportunities you could exploit. Did you find any?

THE COMMERCIAL MODEL: PAY-AS-YOU-GO OR PER-UNIT PRICING

Would you like to get full transparency on what you are paying for as the business owner of a use case? The Use Case Methodology (UCM) provides a way to dissect the costs of mind+machine analytics in very transparent ways. The use case's business issue is clearly defined; the business owners and the end users (i.e., the main beneficiaries) are named; and the output and its client benefits are known quite precisely. These are all the ingredients needed for transparency in pricing.

In addition, the UCM is also ideally suited for pay-as-you-go (PAYG) and per-unit pricing. Of course, I am not saying that every use case lends itself to PAYG and per-unit pricing, but at least 20 percent of all analytics use cases could be priced in this way—probably even much more, if the UCM were universally applied.

There is another important advantage of PAYG and per-unit pricing. Increasingly, analytics solutions consist of several components stemming from different vendors. For example, Evalueserve's InsightBee Sales Intelligence solution uses inputs from a variety of vendors. This is very similar to the tiers 1, 2, and 3 structure of the automotive value chain. If Evalueserve sells one unit of Sales Intelligence, it effectively helps its suppliers sell a proportional number of units of their outputs that went into the Sales Intelligence product. Therefore, a counter will register the number of units sold and the vendors can be compensated accordingly. In this way, the whole supply chain for this use case becomes per-unit based, which reduces the risk for Evalueserve and gives the suppliers a part of the upside like in a revenue-sharing agreement.

So, how can this concept be implemented?

- Rule 1: **Ring fence revenues (if relevant) and costs by analytics use case.** Work with your finance department to figure out how revenue and costs can be charged against individual use cases or groups of use cases. The use case becomes the economic entity around which the ROI can be calculated. Of course, common sense should be applied, as too granular a model would lead to high administrative complexity.
- Rule 2: **Determine the economic model early on and create the menu.** Most analytics use cases are sold internally, while some generate external revenues. Determine if the use case lends itself to PAYG or per-unit pricing, or if an input-based model should be used. In either case, the economic model should be decided early in the life cycle. An explicit menu with prices by unit of output creates transparency.
- Rule 3: **Track the revenues, costs, and client benefits.** The ROI of the use case will depend on these, and the portfolio management will ultimately decide on the use case's fate.
- Rule 4: **Make central allocations transparent.** Ask central units to show their costs and resources for each use case, which will reduce nontransparent allocations over time.
- Rule 5: **Reduce your economic risk by pushing the economic model into your supplier base.** There is no reason why you should carry all the economic risk of your use cases. By having per-unit-based compensation models with your suppliers, you can more flexibly manage your own business risk, especially the volume swings. The suppliers will have the right incentive to use mind+machine more, which makes them more competitive and will give you further client benefits in the medium term.
- Rule 6: **Identify commercialization opportunities for your use case.** Some use cases may have an external commercialization potential. The life cycle discussion should include the standard assessment of such opportunities.

InsightBee with its various solutions is fundamentally a PAYG model that demonstrates the UCM benefits on the commercial side. Each use case on InsightBee is fully PAYG. Another example can be found in banking if you look at comparables and pitch books, and there are many more to come in the future.

INTELLECTUAL PROPERTY: KNOWLEDGE OBJECTS FOR MIND+MACHINE

Intellectual property (IP) can represent both an opportunity, if managed well, and a risk, if undermanaged. This series of interesting situations will show the need for careful IP management:

- Situation 1: **Trading of assets (knowledge objects, reports, models, machines, templates, use cases).** How much would a company save by being able to buy Internet of Things use cases from other companies? The buying company would save a lot of time and money in getting the use case implemented. The selling company would find an avenue for commercializing its investments in use cases and the intellectual property it created. Similarly, a company might benefit from getting access to K-Hive's knowledge objects on a pay-per-use basis.
- Situation 2: **Micro-payments for PAYG or per-unit-priced products.** Imagine a credit card company whose sanitized data packages become part of an analytics product (e.g., retail sales analytics) produced by an analytics company, and sold to local retailers on a per-unit basis every week. Wouldn't it be great if the data issuer could get a micro-payment for each report sold to a retailer? The analytics company would certainly be willing to pay the money, but needs a simple way to count the products and settle the payments in an agreed frequency (e.g., monthly).
- Situation 3: **Origins of data.** For several years, a bank's index team has been using a certain data stream (produced by a data vendor) to produce a special cross-asset-class index on a daily basis. The index was originally produced by another company that was later bought by the bank, which

inherited the data contract. Now, several units of the bank use the same data stream for other purposes. Nobody studied the terms and conditions during the legal due diligence. A clause in the contract says that the data stream is licensed only for the purpose of the cross-asset-class index. The bank has therefore incurred a potentially large legal liability that could cost tens of thousands of dollars.

It is clear that currently no efficient mechanisms exist for such exchanges of intellectual property. Of course, companies can draft contracts for the larger use cases, but this is a very lengthy and expensive process. Moreover, the contract will be stored in some procurement system, and the actual data assets will be somewhere else. In addition, if the use case changes, who will make sure to let the contract owners know about these changes?

Clearly, a refined model for intellectual property in mind+machine analytics is needed: one that allows market participants to interact easily, on a pay-per-use or one-off basis. In this chapter I propose a model on the basis of the knowledge object architecture discussed in Part II. The K-Hive of InsightBee is also knowledge object based. Granted, this proposed model is still a way off, and it might ultimately not become the dominant standard in the marketplace. However, given the increasing Machine role in the analytics space, ignoring the need for a working intellectual property model would be very dangerous. So, one way or another, we will need to agree on a market-based, open-source standard for mind+machine analytics.

In mind+machine, what are these assets (or knowledge objects) that can potentially be traded or licensed? I tend to think of them as "slices" of intellectual property; for example, a best-practice template (not the actual content) for competitive intelligence profiles could be licensed to other companies. Why reinvent templates all the time? Here are nine types of marketable assets:

1. Level 1 data
2. Level 2 information
3. Level 3 insights
4. Level 4 knowledge
5. Reports (or parts thereof)
6. Templates
7. Models and algorithms
8. Machines
9. Complete use cases

The idea therefore is to use the knowledge object architecture to tag the knowledge objects with their ownership information and any information pertaining to the intellectual property rights of the owner (e.g., limitations of usage or payment). Knowledge objects keep all the relevant information with them.

If someone uses one, they can easily determine who owns it and what terms exist regarding its usage, as the tag accompanies the knowledge object, while any contracts might be stored far away. They can also be nested (i.e., consist of other knowledge objects). In this way, a whole value chain can be constructed, and when the final product is sold, the rights of all the tiered suppliers in the value chain can be taken care of. Counters would store the usage history of the knowledge object in the tag. At the end of the month simple programs could then figure out who needs to be paid how much, and micro-payments could be made to the owners.

Of course, the software infrastructure for the aforementioned functionality does not yet exist as I am writing these lines. However, knowledge objects are already implemented and in use. Extending the tags to add the functionality handling the intellectual property is a relatively simple and logical next step.

CREATE AN AUDIT TRAIL AND MANAGE RISK

R isk management is no longer just nice to have these days. Things have become serious, and jobs are on the line.

This chapter is *not* about the analytics use cases of risk management in financial institutions (e.g., the market risks of share portfolios), which is of course a huge area with thousands of use cases. It is about the risks of mind+machine and how to manage them, and what you as a business owner need to know in order to ask the right questions.

Companies can have thousands of analytics use cases with many more to come (e.g., Internet of Things and big data). Machines multiply whatever humans could have ever done, and they do it much faster. But this also means that errors get multiplied much more quickly and distributed more widely in much shorter time frames. Please think back to the Volkswagen analytics software that got multiplied several million times.

Moreover, increasing levels of AI don't reduce the risks, either, given their black box nature. So, it is very clear that portfolios of mind+machine use cases need proper risk management. Ultimately, as recent high-profile cases have shown, the business owner (and not just the technical experts) will be held accountable for whatever mind+machine activities were executed. Given that both the business owners and the analytics staff rotate jobs frequently or even leave the companies, it is essential that any risk management be institutionalized and not just be located in people's minds. Some people still remember the days when payment software routines in banks were written in archaic languages such as Cobol or Fortran, badly documented or not at all, with all the former programmers having moved on long ago, and nobody dared to touch the code for fear of creating a financial mess. Well, a number of analytics use cases we have seen over the years were not much different.

The Use Case Methodology (UCM) provides a great environment to manage the risks and the compliance requirements, as it breaks down the nontransparent blob of analytics into manageable pieces with clearly allocated responsibilities and accountabilities. By doing so, it also helps relax restrictive compliance requirements for individual use cases leading to lower cost and higher speed. The key is that each use case is being managed individually or at least in small homogeneous groups.

Here are some rules that can be implemented on a use-case-by-use-case basis:

- Rule 1: **Check the current and expected regulatory environment wherever we operate.**
- Rule 2: **Check the internal compliance rules**. Are we compliant? Are there any unnecessary restrictions set by compliance?
- Rule 3: **Check the top three risks and potential liabilities downstream.** If something went wrong, what would be the damage for the end users or their clients?
- Rule 4: **Check the top three risks and potential liabilities upstream.** Are we sure we have the rights to all the data and tools we use? Are we compliant with the terms of usage, especially in terms of further distribution to end users or even external commercialization?
- Rule 5: **Check the top three operational risks along the Ring of Knowledge.** Where could things go wrong? Do we have the right quality checks in place, both for the minds and for the machines?
- Rule 6: **Make your use case as future-proof as possible.** Are there any regulatory trends or compliance rules that might affect the well-being of our use case, such as the introduction of General Data Protection Regulation or the EU–US Privacy Shield in 2018?
- Rule 7: **Create the necessary audit trails.** The no-brainer is the log of who did what when in creating, running, and changing the use case. Quality and compliance checks and procedures should be logged as well.

Investment banks are good examples given the increased scrutiny they are under. They run thousands of models that lead to financial products sold in the market. Sometimes these models are not more than complex Excel spreadsheets that are handed over from one analyst to the next over several generations. Most banks are taking model audits very seriously these days, and lots of potential mistakes (e.g., formulas, parameter ranges, programming errors, or lack of documentation) have come to the surface and could be corrected in time.

Within the UCM, the knowledge object architecture provides an excellent framework for the audit trail of knowledge objects, as they can be tagged easily and the tag travels with them. In this way, the analytic history of a knowledge object can be analyzed in automated ways without having to have access to some centrally stored audit trail. As discussed earlier, the knowledge object architecture is not yet mainstream, but its open-source character should benefit everybody as soon as enough software is available supporting it.

THE RIGHT PSYCHOLOGY: GETTING THE MINDS TO WORK TOGETHER

The machines will pretty much do what they are told to, unless, of course, they are black boxes or there are programming mistakes. But at least the machines don't have hidden agendas. If AI becomes so good that machines start having such agendas, I (with the help of my personal AI bot) will probably have to write another book, but this may still be a few years out… I hope.

Minds are very different, as we have seen in Part I. They have strong feelings as well as a surprising number of open and hidden agendas, all affecting the workings and outcomes of use cases in major ways. More often than not, the psychology may make the difference between success and failure. Nobody has the resources to come up with use case psychotherapists. The good news is that there are simple measures that can improve the probability of success significantly. Here are some of the very practical measures that probably already address about 75 percent of the challenge.

- Rule 1: **Use the Use Case Methodology (UCM) approach.** The UCM already resolves most of the alignment problems by defining the use cases precisely. Focusing the use case on a single group of homogeneous end users gives clarity about who needs what and who pays. In fuzzy approaches, the central teams have to simultaneously serve many masters with different needs, which can lead to significant conflicts between different groups of end users working with interconnected "spaghetti" use cases, leaving the central team in a dilemma.

- Rule 2: **Make team members aware of the pitfalls, and provide targeted training.** Already being aware of the psychological issues outlined in Part I can help a lot. It is not just about the analysts who need soft skills and communication skills—the end users involved in the project team need a certain degree of understanding of the analytical and technological challenges to be overcome.
- Rule 3: **Allocate roles and establish the business owner as the decision maker.** It must be clear who ultimately calls the shots. Full stop. Clearly, the most frequent problem is that the business owner is not part of the same organizational unit as the central analytics team. Nevertheless, the business owner is ultimately the budget owner and needs to be able to make decisions quickly. Similarly, the project manager needs to lead the whole team, regardless of where people come from in the organization. A typical mistake is to have a tech team and a business team with two separate team leaders working as peers. This does not work in most cases.
- Rule 4: **Establish a common language for nerds and antinerds.** Try to read through some meeting protocols. No wonder there are significant issues! End users usually aren't fluent in tech jargon, and technical experts are usually not fluent in the specific business lingo. A simple glossary with precise definitions can help.
- Rule 5: **Colocate the development team.** At least for the initial phases of the use case design and again for life cycle management, get the team to colocate in the same room, if possible. This is the only way to iterate designs and analytics rule sets quickly enough, and make the 10,000+ micro-design decisions. Email or shared folders simply don't work well enough. Of course, videoconferencing helps in cases of geographic dispersion, but only if it is desktop-to-desktop. Booking videoconference rooms is far too formal and doesn't occur frequently enough.
- Rule 6: **Get the quants and analysts to work directly with the end users early on.** The central teams need to experience the end user's environment live. They need to spend a few days with the end users to understand how they work, what their daily pressures are, and how they would like the use case to help them. Descriptions, however good they may be, simply cannot match the "felt" context. Questions of user experience design and workflow integration can be addressed much more effectively in this way.
- Rule 7: **Ensure alignment with objectives: repeat, repeat, repeat.** Use cases keep morphing, especially during the design phase. Other units may also want to piggyback on the project. All this can lead to changes in objectives—and the bulk of the work involved in them may be hidden under the surface like icebergs.
- Rule 8: **Crush little power plays and hidden agendas.** Nothing new here, but it is still a neglected area. Sitting on data, feeling superior because of higher levels of education (especially in competitive environments—e.g.,

between MBAs and PhDs in statistics), and other types of power plays can slow things down considerably.

- Rule 9: **The company, not individual departments or business units, owns the assets.** Sometimes this legal fact needs to be explained to various teams working on different use cases or producing some data sources. Efficient sharing helps shorten time lines and costs. Unless there are genuine compliance-related issues (e.g., in the case of hot insights in M&A that might move stock markets), there are no good reasons not to share inside a given company. Moreover, sharing of best practices can also greatly improve the quality of use cases, reduce risks, and improve the client benefits further.

- Rule 10: **Establish use-case-based governance cycle at the use case level.** Most people know how to start and execute projects to create use cases. The launch of a use case is not where this rule is needed most. It is needed in the middle and at the end of the life cycle, where life cycle decisions should be taken formally. Terminating use cases can free up resources, but the actual decision and the reasons need to be properly communicated to the end users.

- Rule 11: **Align incentives and performance management around the use case.** Having done many projects with many different departments, we have realized that the program manager needs to have the ability to provide formal input "with teeth" into the team members' performance assessments, wherever in the organization they may be. If the program manager does not have this leverage at his or her disposal, the execution might suffer.

Some of these rules might sound quite basic to you—and that is fundamentally true. However, these issues are real and crop up all the time, particularly in mind+machine analytics. Why? It probably has to do with the inherent cross-functionality of analytics use cases, as well as the range of personality types involved, which seems to be much wider in analytics than in other functions.

Perspective #14

THE GOVERNANCE OF USE CASE PORTFOLIOS: CONTROL AND ROI

Imagine a forest where the owner has tasked an employee to count the total number of leaves, but then the unlucky individual finds out that the trees and bushes are growing leaves more quickly than they can be counted. This is pretty much what is currently happening with mind+machine analytics. More use cases appear every day, driven by the hunger for more insights to drive decision making and support improved risk management. There is also a growing number of data sources that can be analyzed and, even worse, an exponential growth of potential combinations of sources that could be analyzed, leading to quickly growing portfolios of use cases. This chapter is about how to manage such portfolios, today and in the future.

Let us first look at seven managerial areas where such portfolio management needs to address questions:

1. **Mind+machine strategy:** How do we make operational the overall mind+machine strategy, defining portfolios of use cases at the company and business unit levels?
2. **Resource allocation and prioritization:** How do we allocate scarce central and noncentral resources to use cases? How should we prioritize among individual use cases and various portfolios of use cases?
3. **Managing for ROI and client benefits:** How do we make sure we understand the ROI and the client benefits each use case generates? How do we manage the portfolio ROI on an ongoing basis?

4. **Life cycle management:** How do we decide whether to initiate use cases? How do we decide on measures to extend the life of a use case or kill it?
5. **Knowledge management, transparency, and communication:** How can we communicate the wins internally? How can we create excitement? How do we keep things transparent for everyone?
6. **Risk management and audit trails:** How do we stay on top of the risks? How can we communicate efficiently to internal audit functions, external auditors, and regulators that we are on top of the risks?
7. **Organization:** How should we structure the organization, balancing central, noncentral, and external resources?

There are some notable best practices we have seen in our client base, including a global automotive manufacturer, a big commercial bank in the United States, and the sell-side research function of a large investment bank. What do these clients have in common? They have found operating models that work well for their particular industries, and they manage their portfolios of use cases in very proactive and coordinated ways, maximizing client benefits and consequently ROI.

The following are some best practices that seem to work. However, it must be said that such patterns are emergent at best. Few companies have fully implemented such frameworks at the company level at this point.

- Rule 1: **Establish central governance framework.** Companies should look at their mind+machine use case portfolios like you look at your own securities portfolio (present or future). These are assets that need to be managed effectively, but with as small an overhead as possible. You don't want to create big, cross-functional debating clubs with tons of meetings sucking up everybody's time. Nevertheless, someone needs to be accountable for each portfolio, and someone must be accountable for the sum of all portfolios. There should also be a rules framework and a governance cycle. The rules framework should set the general context, but not stifle innovation. The governance cycle should be frequent enough to be able to make the right decisions, but not become an "art for art's sake" paper exercise, either. At this point, most companies leave the governance to the central analytics units, where successful leaders drive the agenda (e.g., in the case of the automotive company). However, we have also seen great noncentral implementations, as in the case of the investment bank's sell-side research department where the leader is the global COO. The key is that these leaders are extremely business-minded, always focused on ROI and client benefits, and less focused on technology or analytics as such. One of the most important rules in the framework must be that everybody understands that resources will be allocated or taken away based on ROI and client benefits. Another rule centers on knowledge management, where the right incentive structures are required.

- Rule 2: **Focus on ROI and client benefits.** When the benefits get delivered, this will translate into ROI. We have seen many use cases that did not generate ROI, but people were excited about them because things were so cool and high-tech. Initially, this worked quite well, but after a while the business owners and controllers started asking for the client benefits and the ROI. Also, monitor the delivery against the targets. We had one use case using AI, but it simply did not deliver the promised benefits, and we terminated the effort. Another use case used AI and machine learning: it performed really well and was accelerated.

- Rule 3: **Make mind+machine a self-financing concept.** Mind+machine generates ROI by way of improving productivity, shortening time to market, improving quality, and enabling the end users to do new things. The productivity improvements alone usually free up enough resources to fund new efforts. The trick is to create a self-financing engine that can reinvest the savings into new use cases that will again create ROI, and so on.

- Rule 4: **Prioritize use cases and actively influence resource allocation.** To be prioritizable, use cases need to be made comparable, and ROI and client benefits can do exactly that. They are the universal language of comparison. It simply does not matter if something is big data or small data, uses AI or does not. What counts is the ROI and the client benefits. Giving resources is easy, but taking them away is hard: it requires facts and figures.

- Rule 5: **Keep use cases modular and avoid spaghetti architectures.** Simplicity wins. Why was the iPhone so successful? Simplicity and focus. Was this easy to achieve? Certainly not. Being able to manage use cases means that they cannot be intertwined with other use cases in nontransparent ways, or in ways where independent decision making is not possible. If the use case serves several user groups with potentially conflicting objectives, odds are that it will be expensive and complex to manage. Making changes always requires decision-making loops with multiple parties. This can take months or, worse, may result in gridlock. The fewer interfaces and user groups, the easier it will be to make decisions. This sounds simple, but it is surprisingly hard to achieve.

- Rule 6: **Have the courage to kill use cases.** People fall in love with their own use cases. Stopping the effort implies wastage of prior investment. However, the "sunk cost" principle is very clear about this: past investments don't matter for future decision making. Sunk is sunk. What matters is the future return based on which we should invest or not invest. The most effective leaders understand this and kill low-ROI use cases early on. The opportunity costs of sinking valuable data scientists into low-ROI use cases are simply too high.

- Rule 7: **Collect and manage use cases in a portfolio management workflow tool.** If you work for an investment bank with 6,000 models or a corporation with 500 Internet of Things use cases, manual paperwork will drive everybody crazy and proper management of analytics use cases simply won't happen. Some vendors have produced knowledge management tools for their particular analytic software packages. However, the Use Case Methodology (UCM) is supposed to work in a multitool and multi-vendor environment and, more importantly, to provide the key management functionalities for ROI and customer benefits. Evalueserve has developed a patent-pending, cloud-based tool called the Use Case Framework (UCF) for the UCM methodology, which enables the management of individual use cases as parts of overall portfolios. It stores the main elements of analytics use cases, such as the business issue, the analytic methodology and algorithms, the data models, the code, the audit trails, and many other parameters needed to characterize use cases.

- Rule 8: **Balance central, noncentral, and external resources.** We often get the question of central versus noncentral structure for mind+machine. As always, the answer is somewhere in the middle. The center can help define the guidelines and operate the portfolio management on behalf of the business owners. Moreover, it can hold a number of scarce and highly qualified resources with special technical skills that are needed for critical elements of use case design, plus it can help find the right external partners. However, the business-specific resources should be held noncentrally, as close to the business or the end users as possible. Specialized central resources should not be burdened with low-end Level 1 data work (i.e., data stewardship). This can usually be done at much lower cost by external parties.

- Rule 9: **Enforce knowledge management and smart platform architectures.** Minds work together when the incentives are right, as we saw in the previous chapter. The UCM tool will already go a long way to enforcing knowledge management, but Minds ultimately have to share and support each other. Evalueserve has also seen that smart platforms allow the hosting of multiple use cases. The cost for launching the next incremental use case (e.g., Procurement Intelligence or Sales Intelligence on InsightBee) reduces development time lines and investments manyfold.

- Rule 10: **Become an extrovert: communicate the client benefits achieved.** Jobs depend on it. Celebrate the successes. However, communicate them in a language that the end users understand, not just the data scientists. Communicate with the company's leadership to demonstrate the use cases. Use live demos, not PowerPoint presentations that people consider dull. Management and clients will love your demos.

- Rule 11: **Treat risk management in mind+machine analytics as a use case by itself.** Getting transparency is already the first step. The UCM helps disaggregate risks and make them comprehensible at the use case level. The UCF tool then allows comparison of the risks at the aggregate portfolio level. Ultimately, it comes down to who is accountable for which use case. The UCM provides exactly this information. By having the accountability audit trails stored in the UCF tool, the business owner can demonstrate a closed-loop control.

Mind+machine can help generate significant ROI in a noncentral model. If the UCM is additionally applied across the use case portfolio, the benefits for all parties involved more than justify the investments.

TRADING AND SHARING USE CASES, EVEN ACROSS COMPANY BOUNDARIES

Why not trade and share mind+machine use cases across company boundaries? The synergies would be massive. There are about 1.2 million companies with more than 50 employees in the world. According to the MSCI classification, they belong into 156 industries (120 in B2B, 36 in B2C). Of course, there are probably about 10 to 15 subindustries per main category, but this would still imply that there are about 500 to 700 companies per subindustry with the same or similar business issues to resolve, and I haven't even addressed functional topics such as HR or finance, which are pretty much the same for any company. Imagine if these companies could draw on central use case libraries to find their use cases. The costs for creating and running the use cases could be halved and time lines could be cut by 50 percent at least.

Granted, many companies see their analytics as a source of competitive advantage, and that is true for a part of them. However, let's look at the example of equities research valuation models in investment banking. Every bank considers its research to be better than the other banks' research, and *Institutional Investor* publishes the rankings every year. True, but the real source of competitive advantage is not really in the Excel valuation model; it is in the assumptions that are being put into the model and, more importantly, the insights created by the equity analyst. Evalueserve maintains thousands of such models in a highly compliant environment where no model or data ever makes it across to another bank. It is surprising how similar all the models are in spite of the analysts guarding their models as if they were the crown jewels of the United Kingdom.

Every investment bank spends enormous amounts of effort to create and maintain its own models. Wouldn't it be great if a set of trusted and certified model templates with a basic set of input data that is always the same (e.g., quarterly results of companies permanently maintained and fed into the templates) could be provided centrally? These templates would also have a lot of automated quality checks and audit trails built into them. Of course, anyone who knows the banking industry understands that this proposed sharing model might still be a decade out—or it might never happen. However, other industries might not have the same issues, and the productivity advantages would be huge.

How would a vision of a trading place for Mind+Machine analytics use cases look? What would be the main elements? Just to be clear: I am *not* talking about sharing proprietary data or insights, only about the generic use cases, the templates, the models, and some of the generic data feeds. Moreover, I do understand that such a vision is far out at this point. However, given the strong economic incentive for such a solution, it is just a matter of time before such models start emerging in Mind+Machine analytics. Microsoft Azure is already demonstrating a similar model for software.

Seven steps would need to be taken:

1. **Create a model for tradable units.** Before anything can be exchanged, the current entangled model of analytics needs to be moved to a model of modular use cases. The Use Case Methodology (UCM) provides such a model.
2. **Create a common, open-source language for analytics use cases.** Currently, there is no common, open-source language for analytics use cases other than the UCM, and even the UCM is in its infancy. Whichever standard ultimately emerges, it is a precondition for being able to trade analytics use cases.
3. **Create an exchange mechanism for selling or licensing use cases.** Of course, analytics use cases require permanent maintenance, which is why the exchange mechanism would need to work for pay-as-you-go (PAYG) models.
4. **Find ways to compensate intellectual property on an ongoing basis.** Contributors of analytics use cases to the marketplace need to find a way to price their own intellectual property. The UCM provides a way to do so.
5. **Create a certification mechanism for providers and use cases.** Microsoft Azure already provides a platform for certifications.
6. **Create use case workflow platforms.** Once a use case is licensed or acquired, a streamlined workflow platform could support the implementation and ongoing maintenance.
7. **Create an ecosystem of use case maintenance, implementation, and certification providers.** Over time, an ecosystem of specialist providers would emerge.

I am not naive. This vision will take many years to emerge. However, the UCM demonstrates that the vision is feasible. Most importantly, the overall economic benefits justify it.

PART III CONCLUSION

A re you ready for the future?
Wernher von Braun, the creator of the Saturn V rocket and significant contributor to the Apollo program, once said: "I have learned to use the word 'impossible' with the greatest caution." I hope you find inspiration in this quote for the world of mind+machine.

The objective of this book was to equip you with enough knowledge to ask the right questions when you need to. In Part I, we dispelled a set of fallacies about mind+machine analytics. In Part II, we looked at the underlying trends and how they will drive mind+machine in the future. And in Part III, I proposed the Use Case Methodology as a framework to apply mind+machine to the world of analytics.

I hope I have managed to show you that navigating the labyrinth of mind+machine is possible, now and in the future. Think of this book as the equivalent of Ariadne's ball of thread, given to Theseus to ensure that after completing his mission, he could come safely back home.

NOTES

Part I

1. "Gartner Predicts 2015: Big Data Challenges Move from Technology to the Organization," Gartner Inc., 2014, https://www.gartner.com/doc/2928217/predicts--big-data-challenges.
2. Jeff Kelly, "Enterprises Struggling to Derive Maximum Value from Big Data," Wikibon, 2013, http://wikibon.org/wiki/v/Enterprises_Struggling_to_Derive_Maximum_Value_from_Big_Data.
3. Columbia Business School's annual BRITE conference, BRITE–NYAMA Marketing Measurement in Transition Study, Columbia Business School, 2012, www8.gsb.columbia.edu/newsroom/newsn/1988/study-finds-marketers-struggle-with-the-big-data-and-digital-tools-of-today.
4. Vernon Turner, John F. Gantz, David Reinsel, and Stephen Minton, "The Digital Universe of Opportunities: Rich Data and the Increasing Value of the Internet of Things," IDC iView, 2014, www.emc.com/leadership/digital-universe/2014iview/executive-summary.htm.
5. Mario Villamor, "Is #globaldev Optimism over Big Data Based More on Hype Than Value?," Devex.com, 2015, https://www.devex.com/news/is-globaldev-optimism-over-big-data-based-more-on-hype-than-value-86705.
6. Jürg Zeltner, "A Mass of Information Does Not Equal a Wealth of Knowledge," FT.com, January 2015, www.ft.com/cms/s/0/69b0154c-959a-11e4-a390-00144feabdc0.html#axzz491J3nqhQ.
7. Experian News, "New Experian Data Quality Research Shows Inaccurate Data Preventing Desired Customer Insight," Experian, 2015, https://www.experianplc.com/media/news/2015/new-experian-data-quality-research-shows-inaccurate-data-preventing-desired-customer-insight.
8. Domo and BusinessIntelligence.com, "What Business Leaders Hate about Big Data," Domo, 2013, https://web-assets.domo.com/blog/wp-content/uploads/2013/09/Data_Frustrations_Final2.pdf.
9. Aaron Kahlow, "Data Driven Marketing, Is 2014 the Year?," Online Marketing Institute, January 2014, https://www.onlinemarketinginstitute.org/blog/tag/analytics.

10. Infogroup and YesMail, "Data-Rich and Insight-Poor," Infogroup and Yes-Mail, 2013, www.infogrouptargeting.com/lp/its/data-rich-insight-poor/index-desk.html.

11. Dan Woods, "Big Data Requires a Big, New Architecture," *Forbes*/Tech, July 21, 2011, www.forbes.com/sites/ciocentral/2011/07/21/big-data-requires-a-big-new-architecture/#232c3c711d75.

12. Brian Stein and Alan Morrison, "The Enterprise Data Lake: Better Integration and Deeper Analytics," PwC, *Technology Forecast: Rethinking Integration*, Summer 2014, https://www.pwc.com/us/en/technology-forecast/2014/cloud-computing/assets/pdf/pwc-technology-forecast-data-lakes.pdf.

13. Ibid.

14. Gartner, *The Data Lake Fallacy: All Water and Little Substance*, Gartner Inc., 2014, https://www.gartner.com/doc/2805917/data-lake-fallacy-water-little.

15. James Manyika et al., "Big Data: The Next Frontier for Innovation, Competition, and Productivity," McKinsey Global Institute Report, 2011, www.mckinsey.com/business-functions/business-technology/our-insights/big-data-the-next-frontier-for-innovation.

16. Aaron Whittenberger, "The Top 8 Mistakes in Requirements Elicitation," BA Times, January 2014, www.batimes.com/articles/the-top-8-mistakes-in-requirements-elicitation.html.

17. Steven Aronowitz, Aaron De Smet, and Deirdre McGinty, "Getting Organizational Redesign Right," *McKinsey Quarterly*, 2015, www.mckinsey.com/business-functions/organization/our-insights/getting-organizational-redesign-right.

18. Neal R. Goodman, "Knowledge Management in a Global Enterprise," *TD Magazine*, December 2014, https://www.td.org/Publications/Magazines/TD/TD-Archive/2014/12/Knowledge-Management-in-a-Global-Enterprise.

19. https://en.wikipedia.org/wiki/Deep_learning.

20. William Heitman, "How to Vanquish Management Report Mania," CFO.com, 2014. http://ww2.cfo.com/management-accounting/2014/09/vanquish-management-report-mania/.

21. KPMG, *Disclosure Overload and Complexity: Hidden in Plain Sight*, KPMG, 2011, www.kpmg.com/US/en/IssuesAndInsights/ArticlesPublications/Documents/disclosure-overload-complexity.pdf.

22. Heitman, "How to Vanquish Management Report Mania."

23. BusinessIntelligence.com, "5 Reasons Your CEO Prefers Data on a Dashboard," BusinessIntelligence.com, January 2015, http://businessintelligence.com/bi-insights/5-reasons-ceo-prefers-data-dashboard.

24. Timo Elliott, "#GartnerBI: Analytics Moves to the Core," Business Analytics & Digital Business, February 14, 2013, http://timoelliott.com/blog/2013/02/gartnerbi-emea-2013-part-1-analytics-moves-to-the-core.html.

Part II

1. Andrew Bartels et al., "The Public Cloud Market Is Now in Hypergrowth," Forrester, 2014, https://www.forrester.com/report/The+Public+cloud+Market+ Is+Now+In+Hypergrowth/-/E-RES113365.
2. Zachary Davies Boren, "Active Mobile Phones Outnumber Humans for the First Time," *International Business Times*, 2014, www.ibtimes.co.uk/there-are-more-gadgets-there-are-people-world-1468947.
3. Sarah Wolfe, "Smartphone Numbers to Triple by 2019, Report Says," GlobalPost.com, 2013, www.globalpost.com/dispatch/news/business/ technology/131111/smartphone-numbers-triple-2019-report-says.
4. BusinessIntelligence.co.uk.
5. Satya Nadella, "Satya Nadella: Mobile First, Cloud First Press Briefing," Microsoft News Center, March 27, 2014, http://news.microsoft.com/2014/ 03/27/satya-nadella-mobile-first-cloud-first-press-briefing/sm .0000viw9g2sdoe84zd422fmm7wog4.
6. GSMA Press Release, "GSMA Announces the Business Impact of Connected Devices Could Be Worth USD4.5 Trillion in 2020," GSMA, 2012, www.gsma.com/newsroom/press-release/gsma-announces-the-business-impact-of-connected-devices-could-be-worth-us4-5-trillion-in-2020.
7. Dave Evans, "The Internet of Things: How the Next Evolution of the Internet Is Changing Everything," Cisco White Paper, 2011, www.cisco.com/c/dam/ en_us/about/ac79/docs/innov/Internet of Things_IBSG_0411FINAL.pdf.
8. http://www.ey.com/Publication/vwLUAssets/EY-cybersecurity-and-the-internet-of-things/$FILE/EY-cybersecurity-and-the-internet-of-things.pdf.
9. Reform of EU Data Protection Rules, http://ec.europa.eu/justice/data-protection/reform/index_en.htm.
10. Communication from the Commission to the European Parliament, the Council, the European Economic and Social Committee, and the Committee of the Regions, "Safeguarding Privacy in a Connected World: A European Data Protection Framework for the 21st Century," http://eur-lex.europa.eu/ legal-content/EN/TXT/HTML/?uri=CELEX:52012DC0009&from=en.
11. European Commission Press Release, "EU Commission and United States Agree on New Framework for Transatlantic Data Flows: EU–US Privacy Shield," February 2016, http://europa.eu/rapid/press-release_IP-16-216_en.htm.
12. Adobe Investor Presentation, January 2016, http://wwwimages.adobe.com/ content/dam/Adobe/en/investor-relations/PDFs/ADBE-Investor-Presentation-Jan2016.pdf?wcmmode=disabled.
13. PwC, *The Sharing Economy—Sizing the Revenue Opportunity*, www.pwc .co.uk/issues/megatrends/collisions/sharingeconomy/the-sharing-economy-sizing-the-revenue-opportunity.html.

14. Yves de Montcheuil, "43 Percent of Marketing Organizations Sell Data," InfoWorld, www.infoworld.com/article/2851396/big-data/43-percent-of-marketing-organizations-sell-data.html.

15. KD Nuggets, "API Marketplace," www.kdnuggets.com/datasets/api-hub-marketplace-platform.html.

16. Business Wire Report, "Global Process Automation and Instrumentation Market to Reach Over USD 94 Billion by 2020, Says Technavio," January 2016, www.businesswire.com/news/home/20160126005046/en/Global-Process-Automation-Instrumentation-Market-Reach-USD.

Part III

1. Tom Wujec, "Build a Tower, Build a Team," TED, February 2011, https://www.ted.com/talks/tom_wujec_build_a_tower?language=en#t-373412.

ABOUT THE AUTHOR

Marc Vollenweider is the CEO and co-founder of Evalueserve, a global provider of research, analytics, and data management solutions. As a former partner at McKinsey & Company in Zurich and India, Marc developed a deep interest in the world of data analytics, particularly how human minds and smart machines can successfully complement each other. He saw the potential for companies to enhance productivity, shorten their time-to-market, improve quality, and gain new capabilities by leveraging mind+machine.

He studied Telecommunications Engineering at the Swiss Federal Institute of Technology in Zurich, and went on to earn an MBA from INSEAD in France in 1991. He made partner at McKinsey in 1998 and became a geographic entrepreneur by moving to the fascinating growth market of India. It was there that he met his Evalueserve co-founder and decided start the company as a greenfield venture. In the 16 years since its founding, Evalueserve has seen rapid expansion, driven by the growing strategic importance of data, information, insights, and knowledge, and it now has over 3,500 employees, globally serving financial and professional services firms, corporations, and small and medium businesses.

Marc's fascination with innovation has led to the establishment of a series of internal ventures at Evalueserve. He is the co-inventor of the digital model of InsightBee, Evalueserve's new pay-as-you-go research and analytics solution.

Referring to himself as a "self-aware nerd," Marc is well aware of the communication challenges between the technologist nerds and the antinerd end users and decision makers in the global economy. With mind+machine, he is trying to bridge this communication gap by demystifying and simplifying the world of data analytics.

Marc and his wife Gabi have three grown children and one teenager—and a very balanced family in terms of the number of nerds and antinerds. His family is his true inspiration in life. Gabi runs a psychotherapy practice and has inspired this book's section on the psychology of analytics, a topic nobody has written about before. Having lived in Switzerland, Austria, India, Singapore, the United States, and the United Kingdom, the whole family has developed a deep appreciation for other cultures. They also share a love of the mountains and the occasional game of golf.

For more information about Evalueserve and the mind+machine approach, visit the Evalueserve blog, where Marc is a frequent contributor.

evalueserve.com/blog

＊ ＊ ＊

You can find Marc on LinkedIn or follow him on Twitter, or contact him directly via email.

LinkedIn: linkedin.com/in/marcvollenweider
Twitter: @vollenweide
Email: marc@evalueserve.com

INDEX

and data security, 62
future of, 194–195
globalizing (era 2), 180–183
hybrid on-site, near-shore, and far-shore (era 4), 184–185
mind+machine in (era 5), 185, 190
pricing and performing benchmarks in, 190–191, 194
process reengineering and specialization (era 3), 184
sophistication of solutions for, 177

Pay-as-You-Go (PAYG), 108–109, 266
    as commercial model (perspective #10), 264–265
    seismic shift to (trend #5), 123–132
Peppers, Don, 105
Personal data, 120–122, 146
Personality profiles, 79
Per-unit pricing, 264–266
Predictive Analytics: Cross-Selling Support, 224–225
Preventive Maintenance: Analyzing and Predicting Network Failures, 212–213
Primary use cases, 12, 13, 47
Privacy, 101–102, 114–115, 118–121, 137
Private clouds, 90
Proactive Identification of New Sales Opportunities, 130–131
Process, flexible workflow platforms embedded in (perspective #6), 241–244
Process automation:
    for analytics use cases (trend #10), 156–163
    programming for, 40
Procurement:
    InsightBee Procurement Intelligence: Efficient Management of Procurement Risks, 68, 70–71
    managing and developing suppliers, 160–161
    Managing Indirect Procurement Market Intelligence: Efficient Procurement, 64–65
Productivity, 59–60, 191
Psychology:
    of analytics, 78–81

for getting the minds to work together (perspective #13), 271–273
PwC, 26, 144

Quality, in client benefits framework, 59–60

Rapid prototyping, 251
Rate table, 190
Rational process, analytics as (fallacy #12), 78–81
Regulation:
    of Ring of Knowledge (trend #4), 111–122
    of risk & compliance functions, 61–62
Reorganizations, impact on analytics (fallacy #6), 40–44
Reports, larger and fancier (fallacy #10), 66–71
Return on investment (ROI):
    in big data, 3, 5, 8, 219
    and business issue definition, 207–208
    framework for, 208
    in governance of use case portfolios (perspective #14), 274–278
    insight as driver of, 209
    and investment in analytics (fallacy #11), 72–77
    and knowledge management, 45
    in small data, 13
    in technology, 247
Ring of Knowledge, 21–22
    impact of cloud and mobile on, 92–95
    and Internet of Things, 104
    mapping (perspective #2), 214–217
    regulatory flooding of (trend #4), 111–122
Rise of the Robots (Martin Ford), 164
Risk & compliance, 61–62
    central risk & compliance teams, 38–39
    growth in functions of, 111
    intertectonic BCP in, 177–178
Risk management, 278
    InsightBee Procurement Intelligence: Efficient Management of Procurement Risks, 68, 70–71